Two Gryphius Tragedies in English Translation:
Leo Armenius and *Catharine of Georgia*

Janifer Gerl Stackhouse

FIRST EDITION

Printed in the United States of America

Two Gryphius Tragedies in English Translation: *Leo Armenius* and *Catharine of Georgia*

Translations, introductions, and notes © Janifer G. Stackhouse, 2020
All rights reserved.

ISBN 978-1-07-028964-9

Book design and production by Leslie A. Keats

Set in Minion Pro

Cover: Moravian paste paper by Janifer G. Stackhouse

Dedicated to my mother, Ada Bernice Weston Gerl (1914-1969),
whose encouragement inspired my scholarly endeavors,
and to my grandson, Colson Alexander Stackhouse, born in September 2015,
to inspire and encourage his future quest for knowledge.

PREFACE

This book has been in the making for over half a century. My first encounter with the lyric poetry of Andreas Gryphius occurred during my undergraduate years at the University of Chicago. It is with enduring gratitude that I thank Professor Ulrich Gaier, now professor emeritus at the University of Konstanz, for introducing me to Gryphius' *Catharine of Georgia* during my first year of graduate study at the University of California, Davis. His wise counsel also led to my receiving three years of much-appreciated DAAD support for continued study of German Literature at Gutenberg University in Mainz, Germany. While in Mainz (1965-1968), I improved my translation of *Catharine*, begun in California, with valued advice from my venerated professors and colleagues, Willi Flemming and Friedrich-Wilhelm Wentzlaff-Eggebert. I am grateful to Harvard University for the Graduate Prize Fellowship (1969-1971) that enabled me to pursue my Ph.D. in German Studies. At Harvard I was especially fortunate to study with Professors Jack Stein, Reginald Phelps, Henry Hatfield, Eckehard Simon, and others while also benefitting from the rare-book resources and dedicated staff of Houghton Library. With gratefully received support of a Fulbright Fellowship (1971-1973), I began my dissertation on Gryphius' *Charles Stuart or Murdered Majesty* while enrolled at the Free University in Berlin, where I completed my Harvard dissertation, published several scholarly articles on Gryphius, and enjoyed frequent trips back to Mainz to confer with Prof. Flemming on the *Catharine* translation. During subsequent years at Stanford University, UC Santa Cruz, and College of Notre Dame in Belmont, California, I continued my work and publications on Gryphius. I will always remain deeply indebted to my gifted colleague Gerald Gillespie, professor emeritus at Stanford, for his unwavering support of my continued efforts to improve and publish my complete translations of *Catharine of Georgia* and *Leo Armenius*. His generous gift of energy, vision, and guidance, especially during my more recent years as an independent scholar, is without parallel. I am also grateful to my Fulbright colleague, Professor Irakli Tskhvediani, Professor at Akaki Tsereteli State University in Kutaisi, Georgia, for valuable advice regarding evolving political geography in Georgia; to Theodore M. Andersson, professor emeritus at Stanford and my former teacher at Harvard, for assistance in translating Gryphius' Latin dedication of *Leo Armenius*; and to Dr. William E. Petig in German Studies at Stanford, my colleague and friend, for his cheerful and competent editorial review in the final preparation of this manuscript. My dear friend Leslie Keats applied her technical and artistic brilliance to the preparation of the text, the design, and the cover. She deserves full credit for shepherding it through the publication process. For this I will always remain deeply moved and grateful. Finally, I thank my family and friends for their unwavering support. Above all, the love and "Proven Constancy" of my husband, Charles, and our son, Colin Andreas, have added joy and purpose to my endeavor.

J.G.S.

CONTENTS

Contents

Catharine of Georgia or Proven Constancy

Select Annotated Bibliography

Appendix

About the Author

INTRODUCTION

Over four hundred years ago, on October 2, 1616, Andreas Gryphius was born in Glogau, Germany. He entered a world that was about to engage in a war that would last thirty years, find him as an orphan at age eleven, and evolve during his lifetime through political, religious, and social change beyond imagination or belief on the day of his birth.

Before he was thirty, Gryphius had studied in several foreign cities and had traveled throughout Europe. Already an accomplished poet, his talent turned to the theater when in 1646 he completed his first drama, *Leo Armenius or Regicide*. As the first historical tragedy ever written in the German language, his dramatized account of the Byzantine emperor's murder in the year 820 was performed both in local schools and on contemporary professional stages. This first of his original dramas centered on an event so far distant in the past that over eight hundred years separated him from the conflicts and struggles he depicted. He wrote his second historical tragedy, *Catharine of Georgia or Proven Constancy*, almost concurrently with his first. Completed in 1647, it portrayed the 1624 execution of the Georgian queen at the command of Shah Abbas I of Persia. This event was so recent that the geo-political struggles it depicted were still ongoing when he wrote the play.

His first drama, *Leo Armenius or Regicide*, depicts political intrigue and overthrow in the city of Constantinople (modern Istanbul, Turkey), a place never visited by Gryphius. His second drama, *Catharine of Georgia or Proven Constancy*, lauds a captive foreign queen for steadfast loyalty to her Georgian people and Christian faith and for bravely choosing to face death at the stake rather than to submit to her Muslim captor in Persia. Although he traveled to Persia and Georgia only vicariously, through reading the travel accounts of others, his drama about the Georgian queen's sacrifice, suffering, and martyrdom is still well known in Georgia today.

Motivated by an active interest in live theater, Gryphius sought out historical characters and events that could be dramatized in a way that would serve
to proclaim metaphysical truths. Both tragedies deal with moral, political, and
philosophical issues that are not only addressed within the context of the dramatic action, but also in the commentary the poet offered in the between-act
choruses and appended *Explanatory Notes*. Indeed, his *Notes* provided the kind
of contextual material that he believed would assist his audience to appreciate
better the lessons learned in his tragedies. Even his most obscure *Notes* point
to information that the polymath poet believed every educated person should
know. He defined the challenge of providing *Explanatory Notes* in the conclusion
that follows his final reference note to his last drama, *Papinianus*: "And that's
enough for now. But why so much? For scholars this is written to no avail, and
for the uneducated it is still not enough."[1]

Both of his first two historical tragedies written in German now appear in
English translation for the first time. I hope that my translations of *Leo Armenius*
and *Catharine of Georgia* will serve as useful companions to Gryphius' original
texts for those who might not be fully at ease with the German language, in par-
ticular seventeenth-century German. For those who do not read German at all, I
trust that my translations will provide a useful introduction to the dramatic work
of Andreas Gryphius and enable the reader to enter his unique world of German
Baroque drama. His final revised versions of both tragedies, printed in 1663,

---

[1] Andreas Gryphius, *Gesamtausgabe der deutschsprachigen Werke* (Tübingen: Niemeyer,
1963-72), IV, 269. All following citations from Gryphius are according to this edition, here-
after referred to as *Werke*. In 1657, Gryphius published a sonnet entitled "About his Sonnets
for Sun-and Holidays." In the final lines of this sonnet about his earlier sonnets (1639 ff.),
he comments on his own acquired erudition when he compares the "pious" lyric poetry
of his youth to the "learned" content and characters of his first two dramas, *Catharine of
Georgia* and *Leo Armenius*:

> Here, I confess, my brutal *Abbas* does not thunder,
> Nor does *Leo*, whose soul breaks loose on the altar.
> The heroic courage of martyrs can be read about elsewhere:
> You, who only enjoy the errors of others,
> Don't struggle any further: I'll tell you what is missing for me:
> It's that my childhood was not learned, but pious. (*Werke,* I, 243)

serve as the source texts for my translations. Of value to readers of German and English alike, I offer full expositions of the poet's *Explanatory Notes* to both plays and new clarification of his source texts. Although the lofty Alexandrine meter and solid rhyme schemes that Gryphius so masterfully employed to hammer home his messages unleash a powerful dynamic in the original German text, I believe these messages in translation can be most clearly conveyed in the natural tone of free verse.[2] The separate introductions that precede my translations of *Leo Armenius* and *Catharine of Georgia* offer the reader insight that will clarify the content and dramatic action of each historical tragedy. First, however, some background information about the poet and dramatist will illuminate the milieu in which he created both of them.

Andreas Gryphius in Literary Context

The year 1616 might have gone down in the history of European literature as the year when the torch of literary genius passed from the greatest poet and dramatist in the English language, William Shakespeare (1564-1616), to the foremost seventeenth-century poet and dramatist in the German language, Andreas Gryphius (1616-1664). With their lives encompassing exactly one century, both poets received extraordinary honor and acclaim for their sonnets, comedies, and tragedies. But contrary to the dynamic and unfettered Shakespeare, the German poet remained too tightly bound by rigorous rules that restrained the intensity and passion of his lyric poetry and placed unbridgeable distance between the experiences of his dramatic characters and those who experienced his work. Because he was unable to break through contemporary conventions and reveal in his writing the universal mythical elements, deepest emotions, and strongest bonds shared by all of humanity, his work was fated to descend in time to that forgotten realm of period pieces: today it serves to exemplify the elements often labeled as *baroque*. As if self-aware of his limited approach to acknowledge and portray tragedy in the human condition, the poet always referred to his own

---

[2] Additional analysis regarding the original German text of Gryphius and my English translations appears in the Appendix "Translator's Notes."

historical dramas as *Trauerspiele* instead of *Tragödien*. The German philosopher and critic Walter Benjamin (1892-1940) succinctly clarified the gaping difference between them when he defined the artistic core of the *Trauerspiel*: "Historical life, as it was conceived at that time, is its content, its true object. In this it is different from tragedy. For the object of the latter is not history, but myth, and the tragic stature of the *dramatis personae* does not derive from rank – the absolute monarch – but from the pre-historic epoch of their existence – the past age of heroes."[3] To facilitate the following discussion, however, we will refer to his *Trauerspiele* or "plays of mourning" as "tragedies."

Although Gryphius never attained a stature that could approach that of the Bard of Avon, his innovative talents and versatile literary activity secure his unique position in the history of German literature. German poets of the following century would break free from the bondage of Baroque rules to draw more deeply from the mythical wellsprings of the common human experience as they discovered evolving literary forms through which they could deliver better their ideas and passions. Until then Gryphius took possession and held aloft the torch of German letters through his lyric poetry, historical tragedies, comedies, funeral orations, and operatic texts, along with his Latin epic poetry and his translations into German from Dutch, French, and Latin lyric, dramatic, and prose works.

Brief Biography

The poet's first eighteen years present a mosaic of personal hardships against a chaotic background of relentless religious and political conflict. These formative years amidst controversy and confusion served to develop his world view of *vanitas mundi* (vanity, or emptiness, of the world), a conviction that underlies most of his creative effort. Born in the region of Silesia (in present day Poland) as the son of a Lutheran pastor, just two years before the outbreak of the devastating Thirty Years' War (1618-48), young Gryphius lost his father before he was

---

[3] Walter Benjamin, *The Origin of German Tragic Drama*, translated by John Osborne (London: Verso, 2009), 62. Originally published in 1928 as *Ursprung des deutschen Trauerspiels* (Frankfurt a.M.: Suhrkamp, 1963), 51.

five and his mother by the age of twelve. For the next six years he lived first with an older stepsister and was then shuffled between the care of his stepfather and a half-brother, both Lutheran pastors, as they were forced to move from town to town according to changing restrictions imposed upon Silesian Protestants during the course of the omnipresent religious war. In spite of these difficult circumstances, the young orphan demonstrated remarkable literary ability at an early age through his public recitation of original eulogies and his initial publications. At the age of seventeen he wrote his first published Latin epic, *Herodis Furiae et Rachelis Lachrymae* (Glogau, 1634), in just twenty days while his school, the Fraustadt *Stadtschule,* was closed due to an outbreak of the plague.

A new era opened for the budding poet when he set out in the summer of 1634 to begin a two-year program of study at the Gymnasium in Danzig (present day Gdańsk, Poland). His position as tutor in the intellectually stimulating home of Alexander Seton, a Polish admiral of Scottish-Catholic heritage, offered him the opportunity to participate in frequent discussions of the most challenging current religious and political topics. At the Gymnasium he supplemented his academic pursuits with a growing interest in writing poetry and drama. While in Danzig he produced his first sonnets, a second Latin epic that was dedicated to the city councilors of Danzig (*Dei Vindicis Impetus et Herodis Interitus),* and German translations of Latin poetry by the Jesuit poets Matthias Casimir Sarbiewski, Jakob Biedermann, and Bernard Bauhusius. Most probably Gryphius also commenced his first creative work with drama while in Danzig by translating *Beständige Mutter oder Die Heilige Felicitas* (*The Constant Mother or Holy Felicitas)* from the Latin *Tragoediae Sacrae* (1621) of Nicolas Caussin, a French Jesuit. We can be certain that he had been influenced by Caussin's martyrological tragedy at this time, for his personal copy of the Jesuit dramatist's work bears his own inscription with the year 1634. The constancy (*Beständigkeit)* of both Felicitas and Catharine of Georgia is the primary virtue among many qualities shared by these two women who were held captive by powerful tyrants. Gryphius' original drama (*Catharine*) and his translation (*Felicitas*) both appeared on stage at the Elisabeth Gymnasium of Breslau during the 1650s. Finally, the publication of a third Latin epic (*Parnassus Renovatus*, Danzig, 1636), written in praise of his patron and benefactor, the renowned legal scholar Georg Schönborner (1579-

1637), completed his literary activity in Danzig. It also introduces us to the next significant phase of his development: two years at Schönborner's country estate.

While Gryphius served as tutor and companion to Schönborner's two sons, Schönborner himself exerted a profound and lasting influence on the young poet. Gryphius adopted the legal and political views of his patron, and his decision to pursue the study and practice of law was in great part determined by this friend and mentor, whom he called both *father* and *Dicaeus* (a son of Poseidon, whose name δίκαιος means just or lawful). Schönborner encouraged his young friend's literary pursuits as well.

By the authority vested in him as an appointed Imperial Count Palatine, Schönborner rewarded Gryphius in 1637 on the occasion of the publication of his first book of sonnets in Lissa (present day Leszno), Poland, with a title of nobility (never used by Gryphius), conferring a master's degree upon him, and also by crowning him *poet laureate*, an honor that Schönborner himself had received at Helmstedt in 1603. The sudden death of Schönborner in 1637 abruptly terminated this fortunate period of intellectual enrichment for Gryphius. His subsequent departure from the Schönborner estate also marks the end of his developmental years in Germany.

In 1638 the young Silesian traveled to Holland to complete his formal education at the University of Leiden, probably the most culturally diverse and intellectually stimulating center of learning in Europe at that time. He matriculated there on July 26 and combined his own program of study (primarily law, medicine, and philosophy) with offering private courses in such widely diverse subjects as metaphysics, mathematics, philosophy, geography, poetics, astrology, anatomy, and chiromancy (palm reading). During his Leiden years (1638-44) Gryphius published five books of poetry. There he drew from the diverse, tolerant, and lively intellectual atmosphere to formulate most of the decisive political and philosophical views that were to find their artistic expression in his later work. It was also in Leiden that the erudite young German established lasting contacts with such leading European scholars as Hugo Grotius (1583-1645), Claudius Salmasius (1588-1653), Marcus Boxhorn (1612-63), Isaac Vossius (1618-69), Jacobus Golius (1596-1667), and Daniel Heinsius (1580-1665). His years in Leiden also provided the future dramatist with his first exposure to professional theater. The new state theater of Amsterdam had opened just a few months prior to his arrival in Holland, and the production of plays by Joost van den Vondel (1587-1679) and Pieter Corneliszoon Hooft (1581-1647) greatly influenced his own dramatic work. His early enthusiasm for the Dutch theater is evidenced by his translation of Vondel's *De Gebroeders* (*The Seven Brothers* or *The Gibeonites*), to which he added an original prologue and epilogue. Gryphius most likely completed this translation during his years in Leiden, although it was first published posthumously by his son Christian in 1698. According to his son's report, Gryphius had nearly completed an *original* five-act tragedy on this topic, but the manuscript was lost prior to publication. Gryphius' translated version of Vondel's play was performed in Breslau in 1652.

Upon departing from Leiden, he began an extended tour of the continent that took him first to Paris (1644-45), then to Italy (1646), and finally to Strassburg (1646-47), from where he returned once again to his native Silesia. As he moved through Europe, his firsthand observation of ancient and more contemporary works of art, ranging from architecture to sculpture, painting, and public art displays, proved to be transformational for his own artistic sensibilities. His personally recorded encounters with palaces great and small, art galleries both famous (i.e., the Uffizi in Florence) and privately held, gardens, parks, and even extraordinary fireworks with orchestral accompaniment attest to the enduring influence these encounters exerted on his receptive mind. The profound impressions of these enriching experiences, especially in France and Italy, supplemented his contact with dramatic literature and innovative live theater and inspired him to reach new creative heights and to turn his attention to writing for the stage. Recent technological developments in the theaters of northern Italy that enabled the rapid change of scenery and new possibilities for stage lighting also exerted tremendous influence on the future dramatist. His specific instructions for scene changes in *Catharine* (1647), for example, were the first to be included in a German drama. A crucial scene of his *Cardenio and Celinde* (1648) is dependent upon rapid scene change: "The scene (pleasure garden) suddenly changes to a frightening desert and Olympia herself morphs into a skeleton that aims its bow and arrow at Cardenio."[4]

---

[4] *Werke*, V, 148.

While living for a year at the home of the professor and jurist Georg Biccius in Strassburg (1646-47), his legal and political interests were stimulated by frequent contact with lawyers and legal scholars (law and philosophy were the two strongest faculties at the University in Strassburg, which had a total enrollment of about two hundred students during the mid-seventeenth century.) His recent exposure to theater in France and Italy took hold as well, for he not only revised his sonnets and odes, publishing a second book of odes there in 1646, but he also wrote and attempted to publish his first drama, the tragedy *Leo Armenius or Regicide* (1646). Moreover, in his introductory *Letter to the Reader* of *Leo Armenius*, the poet mentions for the first time his intention to write a tragedy about the martyrdom of Catharine of Georgia, noting: "... as soon as possible our Shah Abbas in the *Proven Constancy of Catharine of Georgia* shall abundantly portray that which would not at all suit Leo... [namely, love and courting]." [5] Gryphius completed *Catharine* during his extended visit in Stettin (now Szczecin, Poland) on his return to Silesia in the autumn of 1647, although it did not appear in print for another ten years.

When he finally arrived back in Germany, he found Fraustadt and most of Silesia devastated by events of the Thirty Years' War. In the first few years after his return home, Gryphius maintained prolific literary productivity by writing two more tragedies (*Cardenio and Celinde, or Misfortunate Lovers* and *Charles Stuart or Murdered Majesty*) and two comedies (*Absurd Comedy or Herr Peter Squentz* and *Horribilicribrifax the German*). Although written between 1647 and 1650, these plays were first published together with his initial two tragedies, *Leo Armenius* and *Catharine of Georgia*, in 1657. Now quite renowned and well connected, Gryphius declined professorships at the universities in Heidelberg, Frankfurt on the Oder, and Uppsala (Sweden), choosing instead to serve as *Landes-Syndicus* in his native Glogau. Sworn into office on May 3, 1650, he had been elected to represent the landed nobility as their legal advisor, a highly visible public position that required consummate skill to navigate the tension still existent between Silesian Protestants and imperial Catholics. In fulfilling the duties of this position once held by his esteemed mentor Georg Schönborner, the lawyer and legal scholar Gryphius compiled and published the rights and privileges of the Glogau landed

---

[5] *Werke,* V, 4. See Gryphius' letter *Dear Reader* below, p. 27.

nobility vis-à-vis the imperial authority of the Hapsburg dynasty in Vienna.[6]

Gryphius was greatly admired by his colleagues and contemporaries, as documented not only by their high demand for him to write eulogies and occasional poetry for their loved ones, following the custom then popular to commission celebrated writers for this purpose, but also by the praises they bestowed upon him following his death. He spent his final fourteen years in Glogau, dividing his time between civic duty and continued poetic creativity. Among the most important of his later literary achievements are the *Kirchoffs-Gedancken* (*Thoughts in a Cemetery*), the *Dissertationes Funebres.Oder Leich-Abdanckungen* (*Eulogies*), the extensive revision of *Charles Stuart or Murdered Majesty* (1663), and his final historical tragedy, *The Magnanimous Jurist or Aemilius Paulus Papinianus Facing Death* (1659).

On July 16, 1664, the famed poet, dramatist, and civil servant collapsed and died of a heart attack at the age of forty-seven during an afternoon session of the landed estates in Glogau, the city of his birth. Recognized as the genius of German Baroque drama, his works include some of the highest literary achievements of seventeenth-century Germany. The epithet *"der Unsterbliche"* (the immortal one), bestowed upon him in 1662 when he was initiated into the *Fruchtbringende Gesellschaft* (the Fruitbearing Society)[7] attests to contemporary public recognition of his many valued contributions. His gravestone, decorated with his image and flowers, was inscribed

Illi enim immaturi semper moriuntur, qui immortale aliquid cogitant.

(Those who harbor immortal thoughts always die too soon.)

---

[6] Thorough knowledge of both imperial law and the rights of the local nobility were required for Gryphius to succeed as *Landes-Syndicus* for the principality of Glogau. His careful editing and publication of all relevant legal documents for Glogau from 1490 through 1658 in his *Glogauisches Fürstentumbs Landes Privilegia aus den Originalen an tag gegeben Von Andrea Gryphio,* 1653, demonstrated both his philological proficiency and his civic dedication.

[7] This elite German society was founded by noblemen and scholars in 1617 to promote German as both a scholarly and literary language. It was modeled on Italy's Accademia della Crusca in Florence, with a membership that included a king, 153 Germanic princes, and over 60 barons, nobles, and distinguished scholars before it was disbanded in 1668.

Gryphius' Emblematic Technique of Constructing Historical Tragedies

Although each of Gryphius' four historical tragedies presents the martyrdom of a specific individual within a given historical-political framework, his carefully documented reconstructions of the actual historical events serve not only to exemplify, but indeed to *proclaim* a higher religious-philosophical message or metaphysical truth. The double titles he attached to these dramas provide the audience or reader with a capsule formulation of the drama's dualistic function, for the first half of the title identifies the historical topic, while the second half indicates the ultimate metaphysical message that the poet wanted to impart. Repeated use of the double title typifies the emblematic form of German Baroque drama. Just as seventeenth-century emblematic literature relied upon a specific picture or illustration to suggest a hidden yet higher metaphysical truth to the beholder, so too does Gryphius employ a specific historical-political event (*pictura*) to exemplify and proclaim to the audience an ultimately metaphysical message (*subscriptio*).

The double title of his first original tragedy *Leo Armenius oder Fürstenmord* (*Leo Armenius or Regicide*) identifies the historical topic as the ninth-century Byzantine Emperor Leo Armenius and then offers commentary on this topic that clearly reveals a subjective interpretation (i.e., condemnation) of the actual historical event. Similarly, the double title of Gryphius' second original tragedy, *Catharina von Georgien oder Bewehrete Beständigkeit (Catharine of Georgia or Proven Constancy)*, first presents the historical-political topic by naming the Georgian queen executed in 1624 and then suggests a metaphysical truth proclaimed by this event. The double titles of his final two historical tragedies, *Carolus Stuardus oder Ermordete Majestät (Charles Stuart or Murdered Majesty)* and *Großmütiger Rechts-Gelehrter oder Sterbender Aemilius Paulus Papinianus (The Magnanimous Jurist or Aemilius Paulus Papinianus Facing Death)*, also delineate the historical-political topics portrayed while proclaiming a metaphysical evaluation of the given events.

Literary Pioneer: A Focus on One Brilliant Facet of German Literary History

This introduction has presented Gryphius as the seventeenth-century literary pioneer who first used the German language to create historical drama. His early contribution shines as a single facet of a rich literary tradition that continues to evolve to the present day by questioning and reflecting upon the complexities of the human condition. Specific "complexities of the human condition" identified by Gryphius in his first two plays include the omnipresent power struggle for geo-political dominance and conflicting religious beliefs. The fact that after many centuries these very same struggles and conflicts still remain unresolved will not elude the modern reader. Indeed, this very dimension of timelessness in his work enhances its present value as a commentary that sheds light on current contentious and unresolvable global issues. In retrospect, Gryphius' creative process seems quite straightforward. First he selected a politically significant historic figure as protagonist and then he chose a written source that clearly detailed the story of this protagonist's life. He then transformed the prose of his source(s) into a poeticized drama that not only portrayed the life and death of his protagonists within the context of actual historical events, but also exemplified his own principles and beliefs.

My English translation of his work opens this literary moment to a wider audience. It is my hope that this wider audience will gain new insight regarding the evolution of German literary history through this focus on the singular and brilliant contribution to German drama offered by the poet Andreas Gryphius.

Janifer Gerl Stackhouse
October 2020

LEO ARMENIUS or REGICIDE

Introduction to *Leo Armenius or Regicide*

Over the years that preceded Gryphius' 1646-1647 sojourn in Strassburg, his many significant encounters with mentors, professors, and colleagues had exerted a dominant influence on his belief in the divine right of kings. This conviction would have surfaced in discussions that occurred in the Danzig home of Alexander Seton, a Scottish admiral of the Polish fleet. While serving as house tutor there in 1634, young Gryphius also would have met guests, including Francis Gordon, ambassador from England. Later, from 1635 until 1637, his political and religious views were further influenced and reinforced and through discussion, reading, and debate while residing at the estate of Georg Schönborner, the renowned legal scholar and jurist who ardently supported the principle of divine rights. At the University of Leiden (1638-1644), lasting friendships with Claudius Salmasius and other distinguished scholars immersed in the divine rights issue insured his personal involvement in the intense controversy that was only heightened by the 1642 outbreak of Civil War in England. By 1646, his exposure on the continent to this burning issue had included experiences that ranged from time spent in Angiers, France, during the summer of 1645, just one year after the August 14, 1644, arrival of Henrietta Maria, wife of Charles I, to begin exile in Angiers,[8] to continued

---

[8] See Sonnet XVI in *The Second Book of Sonnets*: "On the Entry of Her Royal Highness Queen Maria Henrietta in Angiers on August 14, 1644." *Werke*, 1, 73. Henrietta Maria of France, Queen of England (1609-1669), married Charles I of England in 1625. In 1644 she returned to France from England on a Dutch ship accompanied by Henry Jermyn, the Earl of St. Albans, with whom she lived in France prior to the execution of Charles I.

concern about hostilities in England waged against Charles I by antiroyalists. In addition to his scholarly interest in the history and politics of England, his association with the courts of the Palatinate and Brandenburg influenced his sympathy for the English king. He was personally acquainted with Princess Elisabeth von der Pfalz (1618-1680), a niece of Charles I, and in 1648 he dedicated the second edition of his *Olivetum* to Princess Elisabeth and her cousin Friedrich Wilhelm (1620-1688), Elector of Brandenburg ("the Great Elector"). Later, his third historical tragedy (*Charles Stuart or Murdered Majesty*) would give voice to his passionate conviction and belief in the divine right of kings. For the duration of his extended visit in Strassburg, Gryphius lived in the home of Dr. Georg Biccius (Georg Bieck, 1572-1657), a legal scholar and professor of law at the university there. Many of the poet's close associates at the University of Strassburg were jurists who strongly supported the theory of divine rights, including Johann Heinrich Boecler (1611-1672), professor of history and constitutional law, and the renowned legal scholar Johannes Rebhan (1604-1689).

Arriving in Strassburg after two years of touring the continent (1644-46), Gryphius began to write *Leo Armenius or Regicide*, his first original tragedy, and his first drama in the German language. In 1632, at the age of sixteen, Gryphius had been highly praised by the citizens and city council of Fraustadt for his eloquence when, as a student at the Fraustadt *Stadtschule*, he presented a public speech about the fall of Constantinople to the Ottomans in 1453 that marked the end of the Roman Empire. Why was his early interest in Byzantine history revived fourteen years later when, at the age of thirty, he turned to a different event in Constantinople that had occurred six centuries *earlier?* What captivated his interest in the legendary ninth-century Byzantine emperor, Leo Armenius (Leo V the Armenian, 775-820), compelling him to write a dramatic tragedy that would examine the fated emperor's murder on Christmas in the palace chapel of St. Stephen in Constantinople?

The immediate stimulus for his choice of topic probably occurred in 1646 when he visited Rome, where he could have seen a presentation of the Latin

Leo Armenius play written by an English Jesuit, Joseph Simon (1594-1671). A comparison of the two *Leo* plays clarifies why the German poet was motivated to write his own dramatic version of this historical event. Simon's *Leo Armenus seu Impietas punita (Leo the Armenian or Impiety Punished)* had been performed at the Jesuit College of St. Omer in the Spanish Netherlands between 1624 and 1629, but it was not published until 1656. The well-known German Jesuit scholar, Athanasius Kircher (1602-1680), whom Gryphius visited in Rome and whose work he cites in his *Explanatory Notes* to *Leo Armenius* and elsewhere, may well have drawn his attention to the English Jesuit's play. It is most probable that Gryphius saw a production of it in 1646 while in Rome. Simon's play condones the murder of the tyrant Armenius as an act necessary to end the iconoclast controversy of the ninth century and thus as an act that was directed toward the greater glory and unity of the Catholic Church. The close of Simon's *Leo* proclaims: "O justa coeli poena! Pro vindex Deus!" ("How just are heaven's punishments! Oh God, what a vindicator you are!")[9]. Gryphius' support of theocratic absolute monarchy, however, sparked his negative reaction to Simon's assessment of the historic event. Thus challenged by Simon's analysis and interpretation, Gryphius side-stepped the entire iconoclast controversy and set out instead to defend Leo as a legitimate monarch, whose murder had to be condemned as regicide. A brief review of the various titles that he chose for his first original drama confirms his politically oriented analysis of the event. The original title (1650 pirated edition) reads: *Ein Fürsten-Mörderisches Trawer-Spiel / genant. Leo Armenius (A Regicide Tragedy called Leo Armenius).* The edition of 1652 bears the title *Leo Armenius / oder Jämmerlichen Fürsten-mords Trauerspiel (Leo Armenius, or A Pitiful Tragedy of Regicide)*, while all editions printed after 1657 concisely summarize his view of the event with the shorter title *Leo Armenius oder Fürstenmord (Leo Armenius or Regicide)*. Leo's doomed support of iconoclasm recedes completely in the German poet's drama while

---

[9] Cited from Josef Simon's *Leo Armenus seu Impietas punita (Leo the Armenian or Impiety Punished)* in Willi Harring's *Andreas Gryphius und das Drama der Jesuiten*, (Halle: Niemeyer, 1907), 126.

attention is directed instead to the theological/political significance of the Emperor Leo's death.

Gryphius' stated purpose for writing the *Armenius* tragedy was to demonstrate the vanity of all human affairs and the transitory state of the human condition in general, as he articulates in the opening lines of his prefatory letter to the Reader:

> Since our whole fatherland now buries itself in its own ashes and turns into a theater of vanity, it is my intent to present to you the transitory nature of human affairs in this present and in several following tragedies.[10]

Before leaving Strassburg in 1647, he addressed a sonnet to the Strassburg printer Caspar Dietzel, who had intended to first publish the tragedy.[11] In this sonnet, Gryphius again suggests that the fall of Armenius demonstrates worldly *vanitas*, or vanity, as illustrated by fortune's quickly turning wheel: "*The prince, who dying, teaches how soon the swift wheel / Of fortune is reversed.*" His sonnet projects a certain historical objectivity regarding the fall of Leo that his dramatic version of the event eludes. Although he recognized the historical Leo to be a feared and hated tyrant in his sonnet, his personal political conviction regarding absolute monarchy and the corollary condemnation of regicide shaped the historical material in his drama. Thus he excused the tyrant Leo for certain excesses in the drama's preface (see *Dear Reader,* below) by noting:

> "…However I just have to remind you that since our Leo was a Greek emperor, he will also reveal much to his reader that is partly not praised and partly not allowed currently ruling princes."[12]

---

[10] *Werke,* V, 3. See Gryphius' *Dear Reader* letter below, p. 26
[11] Sonnet XLIV in *The Second Book of Sonnets, Werke,* 1, 88-89. My English translation of this sonnet is included in the prefatory materials to *Leo Armenius*, below, p. 24.
[12] *Werke,* V, 3. See Gryphius' *Dear Reader* letter below, p. 26.

As indicated by his drama's title, the fall of Armenius serves not only to project the general theme of *vanitas*, but, more specifically, it warns against the crime of regicide as a breach of human and divine justice.

Today the modern reader has access to more information about the attitudes and experiences recorded by Gryphius in publishing this first drama than about any of his subsequent plays. The above-mentioned sonnet written to his intended first publisher before Gryphius left Strassburg in 1647, entitled: "To H. Caspar Dietzel: On the Writing and Publication of Leo Armenius," refers to unexpected publishing delays. He writes of the horrendous event of Leo's murder in Constantinople "in that dreadful and furious night" in his Latin dedicatory poem to his mentor and traveling companion, Wilhelm Schlegel, dated November 1646.[13] (Schlegel had accompanied Gryphius and the two sons of Georg Schönborner, Georg Friedrich and Hans Christoph, on their three-year European tour [1644-1646], departing Strassburg before Gryphius. On his return to Silesia from Strassburg, however, Gryphius stayed at the estate of Schlegel's father in Stettin, where he completed his *Catharine of Georgia* tragedy.) *Leo Armenius* appeared for the first time in a pirated edition published in 1650 (Version A) without the knowledge of Gryphius. The first official edition appeared in 1657 (Version B), with final emendations by the poet in the publication of his collected dramas in 1663 (Version C), which I have used for my English translation. In 1651, the first public performance of *Leo Armenius* was staged in Cologne by the traveling theatrical company of Joris Jollifous (George Jolly, fl. 1640-1673).

---

[13] Gryphius' Latin dedication of *Leo Armenius* to Wilhelm Schlegel appears in the prefatory materials to my English translation, below, p. 25. Gryphius expresses his profound regard for Schlegel in his sonnet "To Mr. William Schlegel / in Castain and Möhringen, on his Name Day." See "An H. Guilhelm Schlegel/ in Castain und Möhringen. Auff seinen Namens Tag:" Sonnet XVII *in The Second Book of Sonnets, Werke,* I, 74.

The Historical Source

Because Gryphius presumed that the credibility of his drama's message depended on the spectator's or reader's recognition of the play's historical accuracy, he was most eager to point out the sources of his dramas. His opening to the preface of *Leo Armenius* notes: "The entire course of his [Leo's] demise is explained in detail by Cedrenus and Zonaras, who write with a pen not merely about his death, but actually also project everything in such a way that it hasn't been necessary to mix in many other fictitious inventions." [14] Cedrenus and Zonarus, the two Byzantine historians to whom Gryphius refers in a majority of appended reference notes to *Leo Armenius*, enjoyed great popularity throughout the seventeenth century. Indeed, their authority in reporting events related to the fall of the Byzantine emperor was considered absolute. Since the work of Johannes Zonaras (twelfth century) is based on material presented in the *Historiarum Compendium* of Georgios Cedrenus (eleventh century), the latter's detailed account of Leo's death contains the basic information available to Gryphius. Although the dramatist provides useful plot and action summaries of his play in the "Contents" section that precedes the dramatic text, the more specific, detailed information presented in his source text provides a helpful resource that enables a better understanding of the play.

The following excerpts from Cedrenus make available the information known to Gryphius when he set out to construct his first historical tragedy. [15]

---

[14] *Werke,* V, 3. See Gryphius' *Dear Reader* letter below, p 26.

[15] My English translation of Cedrenus is based on the abbreviated German translation by Willi Harring, *Andreas Gryphius und das Drama der Jesuiten,* (Halle: Niemeyer, 1907), 53-58, as reprinted in the Reclam edition of *Leo Armenius* (Stuttgart: Reclam, 1971) edited by Peter Rusterholz, 116-21.

Georgios Cedrenus' Text: *Leo the Armenian*

When the Emperor Michael Rhangabe lost a battle with the Bulgarians, the army deserted him and, at the instigation of Michael Balbus, a subordinate general, it recognized General Leo the Armenian as emperor.

Leo exiled Michael Rhangabe and his followers and rewarded his friend Michael Balbus by making him a patrician and appointing him commander of the Imperial Guard. He [Leo] was luckier than his predecessor in battle against the Bulgarians, who, filled with pride over their recently achieved victory, surged anew against the Romans. He conquered them and returned home in triumph. Then he remembered the monk at Philomelium who earlier had prophesied that Leo would someday be emperor. He wanted to reward this prophecy with gifts and therefore dispatched one of his loyal subjects with many valuable presents. That monk had already died, however, and a certain Sabbatius, a member of the Iconoclasts, had succeeded him. He refused the gifts because the emperor followed the icon cult and obeyed the instructions of the Empress Irene and the Patriarch Tarasius. Cursing both of them, he threatened the emperor with a quick end of his rule and his life if he didn't immediately remove the holy images. Terrified by this threat, the emperor discussed with Theodot of Melissen just what he ought to do. The latter, however, was also a member of the heretical faction [Iconoclasts] and he took advantage of this opportunity to win over the emperor. He advised him to request the counsel of a Dagestanian [Russian] monk, who was famous for his amazingly accurate prophecies. Immediately after this conversation, however, Theodot went to the monk and informed him that during the following night the emperor, dressed in simple clothing, would come to him in order to seek his counsel. He should then foretell him of the impending loss of his sovereign power and his life if he didn't destroy the holy images, but that if he did initiate this destruction, then his reign and life would last forever. When Theodot had thus prepared the monk, he led the emperor to him the following night. The emperor, who considered it to be the monk's own amazing power to have recognized him immediately in spite of his disguise, was deeply moved by what the monk instructed him to do, and he hastened to fulfill his wish. The command to destroy the images brought forth great agitation among the nobles and princes of the church. The Patriarch Nicephorus refused to sign the emperor's edict and was deposed. Theodot received his position and henceforth campaigned for his heretical doctrine no longer in secret, but openly and loudly.

Leo, however, had become uncontrollable due to his victory over the Bulgarians and a successful blow against the Arabs. He became mean and inclined towards cruelty, was irreconcilable in anger, and punished crimes most severely. For minor misdeeds he meted out the heaviest penalties. He had the hands of some, the legs of others, and other members of yet others cut off and displayed in the streets to frighten the populace. Because of this, he was extremely hated. And not only did he rage against men, but also against religion and against God. He cared for the welfare of the state, however, in the best possible way; and he executed a just severity against criminals.

Michael Balbus, a man who to be sure was not distorted by vices like the others, but who could not control his tongue, had chastised the emperor by threatening him with the loss of his ruling power and by declaring that his marriage to Theodosia was illegal. He had once already been accused of a crime against majesty, but had been able to clear himself of the charge. When the emperor heard of this he at first tried to change Michael's mind, but when that did not succeed, he had him watched by spies. Wise Exabolius gained Balbus' confidence the most. He often warned him not to get himself into trouble with his big mouth, but since that didn't help, he revealed Balbus' plans to the emperor. And thus on the day before Christmas the trial took place. Michael was accused of plotting to take control. Because of the overwhelming evidence against him, he had to admit his guilt, and thus he was condemned to death by fire.

Just as he was about to be led away in chains to his death, Theodosia, the emperor's wife, rushed forth from her chambers and called Leo a blasphemer of God, since he was not even going to observe the holy day of Christ's birth. Leo was frightened at the thought of insulting God, and he postponed the execution. Michael was held captive in chains. Leo entrusted the watch to the chief guardian of the palace, Papias. But he placed all the blame on his wife in case the matter did not run smoothly.

And he had cause enough for fear, since he had received prophesies of his death in oracles and visions. Thus he is said to have received an oracle according to which he would lose his rule and his life on the birthday of Christ. This was a sybillic oracle that was in a volume of the royal library. In this volume there were also figures painted with the features of the emperor. Here there was the picture of a lion [Leo] on which the letter X was inscribed from his back to his stomach, and from behind a man was piercing the lion with a lance directly through this letter. An interpreter was questioned and said that Leo would someday be emperor, but would perish in a humiliating death on the birthday of Christ. Leo was no less frightened by a vision that his mother had experienced. In her sleep she saw herself as she entered the holy temple of the Mother of God at Blachern and met a virgin who was followed by many boys dressed in white. She saw the temple filled with blood. One of these boys dressed in white told the virgin to fill a cup with blood and to give it to Leo's mother to drink. She refused it with a shudder, however, and the virgin responded angrily: "Why doesn't your son stop covering himself with blood and thereby provoking me and my son?" Thereafter Leo's mother constantly thought about this vision, and she never tired of pleading with her son to drop the heresy of iconoclasm.

Yet a third prophesy frightened Leo. As he slept he saw the ghost of Tarasius, who already had been dead for a long time, as he [Tarasius] admonished and incited someone named Michael to attack the emperor and to knock him to the ground with a deadly thrust.

In addition there was also the prophecy of the monk at Philomelium, who had foretold that "Leo and Thomas would be emperor" but had added that "both, however, would be killed by Michael." And finally Leo remembered the incident that had occurred when he had just come to power. He had at that time wanted to offer God a prayer of gratitude for his successful ascension, and he handed his cloak to the prefect Michael Balbus. The latter, however, immediately put it on. All those who saw this considered it to be a sign that Michael would rule after Leo, and when Leo, dressed in another garment, entered into the temple, Michael carelessly stepped on the hem of the imperial garment. That, too, Leo considered to be an unfavorable sign.

Frightened at the thought of all these things, the emperor could not sleep during the night following Michael's conviction. He rose to see if the prisoner was being guarded carefully. When he entered the house of the chief palace guard, however, he experienced a great shock. He saw the condemned man resting on a splendid, lofty cushion, while the chief palace guard (Papias) slept on the bare floor. It surprised the emperor even more that Michael wasn't sleeping restlessly as someone who is in fear and danger of his life normally does, but that on the contrary, he slept so soundly and peacefully that he could not even arouse him by touching him. Filled with anger, he resolved to carry out not only Michael's death, but also that of his unfaithful guard, who honored the condemned man as if he were the emperor. But the incident did not remain unknown to the chief guard, since one of the guards had recognized the emperor by his red shoes. Papias, beside himself with fear, therefore decided to flee with his family. Dawn was approaching when Michael made the following rescue plan: one of his followers would have to ask the emperor if he could fetch a priest for Michael so that he could confess his sins. With the emperor's permission, Theoctist left the castle with the secret mandate from Michael to his sworn colleagues that if they did not immediately free him from his precarious situation he would inform the emperor of the whole conspiracy. The conspirators drew up a plan by which they saved themselves and secured life and rule for Michael. With daggers hidden beneath their garments, they dispersed themselves among the priests who entered the temple in the morning, and they went in with them. When the hymn had faded, the emperor appeared and sang as he was accustomed, with a powerful voice, the song: "To altogether sing out, that is my wish." Then the conspirators attacked him. At first they struck the priest by mistake, because he looked like the emperor or had covered his head with a similar garment. The emperor hid in a corner of the altar, tore down a chain from the censer, or as others report, the holy cross, and then tried in vain to defend himself with it. He received the blows of the murderers.

As Leo still defended himself, he raised his hand in order to implore the attackers to spare him. Among them was one from the family of Crambonites; he cut off Leo's hand with the words: "Now is not the time to implore, but to murder!" Finally the emperor succumbed to his wounds.

Thus Leo died, who more than his predecessors had been cruel and godless, but who also had proven his concern for the administration of the state and his bravery in war. The murderers carried Leo's corpse to the circus on animal skins. They also drove the empress from the palace with her four sons; Symbatios, Basil, Gregory, and Theodosios. They were exiled to the island of Prote and were castrated. Michael, however, was freed from imprisonment and with the chains still on his feet, he sat upon the royal couch. He was hailed as emperor by all.

And now may you enjoy the comments on the writing and publication of his play, the dedication of his play, and the prefatory program notes provided by the renowned poet and dramatist Andreas Gryphius as you prepare to read his first drama, *Leo Armenius or Regicide.*

XLIV.

To H. Caspar Dietzel

On the Writing and Publication of *Leo Armenius*[16]

The much-hated prince, whom indeed the great city
Of the Bosphorus crowned, yet against whom were united
Earth, heaven, friend and foe; who, through cumulative wounds
  Was toppled from this throne, which he had ascended by force;
  The prince, who dying, teaches how soon the swift wheel
Of fortune is reversed, has, now that he has totally disappeared,
Through the assistance of my hand, again found his life,
  Which the murderers' sword had so quickly abbreviated.
I was wrong; he fell previously when Byzantium killed him,
He falls now through the hand that describes his death,
  He falls now because my writing can't be read.
Yet the one who died three times must live threefold through you,
Mr. Dietzel, whose hand and press can grant him this
  Which Byzantium, my poem, and my manuscript took from him.

---

[16] This sonnet addressed by Gryphius to the Strassburg printer Caspar Dietzel before the poet left Strassburg in 1647 appeared in *The Second Book of Sonnets*, 1650. Dietzel had intended to first publish *Leo Armenius* in 1647. Gryphius, *Werke*, I, 88-89.

Translation of Gryphius' Latin dedication of *Leo Armenius*
to Wilhelm Schlegel.[17]

To WILHELM SCHLEGEL
The heir in Castayn and Mohringen,[18]
In sum, to my master and friend,
Many Greetings!

The furies of sinister night and the unholy crime,
The rule of a crumbling court, rule stained by
Seizure, with the leader trampled underfoot,
The horrid altar alive with the emperor's flowing blood
And the ashes of the realm, these things
You (Wilhelm), whom the prince (Leo) designates as critic with full powers,
A prince, who is the concern of the gods and the shaker of lands,
Consent to approve with your face and the suns of your visage (eyes),
And let no darkness distract the mind of Gryphius
Or the very auspicious light that is yours, and may you sigh
Only at the imagined furies of the night and the crimes enacted on the stage.

Strassburg, November 1646 (Gregorian calendar)

---

[17] I am grateful to my former teacher and present colleague, Professor Theodore M. Andersson, for his invaluable assistance in translating this dedication. Gryphius' Latin dedication appears in *Werke,* V, 2.

[18] These two estates of Wilhelm Schlegel's father were located near Stettin, Germany (modern Szczecin, Poland).

Dear Reader: Introductory letter Gryphius included prior
to the text of *Leo Armenius*

Dear Reader,

Since our entire fatherland now buries itself in its own ashes and morphs
into a theater of vanity, it is my intent to present to you the transitory nature
of human affairs in this present and in several following tragedies. Indeed not
because I don't have something else and something perhaps more pleasant for
you at hand, but because presenting anything different at this time is still as little
favored as it is permitted to me. The ancients, after all, did not consider this manner of writing as unimportant, but praised it as a convenient means to cleanse
human minds of all kinds of wayward and harmful inclinations: as would not
be difficult to prove if others before me had not done this extensively, and if I
didn't loathe to draw notice to that which is hidden to no one. Much less am I of
a mind to praise this work, which will be submitted now to external criticisms,
with splendid and lengthy prefaces. Bad books are not improved by acclaim, and
natural beauty requires no cosmetics. However I just have to remind you that
since our Leo was a Greek emperor, he will also reveal much to his reader that
is partly not praised and partly not allowed currently ruling princes. The entire
course of his demise is explained in detail by Cedrenus and Zonaras, who write
with a pen not only about his death, but also actually articulate everything in
such a detailed way that it hasn't been necessary to mix in many other concepts.

What was present in the above-mentioned references regarding dreams, visions, strange images, and such things is reported in all the accounts of these
nations. Indeed a similar book full of strange pictures still reached me personally a few years ago, out of which, for those whose brains were pregnant with
researching things of the future, several not insignificant things (according to
their fancy) were learned about the recapture of the previously splendid but now
(unfortunately!) servile state, about the fall of the Turks, the unity of Christians

in matters of belief, and the common conversion of the Jews. Therefore no one ought to hold completely in vain what Zonaras and Cedrenus thought and what we have cited from them out of perhaps the same book. Also it's not so unheard of to use secret revelations to wage war and peace, to seize kingdom and scepter for oneself, indeed to flood entire countries with blood like a new deluge. Not only Europe, all of Asia and Africa will offer probably a hundred for one example of this truth, and in the new world no less than among us this pestilence sets into action monstrous murder and knavery, recently under the pretense of serving God (like Michael and his allies). It's undeniable that the dying emperor grabbed a cross during the hovering danger of death right before his eyes: however, the historian did not say that it was exactly the same one on which our Redeemer sacrificed himself, indeed, if you examine his word, he much more said the opposite. But nevertheless, since at that time the remaining bits of the great altar-of-the-Son or (as the Greeks say) the Holy pieces of wood, were safely kept in Constantinople: we have yielded to the art of poetry, which otherwise is not allowed much freedom on this stage, to make it the same. Those who get mixed up in this heresy that no tragedy can be complete without love and courting are hereby reminded that we're not of a mind to believe this opinion unknown to the ancients and we consider the same work hardly praiseworthy, that recently led a holy martyr to battle and, against the basis of truth, assigned a wife to the same martyr, who finds almost more to do with her flirting than the prisoner finds to do with the judge, and through the involvement of her father becomes a bride instead of a widow. However, in order not to lose completely the same favor; we herewith assure you, that as soon as possible our Shah Abas, in *The Proven Constancy of Catharine of Georgia,* shall fully play a part that cannot be suitable for Leo. Who, since he was not created by Sophocles or Seneca, is certainly ours. Another might snatch names from the discoveries of foreigners and put them forward as his own: We conclude with the words, which that well-known and most praiseworthy Welsh[19] poet wrote above his front gable:

> This house may not be grand: yet it knows me alone:
> It owes nothing to others: it is simply fine and mine.

---

[19] The term *Welsh* refers to French speaking citizens in German localities such as Alsace/Strassburg or Switzerland.

Content of the Tragedy

Michael Balbus, Emperor Leo Armenius' supreme commander, after having been charged on several occasions for his disloyalty and libel, swears an oath against the emperor, who often warned him through Exabolius, his (Leo's) privy counselor, to desist from his recklessness. However, because Michael persists with his resolution, he is unexpectedly taken prisoner and condemned to death by fire at the court in which the emperor serves as plaintiff and judge. But as Michael is being led to the stake, the emperor postpones his punishment until after the Christmas celebration due to the fervent insistence of his wife, Theodosia. Meanwhile, Michael seeks every possible means to save himself. Because the emperor is upset by fear and Michael's audacity, he personally visits the prison at night and finds Michael, dressed in purple, sleeping. Michael, in utter despair after being informed of this by a guard who had recognized the emperor because of his embroidered shoes, threatens the conspirators that he will expose them if he is not aided immediately. But the conspirators successfully enter the palace by means of a special ruse, and they mercilessly murder the emperor before the altar.

This takes place in the year 820 after the birth of our Redeemer, in the seventh year and fifth month of his rule, as the ghost of Tarasius had prophesied in a vision shortly before the event. Cedrenus and Zonarus relate the history in greater detail in their *Leo Armenius* and *Michael Balbus*. The tragedy begins at noon before Christmas Day; it continues through the night and ends before sunrise. The setting is Constantinople, primarily the Imperial Palace.

Characters of the Tragedy

Leo Armenius, Emperor of Constantinople

Theodosia, Wife of the Emperor

Michael Balbus, General

Exabolius, Privy Councilor to the Emperor

Nicander, Captain of the Imperial Guards

Phronesis, Supervisor of the Imperial Ladies of the Court

Tarasius, Ghost of the Patriarch of Constantinople

The Judges

The Conspirators, including the Crambonite

Papias

The Trabant Guards

The Highest Priest

A Messenger

Iamblichus, a Magician[20]

---

[20] The name *Jamblich* appears in explanatory notes of Ludovicus Cellotius' conjuration scene in *Sapor admonitus,* a Jesuit play known to Gryphius. Jamblichus (245-325) was a Syrian Neoplatonist philosopher, the purported author of *Iamblichus de Mysteriis Aegyptiorum, Chaldaeorum, Assyriorum,etc.*, published in Lyon (1570) and Leiden (1607).

A Servant of the Crambonite

The Spirit from Hell

A Guard

A Trumpeter

The Choruses of Members of the Court, Virgins and Priests

Silent Characters

Chambermaids of the Empress

Personal Servants of the Emperor

Messengers

A Boy who attends the Magician

A Ghost in Michael's figure, appearing to the Emperor with the Ghost Tarasius

The First Act

Scene 1

Michael Balbus, the Crambonite, the Conspirators.

Michael: The blood that you ventured in vain for throne and crown,   1
   The wounds that you bear openly on your every limb,
   The unrewarded service, the care-filled life
   That day after day you must yield to plundering;
   The cruel intent of the prince, the discord in the state,   5
   The controversy in the church and dishonesty in the council,
   The unrest in the palace: oh, most flourishing of all heroes,
   These matters struggle in my soul and force me to proclaim
   What cannot be kept silent! Who are we? Are we the ones
   Before whom barbarians have so often dropped to their knees;   10
   Before whom Saracen and Persian and even he, who injures more
   When he flees than when he stands firm, are terrified?
   Who are we? Are we the ones, who often in dust and despair
   Yet filled with blood, with courage and spirit, defied cruel death?
   Who covered the broad land with the enemies' hide   15
   And overturned Sidas[21] and set ablaze
   Whatever showed us weapons? And do we now fall asleep,
   Now that everyone wants to be tyrant over us?
   But ye heroes wake up! Can your fighting hands allow
   That realm and land and state will thus go to ruin   20
   While Leo cleanses himself in his subjects' blood
   And always quenches his thirst for wealth with your goods?
   What is the court anymore but a den of murderers?

---

[21] Sidas was a district between Boeothea and Athens.

But a place of betrayers? A dwelling of bad boys?
He who skillfully flatters and squeals on whomever he can,   25
He is presented to princes: a straightforward man,
Who has often forced a well-equipped army to retreat,
Remains unheralded and withers! What does this weak lamenting
                                        accomplish?
Nothing, if a woman's heart beats in your breast!
But much, if a hero's courage that no fear terrorizes!   30
Whoever is hesitant has heard too little from me:
A hero has heard more than enough. And yet a woman destroyed
The imperial power not long ago, as you know.
The mother had her child taken from throne to prison
Where it had to end its life in greatest torture   35
As both eyes were cruelly ripped out.
A weak arm accomplished this. How can we boast of ourselves?
Irene is worthy of praise.

The Crambonite: Ha, long wished-for match!
Look, hero! Here is a sword, and this fist can stab
And cut, if necessary, and can smash the heads of princes.   40
What is a prince? A human being! And I'm as good as he!
Indeed, even better! If it weren't for me, if it weren't for my sword,
Where would his crown be? The dazzling diamonds,
The purple-golden garb, the companies of trabant guards,
The scepter, fancy toy; all are but an empty splendor.   45
It is an unwavering arm that makes the prince
And, when necessary, displaces him.

First Conspirator: Oh, Judge of all things!
Must your revenge at last awaken from its dreams?
So be it! It summons us, when we least expect it.
Who is there who knows not what vexes my soul   50
And gnaws at my heart and life? That honest spirit,
The more than pious prince, the image of gentle goodness,

The trusted Michael,*[22] was forced -- when the lion became enraged

And charged at him with cruel treachery and mad power –

To lay down his staff and crown. He relinquished the royal purple   55

And put on a hair shirt with the intent of dedicating

The rest of his brief time at altars to his god!

But no! Leo, who was impassioned by nothing but murder and ridicule,

Broke his solitude and banned him from church and the realms

Forcing him to yield before him from throne into the dust.   60

Exiled to the isle of Prote, he who once held this great land

Encompassed in his command, is now encompassed by a narrow

                                          isle of sand

That each moment is washed by the desolate sea!

His son Theophylact!* What has he not felt

When his male parts were torn from his loins   65

And his brother's penis was thrown in his face?

Break forth long wished-for day, that so many thousand tears,

The power of so many sighs and so much sorrowful longing

Demand! Oh, break forth! My life may pass away

If only my foot can first trample on your head,   70

You bloodhound! You tyrant! If I can avenge the atrocity

Then a quick spear may pierce me on the spot.

Second Conspirator: Let him suffer what he did!*

                                 Indeed that day is dawning

Insofar as the human spirit can divine the future,

Insofar as the wise soul can escape from the prison   75

In which flesh and adversity and time and labor force it,

And, feathered by reason, can soar through the air

And observe the obscure: thus must the tyrant

Fall by a faithful hand, as booty to the sword.

I think I already hear the trumpets of revenge resound!   80

---

[22] This and following asterisks in the dramatic text indicate that Gryphius appended an explanatory note to the asterisked item in his *Explanation of Several Obscure References* (see below, p. 123 ff.). Note: Brackets [ ] are used throughout the dramatic text to enclose clarifications provided by the translator.

Michael: What does this speech imply?
Second Conspirator: The splendid chamber
    Atop the castle that is constructed from the ground up to the roof
    Of alabaster, precious metals, and marble
    Is not so much embellished by the splendor of gold and riches
    As by writings with higher meanings. Many an old parchment   85
    Presents to us the heroes who knew Persia and Scythia,
    Who sacrificed their lives for their fatherland
    And dampened their proud swords in the enemies' blood.
    What can the pen not accomplish that gives life to him
    Upon whom death and time have executed their power!   90
    The course of the suns, the fleeting essence of the stars,
    The characteristics of plants all can be read on a thousand pages.
    The art of the Greeks, the ways of distant lands,
    And what a human mind conceives is preserved on paper.
    And what is more, how one can know that which is hidden   95
    And how and when a person's life will end.
    Often before, and to be sure not fruitlessly, I have
    Searched through an unknown work filled with drawings
    In which, as is thought, everything that every prince
    Who has occupied this throne has done, is chronicled in symbols.   100
    How long this realm will stand in full blossom:
    How in the future each prince will rise and fall:
    One learns from this book the anxiety, the burden that oppresses us,
    And the means to untangle the distress in which we're bound.
    It tells the cycle of times that violate the church and the world   105
    And also place secure peace in severest misery.
    The synopsis shows us an image of the lion
    Who seems to threaten with inflamed spirit and claws:
    He tosses his front paw into the air as if enraged;
    His hair flies about his head; yes, the portrait shouts   110
    Of his cruel manner; his bright eyes burn,
    Inflamed with mad rage; his jowl can scarcely be discerned
    Due to the foam and fresh blood that flows to the ground

As he begins bite after bite and murder upon murder.

What could be clearer? A purplish red cross embellishes 115

His strong back; the clever hunter guides,

With a more than swift fist, a sharply whetted sword

That penetrates cross, skin, and flesh into the lion's heart.

You know the wild beast: the cross is Christ's symbol,

Before whose birthday passes, our lion will pale and die. 120

Michael: I want to be the hunter. Whoever stands with me

For honor and country and life; whoever pledges his spirit

As security for fame and freedom; whoever has the courage to dare;

Whoever is reluctant to bear any more the burden so bitter;

Whoever desires revenge and reward; whoever can trample

death and eternity 125

With his feet—let him contribute at this time

With counsel and action, and help seek out the means

To carry out the attack without delay and suspicion.

The Crambonite: We'll go wherever you command.

Michael: I swear to venture

Body and blood for the realm and the common welfare. 130

Do what you consider necessary.

The Crambonite: Hand over your sword. We swear

To transform the cruel power of the prince into powdery dust.

Scene 2

Leo Armenius, Exabolius, Nicander.

Leo: So he no longer heeds advice or warning?

Exabolius: That's right! Reprimands, requests, and threats are scorned.

He races like a horse that has snapped the reins; 135

Like a powerful river, when the streams pour out

And sweep houses, trees, and cattle into the sea.

His audacity grows more and more; he (if I understand it right)

Has now taken upon himself such an act

As the greatest perjury rarely has devised before now. 140

Leo: Faithless fool! Man misled by delusion!

    Ingrate, more depraved than depravity itself!

    Bedeviled spirit! Cursed senses,

    That no honesty or beneficence can win over!

    I brought you, mad dog, from the gutter to the court   145

    And here, on my own lap, made you famous and great!

    Has the cold snake, which now bites, cheated us?

    Was this basilisk raised at our breast?

    Why weren't you strangled for this insolent deed

    Before your treason was eventually revealed to the great council?   150

    Have noble courage and reason befooled us?

    Did I strengthen the arm that now rises against us?

    But what is a prince beyond a crowned servant,

    Whom every moment something high, something low, something evil,

    Something powerful defies and scorns. Whom always,

                        from both sides,   155

    Envy, faithless suspicion, hate, pain, anxiety, and fear embattle.

    To whom does he entrust his body, when he spends the long night

    In ceaseless worry and remains alert for the states,

    Who observe his trappings more than his bitter anguish,

    And (because he is no longer free) scorn that which

                        deserves glory?   160

    Whom does he accept at the court? The one who risks his life

    First for him, and then against him, and chases him from the court

    When the game changes. One must honor his mortal enemy,

    See with blind eyes, hear with deaf ears.

    No matter how his heart burns with anger and zeal,   165

    One must be courteous in words, and elevate to honorable offices

    Him, who tramples regiment and crown with his feet.

    How often the perpetrator has been forgiven for this crime!

    How often! What do we lament? No lamenting will help here,

    But only quick counsel.

Nicander: Crush him before he lashes out.   170

Leo: If he should die without a verdict, who would not mourn for him?

Nicander: The Sovereign must not question simple words so much!

Leo: A simple word often wreaks not-so-simple havoc.

    The populace, officers, steed, and knave look only to this man.

Exabolius: Let him be bound and arraigned at the palace.   175

Leo: How? What if, as before, he reduces the complaints to nothing?

Exabolius: The sanction is too clear!

Leo: So was the last one, yet he got away.

Nicander: That is why he breathes revenge and murder.

Leo: His following is too great.

Exabolius: If his head is cut off, then no limb can cause any more damage.

Leo: We would burden ourselves with the hatred and malice of many.   180

Exabolius: Hatred is not heeded if it is a matter of crown and scepter.

Leo: He has filled South, East, and West with his fame.

Exabolius: Now South, East, and West will curse his crime.

Leo: If only East and West do not avenge his punishment.

Exabolius: A bird flees the tree upon which thunder strikes.   185

Leo: The great, desolate forest is moved by the strike.

Exabolius: Moved and also shocked. One learns to avoid the cliffs

    On which someone else's mast has had to suffer shipwreck.

Leo: He has the sword's hilt; unfortunately we hardly have the sheath.

Exabolius: So move your hand before he stabs! It is time to strike or suffer.   190

Leo: Who will be able to fasten his audacious fist in irons?

Exabolius: Where strength is useless, one must resort to cunning.

Nicander: Let him be seized unexpectedly as soon as he comes this way.

Leo: Reluctantly we support what cannot be changed.

    We feel our soul compromised by his guilt;   195

    We hear his long service plead for his crime.

    The excessive favor that we often have granted to him,

    His marble-firm audacity, which no warning can bend,

    Inflame our wrath. We regret his strength.

    Yet our spirit becomes enraged if we even superficially   200

    View his deeds! It will have to thunder,

    Since no lightning frightens him. Tell him once again

    He is to appear upon our summons in the palace.

If he can be changed, if (as we hardly suspect)

He confesses his guilt and honors the one whom he injured   205

In pious humility, no sword will be sharpened here.

Insofar as he (as is customary) wants to sing the same old song,

Nicander, tie him up. Let the proud head roll

That cannot bow.

Scene 3

Nicander, Exabolius.

Nicander: A not unhoped-for conclusion!

    Yet a gravity that is much overdue. Pardon me, but I must   210

    Make known what oppresses me. The emperor is too mild

    And jokes with his well-being: whoever wants to watch the flames,

    When the raw winds set up camp around the embers

    Until the gable and the highest roof are involved,

    Unfortunately cries out in vain when the walls and pillars crack   215

    And stone and marble falls. The arch-traitors stay awake;

    We fall asleep, assured. They seek our death;

    We worry about their fortune and now that dire necessity

    Already begins to embattle us with a bare sword,

    We think of lulling them into a dream with words.   220

    But why, Exabolius, does one speak to the deaf?

    The snake plugs its ear. The sword alone will bring peace

    To the emperor, to you, and to me. I'm supposed to tie up the murderer!

    Why not penetrate his breast with this dagger?

    That is how to end his defiance. This is Nicander's advice!   225

    A great act is lauded only when the deed is done!

Exabolius: I'll gladly confirm that his damaged conscience

    Can atone for all his atrocities with nothing except blood and death.

    Yet if punishment is meted out to a man without a hearing

    He is always revered as righteous, no matter how tainted he may be.   230

Nicander: Do you intend to extinguish the rapid pestilence that

                                         spreads this moment

With an extended trial? Do you intend to fight using the law

When he is grasping the pike? He errs, who tolerates

But for a day the one whose neck he might soon break.

Exabolius: A long time will not be lost with lawsuits here!   235

Nicander: I can execute a quick sentence with this sword.

Exabolius: The emperor's reputation doesn't allow such quick judges.

Nicander: The emperor's welfare begs for and condones what I am doing.

Exabolius: Why would you want to give envy cause to blaspheme?

Nicander: Why should this leader of the revolt live on?   240

Exabolius: His demise is certain if he does not reverse his ways at once.

Nicander: If his sword does not pass through our hearts first.

Exabolius: Your zeal is indeed good, Nicander, but too heated.

Nicander: Exabolius, do not make the accusation all too pointed

Or he will stab us yet, himself.

Exabolius: Do what the emperor bids;   245

Station a guard in the hall and court; in the event the cocky soul

Will not keep within his limits, then let him be seized straightaway.

Nicander: The strongest contingent must be brought to the

adjoining chamber!

Exabolius: Stay behind the tapestry with the body guards.

Nicander: Right you are! Thus I will hear how this game will play out.   250

Scene 4

Exabolius, Michael Balbus.

Michael: Exabolius, where might I be able to find the emperor?

Exabolius: I believe he will be granting you an audience right away.

Michael: What is this "I believe?" What does he do without you?

Exabolius: He does whatever occurs to him. The emperor rules by himself.

Michael: Why so crestfallen? So still? So forlorn? So aggrieved?   255

What is that sigh about? Has he, whom you loved,

Has Leo, who now spares no friends at all,

Rewarded your long service with disfavor, as is his custom?

He is silent! He turns away! I have hit on what is the matter!

Does one thus have no more to hope for than such gratitude?   260
One who plunges himself into burning danger and deep distress
Even as the prince passes time with a thousand pleasures.
He swims in a sea of bliss beyond desire
While we stand in armor and suffer dust and sun
And take to the field against enemy and air and land.   265
We risk our lives when armies flee before us
But then it is said: the emperor did it. The trophies are engraved
With his titles when we pale in the grass;
For our fame and strength and courage and rank
And deeds and service are covered with a handful of sand.   270
If one brings his tired body, his wounded limbs,
His half-mangled head and chest, back to court again,
Then he beholds us as those on loan to him.
And wherever there is a wretched job that no one can do,
Wherever there is a desperate place that no one knows how to save,   275
Wherever there is a dangerous office—that is what we are
                                                  sent to manage
And he staffs us with traitors to keep himself informed—
So that here there is more fear and adversity than in the worst conflict.
Until we make a mistake or the prince takes a certain notion,
And then we are robbed of honor and possessions
                                                  together with our head.   280
Exabolius: My friend! Your loose mouth will bring you to greatest distress.
     If anyone should hear us, you are a living corpse.
Michael: I protest that it is no longer permitted to say aloud
     What unfortunately is more than true. A careless word
     Is treated like a crime worthy of sword and pillar.   285
     Where has freedom fled? Freedom, whose place
     Has been taken by a mouth as sweet as honey, a flatterer,
     Who by maneuvering has arrived at this place
     That my fist earned. I spit upon myself
     For being able to watch this crooked game so long.   290
     The man who pushed himself onto the throne by fraudulence

(As earth and sun well know); who puts down no enemy

Except with a foreign sword; who hears no proposal

That is a bit unpleasant; who honors gossips

And suppresses virtue and suspects honesty 295

And aggrieves himself with strange fear and false suspicion:

Who never laid waste a foreign nation with steel and fire

And constantly dyes his claws in the blood of Byzantines;

Who lets himself be ruled by every knave and lad

And scandalously lets himself be led around the light,

                                     as if by the nose. 300

He is the one, whom you and I must behold with trembling!

He is the one, to whom we entrust our realm, our goods, our lives.

How long will fear, illusion, and terror still blind us?

Insofar as you want what I do, then in these hands exists

The end of tyranny.

Exabolius: The beginning of new pain. 305

    I will request what I may.

Michael: Withhold all requests

    And do what suits your honor and bravery.

Exabolius: I do what friendship bids; whoever shows to one who is misled

    The proper way, whoever restrains a man

    Who is dashing towards the chasm, and

                        whoever subordinates himself 310

To this one who now falls, does more than just wishing.

You seek what is hardly found by blood, by strangling and laying waste

And flame and death; sooner would the proud calm

Of the safe countries shrink! Call forth shield and spear!

Engage all swords! Can you believe without doubt 315

That all rob not for themselves, but just to benefit you?

And another thing! Who will join us? Four hands cannot do it!

Many hands could, if one mouth did not break the oath of all.

Given, too, that we already press with a thousand armies

Into the imperial palace and occupy the court and city: 320

Would Leo most likely stand alone without sword and shield?

Certainly not! Those who now walk at his side,

Whom his power elevated, and who live only through him,

They must give their hearts and necks for his crown.

Why? His fall would be their ruin.   325

Also the one for whom he does something bitterly responds:

Who always pleads for a new age and new masters,

And only lauds what is hoped for; and curses what is at hand,

Who boasts of nothing except his strength and of rusty red spikes,

And what the strong Persian lost in such and such a battle,   330

He is bold enough to kill the tyrant and prince.

When the reveling at midnight banquets with glasses

Melts away full of heated fear, when the trumpet sounds,

When swords are grasped and the armor rattles,

Many wish only to curb the power of the prince,   335

Not to do away with him entirely. Many can put up with strangers;

More can tolerate only their own blood! The uncertain power

Of weapons is not steady. Whoever in a game

Wants to play for thrones can disappear in a battle;

This, what he seeks and hopes and already holds in his hands,   340

Will find fear and woe and pain-filled despair,

And after experienced torture will find the port of lamentation: death.

Heaven itself watches over crowned heads

And supports the scepter. They struggle towards their bier

And reach, unexpectedly, a quick and horrible end   345

Who are bedazzled by the jeweled gold of a heavy crown.

Consider also what it is like to always move as a captive

Of so many thousand worries. When the confounded morning

Exposes the world's anxiety, to hear what

The Persians' sword suppresses; in what direction the

                                        Scythian[23] horse   350

---

[23] Originally a large group of Iranian Eurasian nomads, the Scythians were among the first masters of mounted warfare.

Deploys its swift foot; what Susa[24] has undertaken;

How far the Barbarian might be, how far the Goth has come,

That now the Huns' wrath already penetrates the Danube,

That Cyprus is estranged, that Asia is offended,

That Colchos[25] conceives new intrigues and Pontus[26]

                               invents new cunning,   355

That soon the proud Frank will gain in Greece;

That Taurus[27] is no longer loyal; now the great city,

The queen of the world, dictates what can be hoped for;

Now Illyria[28], soon Sparta, send us emissaries;

Soon Egypt will demand aid, and our allies   360

Will make known what oppresses them. Soon the army

                                will call for pay,

The nations will withhold grain, the cities will lack gold.

Now the foamy waves want to roll right up to the walls;

Now the envy of heaven doesn't want to water the fields:

The severe Titan singes away the dry sheaves   365

With glowing-hot light; the earth itself breaks

And can no longer stand when the peak of Mt. Hemus[29] trembles;

When the great burden of the heavy tower collapses

And temple and altar and castle and court and house

Are covered in a moment with dust and rubble.   370

Now the foul breeze hastens to sweep in diseases

And infects the nations; soon the borders will be surrounded by those

---

[24] One of the most important cities of the Ancient Near East. The modern Iranian town of Shush is located at the site of ancient Susa.

[25] In Greek legend, Colchos was the place where Jason stole the Golden Fleece.

[26] Region on southern coast of the Black Sea, located in modern Turkey.

[27] Region defined by its proximity to the Taurus mountain range, including Anatolia (Asia Minor), home of several major civilizations, including the Byzantine Empire (359 BC-1300 AD) and the Ottoman Empire (ca. 1300-1922).

[28] As the Roman province *Illyricum* located along the Eastern shore of the Adriatic Sea, the region was known for its military prowess. After the division of the Roman Empire, the bishops of Thessalonica appointed papal vicars for *Illyricum*. In the 8th century, the patriarchs of Constantinople brought Illyria under their jurisdiction.

[29] In antiquity, the Balkan Mountains (Thrace) were known as the *Haemus Mons*.

Who are nourished only by robbery; soon an unknown doctrine,
Aroused by superstition and dark delusion,
Will be brought into action (oh, pestilence of these times!),   375
That holds the power of misleading the whole realm and its people
So that the base of the pillars that bear the crown and royal symbols
And support cross and scepter, will tremble and move.
This does not affect everyone, yet everyone must suffer
His own part for himself. The prince can avoid nothing;   380
He feels the entire burden. When someone commits a crime
Who works in his service, the rabble doesn't fear
Ascribing the guilt, no matter its size, to the prince:
Can anything he does remain unrebuked?
He is fearful of his sword; when he goes to dine,   385
The mixed wine, served in crystal,
Is transformed to gall and poison. As soon as the day fades,
That blackened band, the army of anxiety, comes creeping
And keeps watch in his bed. In ivory,
In purple and scarlet, he can never be as peaceful   390
As those who trust their body to the hard ground.
If brief repose be granted to him,
Then Morpheus attacks him and in the night paints for him
With horrible images, what he thought by day
And frightens him first with blood, then with a toppled throne,   395
With conflagration, with sorrow and death and a snatched-away crown.
Do you want to exchange your peace for this burden?
Why? The stream of highest goods rushes toward you!
Do you also yearn for fame? You have climbed so high
That you see the entire empire lying at your feet.   400
The immense power of war rests in your hands.
Whoever is sent to the emperor's palace by princes
Has himself presented to you and then by you to the court.
The Prince can command others; you can command the Prince.
Tolerate something above you! He whom vanity chases,   405
Who ventures into the wide expanse of light breezes

With wings that illusion and pride have bound to him,
Is, before he has reached the goal toward which he struggled,
Drowned in the sea. Indeed Phaeton grabbed
The reins, but as the strong chariot coursed   410
And singed the Niger, Euphrates, and Nile in bright flames,
Even as the thunderbolt exploded on his head
He cursed, although too late, the greatly desired power.

Michael: Tell this to children! A heroic spirit laughs
    At this feeble scare. If a man may live crowned but only a day   415
He will place himself in the greatest danger.
This which seems impossible becomes possible if one dares.
The scepter is considered to be oppressive, yet the one who complains
Does not lay it down freely. Indeed, can a social class be found
That does not have to encircle its own pain with worry?   420
Fear hovers both around straw and sackcloth as it does scarlet.
If Phocas,[30] if Irene[31] sanctioned your counsel
They never would have seized the crown.
If Leo himself delved so deeply into each matter,
If feeble fear intimidated him so effeminately   425
Would Michael likely now be garbed in armor?

Exabolius: If Phocas, if Irene had been more cautious
    Would he have been killed, would she have entered the cloister?
If Leontios [32] would have paid more frequent attention to this,
He would not have had to give up the ghost in the public square,   430
Surrounded with disdain and scorn and martyrdom and fear!

---

[30] Byzantine Emperor 602-610, who usurped the throne from Emperor Maurice (Byzantine Emperor 582-602) but was overthrown by Heraclius (Byzantine Emperor 610-641) after losing a civil war. See *Note* to *Leo Armenius,* III.279, below, p. 125.

[31] Byzantine Empress 797-802. Irene's daring rise ended with a palace revolution and year of exile before her death.

[32] Byzantine Emperor 695-698, Leontios, military commander under Emperor Justinian II (see I.432), usurped the throne of Justinian II (685-695), who returned to power (705-711) until murdered. Prior to Leontios' public execution in 705, Justinian humiliated him by placing his feet on his neck. See *Leo Armenius,* I.432, p. 46, below.

Michael: Would Justinian ever have crushed him with his feet?

    Would he have moved the Bulgarians to aid his recovery

    If he had laid his feeble fist gently in his lap?

Exabolius: He aspired to his empire, from which he had been exiled.   435

Michael: Whoever followed your advice would have remained in misery.

Exabolius: He was driven out by false cunning and turmoil.

Michael: Is it believed that Michael doesn't complain about turmoil?

Exabolius: He willingly gave up that which stifled him too much.

Michael: Yes, when Leo virtually confined him to the palace.   440

Exabolius: He, unarmed, could withstand no enemy.

Michael: Thus he learned to go from the court into the desolate cloister.

Exabolius: Then a hero had to shore up an empire that was

                                      already exploding.

Michael: Why not right now, since the supports will be of no use?

Exabolius: What is it that can justly and truthfully be rebuked?   445

Michael: This: that the emperor never did anything that was praiseworthy.

Exabolius: The vast empire is seen blooming in tranquil peace.

Michael: Because I, not Leo, must wage armed campaigns.

Exabolius: Provisions enter the country with the sail-billowing wind--

Michael: Because the Danube and the Hellespont are secured by me.   450

Exabolius: The Persian gives us gold.

Michael: That I have forced from him.

Exabolius: The primitive Shiite is peaceful.

Michael: He is subdued by me.

    What all is attributed to others, that I have brought into being?

    His life, his crown, exist under my power.

Exabolius: Please don't exaggerate!

Michael: Yet more! Should I keep silent?   455

    Before me, the Franks and Thracians must bow their proud heads;

    The Hellespont fears me. The world which ever-present frost

    Holds imprisoned in ice recoils in fear before me.

    The white-toothed Moor is terrified of the deeds

    That my hand committed. Those who roast in Cyrene   460

    Tell of my deeds and my palm of honor.

What would you have (if it were not for me)? No more emperor.

I raised him to the throne, when Michael (*Rhangabe*) was defeated:

I forced him, so that he had to enter the fray

And am I no longer the one who I was before all of this?   465

My life is his salvation, my threat his funeral bier.

His scepter, crown, and blood rest upon this sword

That has the power to lay his corpse in a cold grave;

That, now that he has become a tyrant and is filled with dark suspicion,

Shall penetrate the cruel fountain of his veins.   470

Scene 5

Michael, Nicander, the Trabant Guards, Exabolius.

Nicander: Surrender!

Michael: What do you intend to do?

Nicander: Upon command of the emperor!

Michael: Traitors!

Nicander: Accuse us of what Michael has committed.

Michael: What?

Nicander: Take away his sword!

Michael: From me?

Nicander: Right now!

Michael: My sword,

That protects your body?

Nicander: And desires our death.

Michael: Heaven help us! What is this?

Nicander: What you had planned to do   475

Has now, doubt not, reached its final goal.

Bring chains!

Michael: Chains? For me?

Nicander: For you, murderer.

Michael: Chains? No!

I want to be unfettered, even if I should die.

Nicander: The emperor desires something more.

Michael: Ha! Your desire has an end.

    Go, executioners.

Guard: Murderer, come.

Michael: Do you want to put in shackles   480

    The one who kept watch over your blood and freedom?

Guard: Now he's struggling with sleep.

Michael: Alas! Am I ridiculed here?

    Before whom the earth trembles? Do you know whom you scorn?

Guard: The one who too soon had himself crowned in Byzantium.

Michael: What incites you against me?

Guard: Your wrongful splendor.   485

    Your own mouth.

Michael: Cursed is he who makes himself a slave

    When he can rule. You lead me into bondage,

    Thoroughly embittered soul. Abyss of the grimmest shame!

    Court hypocrite! Ambiguity! Assassin! Smithy of lies!

    What prevents me from tearing you limb from limb in a rage,   490

    You basilisk, and from rushing to stamp in the dust

    Your sly viper's head? What prevents me?

Guard: The chains.

Exabolius: I showed you the snares.

Michael: You showed me death

Exabolius: I warned you, yet in vain. I threatened you with danger,

     Yet my rescue attempt did not prevail

Michael: So your chicanery must prevail.   495

Exabolius: When one is free of vices, one can rebuke virtue itself.

    Innocence acquits me.

Michael: Ha! Be silent, tyrant's knave.

    Where am I? Heaven help! Where is great justice sleeping?

    Bound, not accused! Condemned, yet not tried!

    Betrayed, by my friend. He, whom the barbarian honors,   500

    Is strangled by the prince of his own race. Alas!

Guard: Away! Away!

Other Guard: Here no escape succeeds.

Guard: To the imperial throne!

Michael: One should sooner draw and quarter me
    Than drag me if I do not go by myself.

Guard: Stab him.

Michael   Yes, stab the dagger,
    Hangman, stab through my heart, as long as my limbs are moving
    Michael is still free. Drag along! Strangle! Press and smash!   505
    Beat! Bind! I am free. Suppress! Martyr! Wrench and tear!
    Even if I stood in glowing sulfur, I will proclaim this:
    That this is the reward of virtue and final gratitude given heroes.

Chorus of the Courtiers

Strophe

The miracle of nature, the wise and then some creature,

Has nothing comparable to his tongue.   510

A wild beast makes known with mute signs

The meaning of its inner heart: we rule through our faculty of speech!

The weight of towers and all that burdens the land;

The building of ships and all that crosses the sea;

The majestic power of the stars,   515

Whatever creates air and flame,

Whatever Clovis displays in her gardens,

Whatever established law requires of all nations;

Whatever God revealed of himself to the world;

Whatever now bursts forth in blossom, whatever has
                        perished through time   520

Will be discovered by this device alone:

Friendship, which abhors death and finality,

The power that has forced wild tribes to civilized ways,

A person's life itself depends upon his tongue.

Antistrophe

And yet there's nothing quite as sharp as a tongue!   525
Nothing, which can cast us poor ones so low.
Oh, would heaven but grant becoming dumb
To him, who is much too free with words!
The rubble of cities, the corpse-strewn field,
The burning of ships, the sea discolored by blood,   530
Black magic,
The vapor of vain doctrine,
The power to thwart the fates by poison,
Bitter hatred among nations, that monster war,
The quarrel that engages church and souls,   535
The decline of virtue, the victory of raging depravity:
All are borne by the power of the tongue,
Through which love and loyalty are lost.
How many a soul the tongue has forced into his grave!
A person's death depends upon each person's tongue.   540

Epode

Learn, you living, to keep a tight rein on your lips,
In which salvation and doom reside,
And that which condemns and rewards.
He who seeks advantage in words should ponder each word.
The tongue is this sword   545
That protects and wounds;
The flame, which so consumes,
And yet so well delights;
A hammer, which builds and breaks;
A rose branch, which perfumes and pricks;   550
A stream, which refreshes and drowns;
The medicine, which revitalizes and sickens;
The track, on which there's often failure and success.
Your life, man, and your death, always depend upon your tongue.

The Second Act

Scene 1

Leo, Michael, the Judges.

Leo: Whoever sets out upon the rigid course of honors
      And loves the righteous appearance of true virtue;
      Whoever wants to live and die only for his fatherland,
      And expects to earn well-deserved gratitude from someone;
      Whoever supports himself on the weak gold of the weighty scepter,   5
      And builds upon hearts that he protected in adversity,
      That he raised from wretched dust to highest eminence,
      Let him come and behold us! One light had brought us joy
      From earliest youth on! When one seized the spear
      And charged into the dense band of fierce enemies.   10
      When we, bespattered with blood, covered with fame-worthy wounds,
      Intertwined with steel and death, found our first name [Leo=Lion]:
      There we also found envy. He who with bared sword
      Defied the Romans' army, he, who turned back nations
      That our defense covered, was terrified at our victory.   15
      Whoever was next to us in praise had to lie low in their tents
      And seek out what had become of us; they minimized the battle
      That brought victor's palms and laurel wreaths upon this head.
      Thus is the first flame, before it can raise itself up,
      Engulfed with dark saturated fumes and black smoke,   20
      Until it heats itself up and spreads to the trees,
      So that the forest, still green, crackles in bright fire.
      Yet, like the strong north wind tends with wild speed
      To stir up the blaze more strongly even as it tries to
                              extinguish it by blowing;

Like a noble horse, when it feels the blow,   25
Runs through the sand and barriers; thus did the strong wind
Of disfavor (although unfortunate) drive us so far
Until both friends and enemies were under foot.
Until Thracian and Saracen and Pontus looked upon our diligence
And ever-equipped arm and melancholy sweat   30
With judgment: the mobs of Ishmaelites
(The terror of these times) joined together to charge
Whoever declared themselves Roman; the greatly distraught land
Trembled with fright as the rapid blaze
Of weapons seized us! Who was not terrified   35
When even a hero paled? Yet no flash of fainthearted fears
Has ever hurt us. Oh, day! Oh, splendid day!
That whoever draws a breath now or in the future will praise!
(The day) on which this hand received the trophies of the fathers
In the same instance, when with two thousand corpses   40
This arm wiped out the evil plague on earth,
That virtuous fortune stays beneath our banner.
Yet: as this mild hemorrhage improved the great nation,
The emperor himself looked upon us with disfavor:
And when the empire sent us out against the Bulgarians   45
And supported us with pay for the army, he[33] abdicated the throne.
It is true: Crum[34] had sullied the field with murder
And kindled flames in the crops and set fires in the cities
Yet not through our fault. From then on it started to happen
That the suppressed army began to look up to us.   50
The one who now stands before you forced us, with drawn sword,
To put on this bejeweled garb, the royal purple,

---

[33] Michael I. Rhangabe, 770-844 (Byzantine Emperor 811-813)
[34] Chan Crum, Bulgarian Prince, 814-831.

No matter how much we resisted! The emperor agreed
And personally sent us embroidered shoes [*symbol of royalty*].
We then loaded the burden on our neck   55
That seemed unbearable. We did away with shame and adversity
And riots, made peace with the Bulgarians,[35]
Suppressed the Ishmaelites, and chased out the Scythian army.
Proud Crum [*Bulgarian Prince*] came with so many thousand armies
As if he wanted to consume sea and land like that Persian.   60
But our sword taught him that the courage of a hero
Is more powerful than lighting, or than the harsh Ister's [*Danube's*]
Swift current runs; so that even twelve thousand brutes,
Frightened by one man, tried to run away.
His misery showed him what it meant to fight the Romans.   65
When, full of wounds, he fell; when fainting freed him
From the power of our sword, whom did we deny
What convention and justice promised? Who complained in vain?
Because this head was crowned, was anyone not delighted
Who realized his dire straits? Whom did this sword harm   70
Whom it found innocent? This sword, that I often spared,
For whom punishment reached out! Was anyone left unrewarded
Who served us? And yet our death is sought!
And the sword is sharpened on him, to whom, in the nation's dire need,
God, priest, and visions promised the lofty throne.   75
And you, you Michael, have broken oath and fidelity
With him, to whom you owe gratitude for your rank and honor
                                                     and your life.
Unfaithful one! Did we take you into the fold?
Betrayer! Did this arm raise you up out of the dung?
Ungrateful heart! Did this hand bestow a thousand gifts upon you, 80
Perjurious man? You dog, did I give you the sword,
That you, before my enemy, turned on this breast?

---

[35] A peace lasting thirty years followed the Battle at Mesembria in 817.

Were you, murderer, often forgiven for your brash raging

That permitted you to eliminate your anger all at once?

Has our patience, our favor, deserved this,   85

That you, cursed one, have emboldened yourself to this deed,

That even our enemy doesn't praise? Well, fine! Because goodness

So poorly invested, because your obstinate mind

Can't be forced by any friendliness, because this disease

Doesn't let itself be driven from you by any gentle means,   90

Because benevolence corrupts you, feel instead fire and iron.

The whole wide world shall be shown a new spectacle

How severely injured favor and often forgiven guilt

And hushed revenge and highly touted graciousness

Are shaken and broken to bits when the right time arrives!   95

What is the dog stammering now? Pay attention to what he says,

He who can only blaspheme! What can he bark? *Michael:* Listen!

It's true that Michael was never taught to speak well!

It's also true that I never endeavored to mislead.

Yet your conscience will realize the usefulness of my fist to you,   100

Even if I'm silent. Tell of your deeds,

But also tell that his fist advanced your counsel

Who stood with you and for you in steel and dust

And sweated in battle; lower class and poor parental blood

Should not be scorned as grievous blemishes.   105

My soul, my undaunted courage speak for me.

Virtue is not only innate to us:

How many heroes' fame was lost in oblivion?

The father's prized acclaim vanishes with his spirit.

When pale death drags us into the grave,   110

The noble son inherits our weapons but not our strength.

Don't bear in mind my words; behold the works of the poor,

Of the poor who supported this empire with strong power.

The poor have protected you (just contemplate it,

Just contemplate it, my prince!) When so many thousand swords   115

Encircled your tents, who helped to move the army

That raised you up as its leader? Who elevated you to the throne?
Who didn't allow you to doubt, when you almost withdrew your head
From the great crown? The emperor bade you to come
And he slinked out of this castle, which indeed *you* captured   120
But as *I* stood beside you. If you terrified the enemy,
Keep in mind that my sword stuck in his breast.
I'm also glad to admit that I, through your elevation,
Have come a bit higher! Yet, can you give something to him
(Excuse what necessity teaches me to speak out matter-of-factly)   125
That is worth this rise in rank, who increased your assets so much
That you are able to give this? Let it be told openly
What I received from you. It still will be substantially wanting
That my office is equal to your empire,
And my helmet to your crown! And both were available to me!   130
When I ceded to you what I could have seized,
When I wanted to grant this throne to you and not to myself:
And even now I grant it to you: nonetheless I am accused.
Why? Because often I can't hold back a word
If a betrayer snatches and baits me like a dog.   135
Whom has slander not driven to commit murder?
Can anyone stand on slippery ice without a fall?
If envy shoves him? Who must not go under
If the infuriated winds of fervent falsehoods gust?
If the angered storms of untruthful tongues squall?   140
They rage against me! They impair my honor!
And slay my glory! Do you require a hearing?
Is true service rewarded with disdain and strong chains?
Will the prince trample to the ground the one through
                                        whom he stood?
That's what has happened to me, and a tongue strikes down   145
The one, whom no cruel sword, no sharp arrow slays.
I. Judge: What tongue? Slander? Cunning? What paid-off ears
   Have you, murderer, not sworn to the emperor's death?
   The court, the great city, the whole camp informs

What you are heard hourly rambling about regicide.   150

II. Judge: What does his trap not drivel? Ought this to be excused? [36]

    Shouldn't your tongue be ripped right out of your throat?

    Doesn't his speech expose to us his raging blood?

    What's holding us back any longer? He brings his sentence with him!

Michael: Granted that due to anger and rashness

    That which is so fiercely rebuked escaped me: yet my desire

    Never really craved your throne, nor your death:

    My steady loyalty has been burdened with unknown guilt.

Leo: Oh, ever so perverse loyalty! Where did loyalty remain?   155

Michael: My blood has written this loyalty in the book of time.

Leo: Your blood that's out after our blood every day.

Michael: My blood that has looked out for your blood for so many years.

Leo: Looked out for my death. *Michael:* Which I was willing to bear for you

    At all times. *Leo:* Doing and saying are not the same thing.   160

Michael: I said it and did it when I spilled my blood for you.

Leo: From necessity, for your own glory. *Michael:* It flowed for you.

II. Judge: That doesn't advance the case. Respond to what we're asking about!

Michael: Then ask the wounds that my chest bears.

    Ask enemies; ask the Parthians, the Bulgarians, the Scythians,

                   and the Franks.   165

III. Judge: This vice nullifies previously earned gratitude.

Michael: This vice does nothing here; character assassination will crush us.

IV. Judge: Character assassination, which your mouth alone knows how

                     to produce.

Michael: No mouth loves character assassination that

                     loves unrestricted freedom.

V. Judge: The arm is firm that easily gives applause to the mouth.   170

Michael: A person often blurts out in anger what was never intended.

VI. Judge: We know, without anger, how to find malice of forethought.

Michael: Who lives without any venality? Who has always

                     thought things through?

---

[36] Version C, 1663, adds four lines here between II.150 and II.151.

VII. Judge: He, who does not boast too much about the

strength of his hands.

Michael: Whoever lives also errs and falls.

VIII. Judge: Whoever commits a crime has to suffer.   175

IX. Judge: We can, indeed, differentiate vice from error.

Michael: Yes, vice! If it is sought out in every corner!

Leo: Are you then the one who curses us only in the corner?

I. Judge: What is the use of searching if no place can be found

That is clear of your guilt, of your obvious alliance   180

With your whole band of witnesses; your gang brings to light

What lies deep in your bosom. *Michael*: What hate ascribes to me.

Leo: Who is it that wants to drive his sword through my veins?

I. Judge: Who is it, without whom the empire cannot keep its power?

II. Judge: Who is it, upon whom the burden of the heavy crown rests?   185

III. Judge: Who is it, without whose action the well-being of

the emperor would pass?

IV. Judge: Who is it, who can crush princes with his attack?

V. Judge: Who is it, who knows how to send princes into the cold grave?

VI. Judge: To whom Phocas, to whom Irene, impart such great ideas?[37]

VII. Judge: Before whom the deep fundament of the great earth

cracks open?   190

IIX. Judge: Who would prefer to live one day crowned

Than to hover in highest glory and most profound joy!

IX. Judge: What didn't your mouth say right out when you were ambushed?

Michael: Nothing bad, if you don't want to interpret it for the worst.[38]

X Judge: Nothing bad! Every word has earned tongs and pillar.[39]   195

Michael: Only because I emboldened myself to speak a bit more freely.

II. Judge: And aspired to the prince's throne and to his death.

---

[37] See Act I, 422-428, above, p. 45.

[38] Version C (1663) replaces original lines 195-98, and then adds eight new lines before continuing with original line 199.

[39] Note that only *nine* Judges appear in the earlier versions of *Leo Armenius*.

Michael: The strongest poison is rampant suspicion.

III. Judge: Did no one promise you assistance for this desire?

Michael: One seeks assistance who has broken oath and loyalty.

IV. Judge: Do you think it has not been discovered who is

                            with you in the coalition?

Michael: You seem to know more than I do.

                  VI Judge: Assure yourself, the ground

Is not so deep that our plumb won't find it.

Michael: There's a ground to this: that here my ruin is the target.

I. Judge: Quickly! Torture rack, noose, and fire!

                     Michael: Fine! Do you want me to lie,

Play with feigned innocence, and cheat justice and the world?

I. Judge: Pressed with pain, one says what one doesn't say out of goodness.

Michael: Torture has never overcome an undaunted mind.   200

     Do you weigh carefully what you're doing? I'm trapped in such distress

     Into which you might sink; my life, well-being, and death

     Rest in your hands. Yet if I should die because of words

     Then let me, myself, secure my oath with my own hands:

     And, in fact, for the benefit of the empire. Let the enemy go at me!   205

     I will stand for you in steel at Pontus on the Black Sea,[40]

     I will fight with the Scythians and Parthians until death.

     I will deflate the defiance of the Bulgarians with my blood.

     Thus let break whatever comes out against you, my emperor!

     Thus let disappear whatever harms your empire or this state.   210

     Thus, when I'm gone, let my pale corpse also serve you,

     Thus may your house and line bloom forever and ever. *Leo.* Get out!

Scene 2

Leo, *The Judges.*

---

[40] Pontus here refers to the region on the southern coast of the Black Sea, located in the modern-day eastern Black Sea Region of Turkey.

Leo: The wild beast is in the trap! His disloyalty, anger, and guilt
    Rumble even in chains and captivity. Our benevolence, patience,
    And rejected mercy call out with strength for justice and revenge.   215
    What do you think about this case? *I. Judge:* It is a serious matter
    And worthy of deliberation. If his word is considered,
    Which he cannot deny; if the power of the weapons
    That stand ready to serve him and his frequent blaspheming
    And often-pardoned venality are examined a bit more closely;   220
    It is only more than clear that he is risking his neck.
    If, on the other hand, his great bravery and undaunted mind
    Are taken seriously; the glory of the wounds he received,
    Through which he found so much favor among so many souls;
    Indeed, because it is not yet discovered, who joined with him [and]   225
    Because he has only committed a crime with words,

                                 not with an armed hand,
    I think it is of more than great necessity
    To think of how, and where, and when he ought to be killed.
    Should the simple people see him going to the place of execution
    Bound and dragged? Should he stand shackled   230
    There, where a thousand military and a thousand more would hear
    His often-wreathed head praised, since with highest honors
    He did everything but mount the throne? This looks dangerous!
    Will the emotional populace and those who are linked to his line
    By favor and advantage observe this without horror?   235
    What will the camp, in which he is used to trusting,
    That stands in his service, not do? What will the foreign power
    That carries out whatever he bids, and that keeps watch all around us,
    Not do at such a time? What will those not venture
    Who, without doubt, are obligated to attack with him?   240
    Believe this: whoever stands by him, whoever is firm in the alliance,
    Will seek whatever necessity, whatever hope, allows them to seek.
    And why will he not be forced beforehand, by severe stretching

                                   on the rack,
    To reveal to us the reason for the attack?

II. Judge: He deserves death. Everyone agrees!   245

Let him die! Tomorrow? Yes! You say it! Why not this instant?

We are not acting too quickly here. When one is so heavily laden,

Even a moment more can wreak unbearable damage.

He still is convicted of no deed (so it is said)!

He is in custody because of his word. He whom smoke fools   250

Errs just fine without light! If you want to behold his work,

Then look at his mouth. What can be trusted of this man

Who, facing the judiciary itself, still attacks the emperor and the judges[41]

And brews pure gall and poison in his malicious heart?

Has such a thing as this ever been heard of, that still no one strikes back

At his stubborn blasphemy? If what has happened previously

(Happened and yet pardoned) cannot embolden you

Then take a look at the emperor's head and your own bodies.

Do you want to postpone the long trial until the emperor is left   255

With his death, until you are strangled with him?

Yes, tarry until Michael really deserves the punishment!

Will you not believe there is a rebellion until the empire

                     and scepter are gone?

III. Judge: The populace, it cannot be denied, is easily moved.

Yet no public blood vendetta should be fostered in the state.   260

The place allotted for pain is the corpse-filled field,

Where stake and wood are erected for common guilt.

The gloomy sound of horns, the murderous pomp of the executioners,

Scares people out of their minds. Is the court too small for us?

Let punishment occur where the error was made.

                 The emperor,[42] whom few equal,   265

In virtue, victory, and renown, who relocated this great empire,

The throne, this new Rome, on an ancient horror.

When his lustful wife[43] aggravated him against his own blood[44]

---

[41] Lines 253-54 of Versions A and B are replaced with lines 253-58 in Version C, 1663.

[42] Constantine the Great (272 -327, Roman Emperor 306-327).

[43] Fausta (289-326), second wife of Constantine the Great (betrothed to him in 293; married in 307).

[44] Crispus, (c.300-326), son of Constantine by his first wife Minervina.

He, enraged with holy anger, secretly perpetrated revenge on

The mother who had loved her child in an un-motherly way.   270

At his command, she perished in a scalding hot bath,

This fiery scene of wild sexual desire; this woman,

> the spoilage of nations,

The scorn and curse of humanity, the blemish of her time,

The horror of nature, upon whom everyone spits

And every child curses. What Constantine ordered to be carried out   275

Cannot be chastised as heavy-handed, as new or unheard of.

I. Judge: Does it not plead for torture? *IV. Judge:* Is his guilt not clear?[45]

What would we discover through anguish that is not

> already more than obvious?

I. Judge: The heavy-handed question can deflate the defiance of minds.

IV. Judge: A high spirit is often used to struggling with distress and agony.

I. Judge: To struggle, but only until fierce pain conquers him.

V. Judge: If pain does not lose out to immovable courage.

VI. Judge: Thus it is here, too, I believe: glowing steel,

Pitch, torch, boiling oil, and lead will show us no means   280

To discover what is sought. *I. Judge:* Many have confessed much

When forced by flame and rope. *IV. Judge:* Many have disdained

> blows and burning

And screws and stones. Have him stretched on the wheel!

I doubt that he is honestly going to divulge

What we need to find out! *VII. Judge:* You can't proceed with certainty   285

On grounds that firmly rest only on torture.

Who does not know that often out of hate, out of desire to live,

The most honest innocence itself has been most evilly accused?

I. Judge: Philotas, when blood flowed from all his limbs,

Showed weakness from the fierce slashing, as courageous as he was.   290

---

[45] Lines 277-79 of Versions A and B are replaced in Version C, 1663, with seven new lines inserted before line 280.

VI. Judge: Did not Hippias[46] rob himself of his friends

When he believed the false oath of the one severely tortured?

The woman from Rome is vaunted who let herself be torn to bits

And who, in the ordeal, bit her tongue into pieces.

VIII. Judge: What if he would withstand all the ferocity of the martyrdom   295

And would stand firm and undaunted in defiant silence?

Think what that would mean! *IX. Judge:* It also seems when torture

Grasps for lofty heads as if doubt comes to mind,

Strengthened by false hatred. Why are we struggling here

To mull over the guilt that is seen right before our eyes,   300

That he cannot deny? If anyone stands by him,

He will be shown his [*Michael's*] demise to frighten him:

That has the power to bring back on track what has gone astray,

That his discovery can easily penetrate into despair,

Despair to something more. *III. Judge:* In brief, whatever you do,   305

Do it immediately. A quick start wipes away a drop of blood

much better

Than a flood in the long run. *I. Judge*: I agree. *II. Judge.* Me, too.

III. Judge: We all do.

IV Judge: And we. *V. Judge:* Let fall whoever wants to lift himself too high.

VII. Judge: Set up the scaffold for him. *VIII. Judge:* For the murderer.

IX. Judge: Onto the blaze!

I. Judge: Let him burn and let his pomp, his corrupt boldness,   310

Dissolve in ashes. *II. Judge:* Let him burn! *III. Judge*: Let him burn!!

IV. Judge: Let him burn and vanish!

V. Judge: And let him become a vapor of air and a ruse of the winds.

Leo: You're signing off on his death. *VI. Judge:* His long-deserved reward.

Leo: Write the verdict! Let him die right here with less mockery

And greater security! He, Who gives us life,   315

Who sees into hearts, knows how we have loved him:

---

[46] Probable reference to false oath given to Hippias, commander of the Arcadian mercenaries stationed at Notium, by the Athenian General Paches, as retold by Thucydides in *The Peloponnesian War* (3.34). See Alan H. Sommerstein and Isabelle C. Torrance, *Oaths and Swearing in Ancient Greece* (Berlin and Boston: Walter de Gruyter, 2014) 262.

He knows, He, Who knows everything, how greatly we

                have rewarded him!

How often out of loyal favor we have spared his guilt.

How proudly he has struck out at us! How impertinently he

                has cursed us,

How often he has sought his glory through our dishonor.   320

How heavily his downfall weighs on our spirit,

How sharply his bitter death will consume us, heart and soul.

Yet you [*Judges*], this empire, justice, and our blood and life

Compel us to give the man up to the flames!

The Judges: The verdict is proclaimed! Summon the accused!   325

Leo: Thus do time and justice alternate and honor is restored in clarity.

Scene 3

Leo, the Judges, Michael.

I. Judge: After the high council has deliberated Michael's crime

    With careful consideration . . . *Michael:* Now, God, Thou willst avenge,

    Allow me one word more! *II. Judge:* You've been heard enough!

Michael: Oh heaven! *I. Judge* . . . it is found: because he often revolted,   330

    Reinforced defiance with suspicion, opposed the crown,

    Vilified the sovereign, offended his majesty,

    Sought the emperor's death! That he, with foot and hand

    Bound to the stake, burn alive on open sand.

    However, the sovereign, in order to relieve him of the dishonor,   335

    Has conceded that the punishment should take place in the castle.

Michael: Alas! I have been afraid of this harsh death!

VI. Judge: No harsher than the guilt! *Michael:* Oh, undeserved misery!

    Alas, delivered service! Alas, hoping too much in vain!

VII. Judge: Revenge has unexpectedly struck the right branch.   340

    What's holding us up any longer? Hurry, execute the sentence!

Michael: Heaven help us! Am I the one who can die like this?

    Where is my great glory? Has all favor disappeared?

    Does the sovereign no longer know me? Is there no friend found now

Who can plead for me? Come, enemies! Come and see   345
How this poor soul is doing, before whom you were petrified
As he, who moved your empire with terror,
Who stirred up fear in your celebrations and souls
So pitifully expires. Call out, you horrible spirits,
Call out joyously above me! Break open the solid tomb   350
In which you dead ones are enclosed! Come, long-since paled heroes!
Whom these hands killed! Help proclaim through all of Persia:
That all-too severe justice! That hate and furious envy
Set up the woodpile on which bravery,
And virtue, and what we call the purpose of thrones,   355
A courageous heart, will now burn up with me.
I. Judge: Away now! *Michael*: Alas, one more word. *I. Judge*: To no avail.
                                   Michael: A word, my sovereign.
A word. *Leo*: Speak. *Michael*: Your servant, --whom you will exterminate,
Formerly your right arm! Formerly the trepidation of enemies,
Before heaven's anger so cruelly attacked him   360
With fierce thunder storms, -- falls before you on his knees
And would not wish that his demise would be withdrawn,
(But oh! What am I dreaming of?) he would not wish that
The horror of extended martyrdom be lessened, nor that the pain
                                   would be alleviated.
He would wish in exchange for so much service only a brief respite! 365
Let it be granted that while my grave, the flame, is being prepared
I may write to my children for one final time,
And inform them on paper where I, their father, am left,
In the event that your great anger will not allow it to happen
That I see the sweet gathering before my demise.   370
II. Judge: This is heading towards postponement, and
                                   postponement to escape.
III. Judge: So it is. He's seeking to escape anguish by delay.
Michael: Time and place are too limited for such an act.
III. Judge: Evil often finds counsel in an instant.
Michael: He, whom evil frightens, must always hesitate in suspicion. 375

IV. Judge: Whoever already has succumbed to despair risks

whatever he can risk.

Michael: If love awakens nature in your blood,

If true father-devotion, sovereign, ever arouses your heart,

Insofar as you happily think of seeing the wonderful day

On which you will entrust the crown to your son: 380

Then don't deny your servant his last request.

Leo: It's not unknown to us what your mind is thinking up!

Punishment is weakened through postponement, because revenge,

Lingering as if asleep, seeks an evil object:

Here a plea, there an accessory, and it infects more hearts 385

Than can be healed with gentle kindness or hostility.

Nevertheless, so that no mouth can say in truth:

It is out of hatred that you were denied such a short respite,

Let him be brought into the secure prison for one hour.

In the meantime, pay close attention to the gate and locks. 390

Scene 4

Leo.

Leo: It is this that we and he have sought for such a long time!

Now his spirit feels what his brash mouth cursed us of!

Just as well! He has fallen! That means the throne has been strengthened,

The enemy crushed in horror, myself and my blood protected,

Ingratitude punished, iniquity overcome, 395

Envy pressed into the dung, and blasphemy contained.

Now we are lord and sovereign, and control crown and scepter,

And hold in our hand what the title gave to us;

We, who were formerly a knave and the servant of our slaves.

Now his boat sinks to the bottom, and Leo finds safe haven! 400

Thus it thunders when your crown and scepter are pursued,

Ye, who move below God but above people.

See here the reflection of those who are born to serve you;

And who want to lead by the ears the one who ought to rule.

Audacity often grabs the lion by the hair,   405
But when it becomes confident, and fully and completely
Considers him to be only a hare, he bares his sharp claws,
His cavernous throat, and his sharp teeth
And seizes what tramples upon him! How foolish is he, however,
Who rules over thousands but selects a single one   410
To whom he reveals his whole heart and all his wishes,
And entrusts with the force through which he subdues nations
And ultimately sovereigns themselves; whoever places someone
                                                        on the throne
At his side deserves that the crown
And royal purple be withdrawn from him. One sovereign
                                        and one sun   415
Can exist in the world and the empire. Did an army ever win
That was led by more than one? But what are we saying?
Who can be trusted? Do we stroll here, as if free of anxiety,
While he, through whose death we live, still draws a breath?
It is essential that we ourselves pay closer attention   420
To how this plague goes away: time has taught us
How quickly he errs, who doesn't see more than he hears,
And that no spectacle is so fine in the whole world,
As when what plays with fire must turn into ashes.

Scene 5

Leo, Theodosia.

Theodosia: My light! *Leo:* My comfort! *Theodosia:* My sovereign!
                        Leo: My angel! Theodosia: My sun!   425
Leo: My life. *Theodosia:* My delight! *Leo:* My abode and bliss!
    Why so unhappy, my heart? *Theodosia:* What has my sovereign resolved?
    Alas! Unfortunately! Hasn't enough blood been spilled by now?
Leo: Not enough blood, if they're out for our blood.
Theodosia: Blood will make our throne tarnished and slippery.   430
Leo: Thus will a newcomer be afraid to mount it.

Theodosia: Thus eventually he will have to bow on wet ground.

Leo: Wetness is dried out with flame and ashes.

Theodosia: That easily would turn our house into dust and horror.

Leo: This house will stand in exchange for the enemies of

the house falling.   435

Theodosia: Unless their fall injures those who surround this house.

Leo: Surround with swords. *Theodosia:* With which they protect us.

Leo: That they have drawn on us? *Theodosia:* That support our throne.

Leo: Who under this ruse seek to topple the throne.

Theodosia: Who can shorten the lifespan of the sovereign

if God does not will it?   440

Leo: God watches over us and also bids us to be watchful ourselves.

Theodosia: If God himself doesn't keep watch, every watchman falls asleep!

Leo: Yes, certainly the sovereign sleeps who doesn't reveal a serious matter.

Theodosia: Where a serious matter is absolutely too great, there's nothing

but fear and terror.

Leo: That serious matter is not too great without which

no empire survives.   445

Theodosia: That serious matter is much too great through which

the empire perishes.

Leo: Not by the death of the rogue, whom only death can better.

Theodosia: A bandage often heals more than a profusion of flames

and swords.

Leo: No bandage can help here anymore! What haven't I tried?

Theodosia: The Highest doesn't strike immediately if someone curses him.   450

Leo: Who doesn't say that I have given only more than too much of a break?

Theodosia: The one who doesn't prefer to punish than to praise great virtue.

Leo: I have rewarded more than there was to be rewarded.

Theodosia: A sovereign doesn't give too much if he gives the same

amount every year.

Leo: Might there be anything left that I didn't give to him?   455

Theodosia: Alas, yes. *Leo:* Say what it is. *Theodosia:* A lot.

Leo: What is it? *Theodosia:* His life.

Leo: Life, to him who seeks with serious zeal nothing but the anguish

Of my dearest ones, the ruination of my children, and the death of

his sovereign,

For whose dreadful sins it isn't really known how to find

An appropriate punishment and sentence?   460

Theodosia: Grace outweighs what punishment cannot impose.

Leo: The scale breaks in two if no justice is regarded.

Theodosia: Justice has its course, now let grace encounter it.

Leo: Heaven will bless the leader who has punished vice.

Theodosia: And will be favorable to the one who easily forgives guilt.   465

Leo: Not of one who so deeply distresses God and me and you.

Theodosia: How magnificent it is if one does good things and suffers evil!

Leo: How foolish! If you cut your own throat by yourself:

If you take the wild boar, chased with so much sweat

And entangled in the net, and set him loose on the open meadow.   470

Theodosia: You can move a snake itself with kindness*

So that it's accustomed to divesting itself of the dreaded poison.

What's bred in wild caves, the manner of strong lions,

And what the desolate crag keeps in its bosom

Puts aside – if a gentle person doesn't treat it too roughly—   475

Its ferocious bad behavior and transforms into something tame.

Leo: You can train a blood-thirsty animal, unquestionably,

So that it obeys and kneels down before you:

And what is even more, you can reverse the powerful flood,

Resist rivers, and dam the raging waves.   480

You can quell the power of flames, you can sail against the wind,

You can collapse the cliffs where there are valley and caves.

You can cover the rocks themselves with wheat,

And train the wild branch to bloom on noble stems.

You can do this and even more, only this is unheard of: 485

Skill is a stranger here; no knowledge has ever taught

How a stubborn spirit, whom pride has blown up

And the desire for a crown has bewitched, can be healed

from this rage.

Theodosia: The doctor hopes as long as the soul still moves in the sick.

Leo: For the dead, the hand is put to the task in vain.   490

Theodosia: For the dead, who gave their soul at our word.

Leo: For overwhelming guilt and all of our lives.

Theodosia: Revenge rashly overtakes counsel. Consider carefully

                  what you are doing.

Leo: Revenge asks much too late for such greatly stained blood.

Theodosia: Alas, blood! Consider the dream* that scared your mother.   495

Leo: Consider how this blood often woke us up in fright.

Theodosia: Consider the high (holy) day that gladdens the whole world.

Leo: And me, if the wind now scatters the enemy's ashes.

Theodosia: Do you set up the scaffold, now when JESUS is born?

Leo: For him who has sworn himself against the church of JESUS

                  and its members.   500

Theodosia: Do you want to approach the table of JESUS soiled

                    with murder?

Leo: Enemies are executed who stand at altars.

    My light! No more! Can it be? Can she venture

    To plead for the man who plans to bind up her and me,

    And to stamp me and her into the dust after my death and

                  that of her children   505

    With a new kind of new pain and atrocious despair?

    Who fearlessly dares to say

    That through his favor we wear gold upon our hair

    And royal purple round our bodies? And do I listen any longer to this?

    The demise of this man is my and your peace;   510

    His life is the grave for both of us. *(Leo departs)*

Theodosia: He departs from here in anger.

    But how? Should I tolerate what with heated thoughts

    The Emperor bids to be carried out? Shall the day so holy

    On which God and Man lay low in the manger,

    On which we hasten to unite ourselves with God,   515

    Find the execution-stake at the castle full of spectators?

    Shall the odor heavy with corpses overpower our incense?

    Shall his cry appear before God next to our praying?

No indeed! No! I must, if possible, prevent this!
I will surpass the stubborn courage of the sovereign   520
So that he doesn't carry out harsh justice on the day of celebration.
I know that he won't refuse so little to God and to me.

Scene 6

Michael, the Trabant Guards, Leo, Theodosia.

Guard: Now move: time is wasting. *Michael:* Well, then! Let's go!
    And, indeed, alone, since no friend wants to stand by us.
    Alas, friends without fidelity! Alas, names without deeds!   525
    Alas, title without use! Alas, support without counsel!
    Alas, friends! Friends in fortune! Alas, that we honor you still!
    Cursed is he who lets the illusion of friendship fool him!
    Cursed is he who builds on the oath of fickle men!
    Cursed is he who places trust in what is spoken and promised!   530
    I am dying because I deemed them to be more than honest,
    They, for whom I ventured forth! The one whom my sword placed
    On Constantine's throne places me on this woodpile.
    The prince for whom my blood flowed out of every vein
    Grants me this woodpile as a reward! How high I have climbed   535
    That even the ashes themselves will fly through the air!
    How well I have used time and wounds!
    Alas! If only the bright arrow of thunder had burned me
    When I, then still a child, was torn from home!
    Before I learned to enclose my limbs in hard steel.   540
    Before I grasped the sword and pressed through weapons!
    Before I ascended the enemy's wall with flame and spear.
    Alas! If only a hero, if only a man would slay me;
    Alas! If only my wish would move you, who behold me.
    Come friends, thrust a sword, thrust through this bare breast,   545
    This I ask; come enemies, satiate your desire
    And thrust a sword through me; I will thank you both for it.
    He wishes in vain, who already moves within the crushing limits

Of bitter death. Well, then! Come and teach—
You, who honor your princes as exalted and equal to the gods,   550
You, who want to climb to heaven through the favor of your lords—
How quickly our glory must lower itself in the ashes.*
(Note added in Version C)
We rise, as a man whose neck has been condemned,
On the piercing pole that impales his body.
We rise like smoke that vanishes in the air: 555
We rise towards the fall, and whoever finds the summit,
Finds what can topple him. *Guard*: Death teaches this wisdom!
Michael: Which my scaffold teaches me. Let that teach you my anguish.
Who stands upright can perish! I will disrobe myself.
So let us suffer undismayed the decision of heaven!   560
Thou, adornment of all places! Ruler of the world!
Whom I placed in proud peace through so much anguish:
Farewell! Your hero is dying! Thou witness of my victories
Thou golden light, farewell! Thou country, often in war
Covered by me with flesh, which my hand filled   565
With corpses, brains, and bones, that I often plowed with
                          spear and armor
And shield. Now that death approaches,
Be greeted with good night; be blessed with a good night.
Thou spirits, whom revenge has chosen to serve her,
Insofar as something can be gained by a final wish,   570
Insofar as one who is now dying can move you,
Insofar as you are powerful to arouse fear and terror:
So do I call you together out of the hell of your martyrdom;
Where nothing but fire and woe is granted to the miserable soul,
Which cannot be refused: the one who is causing my pains   575
Must lament them, and with a frightened heart
Seek out the one whom he is burning. My embers must
Set fire to his castle; out of my blood,
Out of the ashes of these limbs, out of these cremated bones
An avenger must arise, and a soul must appear   580

Who is filled with my courage, armed with my hand,
Empowered with my strength, who will blow into the still glowing fire
That must consume me, with taut cheeks,
Who will fume with the flame and rage with the sparks
No differently than that the brimstone-bright power   585
Will break through the populace and the palaces;
                             heavy thunder will crack;
(A soul) who with the blood of princes will set me such an epitaph
That even eternity will not destroy it in the future.
Guard: Make way for your king! *Leo*: Your wish shall be fulfilled.
My life! But, alas, that here no warning prevails.   590
You will yet curse the hour, you will curse the favor
And rebuke what we are doing in response to your demanding request.
Bind up the condemned man in strong chains
Because the celebration is already starting; staff the rough stone
Of the prison all around with the best guards: 595
Traitors cannot be safeguarded too firmly.

Chorus of the Courtiers

1. Oh, thou transition of all things,
     Ever-enduring vanity!
     Does nothing course through the spheres of time
     With constant certainty?   600

2. Does nothing count but falling and standing,
     Nothing but crown and hangman's rope?
     Between the depths and the pinnacles
     Is there barely one sunset?

3. Eternally fluctuating fortune!   605
     Do you respect no scepter?
     Is there nothing in the world
     That can escape your rope?
4. Mortals, what is this life

But a totally mixed-up dream? 610
This, which hard work and sweat give us,
Vanishes like foam on the waves.

5. Princes! Gods of this earth,
    Behold what must kneel before you!
    Often before evening can come 615
    You will kneel beneath foreign power!

6. Even just a moment upsets
    Yours and the enemy's throne:
    And it's a brief instant that adorns
    The ones you hate with your crown! 620

7. You, who with collected honors
    Make yourself beholden to a prince,
    How soon it can be heard of you,
    That you've been bound in chains.

8. Poor ones! Seek yet to climb high! 625
    Before renown rightly glimpses you,
    You must lower your head and eyes
    And death will have ensnared you.

9. Boast, you who convulse the world,
    Boast about the power of your weapons! 630
    If the air thunders somewhat turbidly
    That will scorn your weak fist.

10. The one to whom precious metals flow,
    The one to whom the Tagus offers up treasure,
    Often begs before the day is done, 635
    For pieces of moldy bread.
11. Beauties! Those snow white cheeks,

That entice souls after them;
The noble splendor of the face
A heavy frost bids to wither.   640

12. While we count the years
    And look back at a hundred harvests,
    We must be wanting at the hour
    When Clotho calls: "It's over!"

13. Frame up castles! Build palaces!   645
    Sculpt yourselves from hardest stone!
    Alas! Nothing is too firm for time!
    What I build, another will destroy.

14. Nothing! There's nothing that yet today
    Couldn't rush to ruination!   650
    And we! Alas! We blind people
    Hope to exist forever and ever.

The Third Act

Scene 1

Leo, Papias, Chorus of Actors and Singers.

Leo: He is secured? *Papias:* Yes. *Leo:* Guarded? *Papias:* Strongly.
 Leo: Who stands guard?
Papias: I myself. *Leo:* Don't let anyone he favors
    Get through to the castle: have him bound firmly, too;
    With chains on his arms and shackles on his feet.
Papias: My sovereign, it has been done. *Leo:* Where are the keys?
                                 Papias: Here!   5
Leo: Withdraw. Call the singers to the door.
    We wish to be alone! Oh, trouble-rich life!
    Who is more surrounded with guards, we or he?
    He trembles before his plight; we ourselves (tremble) before our sword.
    Is this scepter's gold possibly worth such worries?   10
    How this delicate garment oppresses! Oh blessed he who spends the years,
    The short balance of time until his hair is grey,
    Far from the castle. Who knows only the forests
    In which he is nourished, who names no servants,
    Is resplendent in no royal purple, he may indeed go safely   15
    Whenever and wherever he wants: those who serve us
    Are often after our hide. Gentle night beds him [*Michael*] down
    On humble straw until Titan is awakened [*the sun rises*]:
    We're disoriented without rest. When we stretch out our body
    The pillow morphs into an evergreen hedge.   20
    Thus does a green bush remain undamaged by lightning
    When heated fierceness strikes in tall cedars

And knocks down trunk and branches, when the winds rise
And demonstrate signs of their strength on tall oaks.
Heaven, which gives us nothing without some melancholy,   25
Has circumscribed the proud throne with ever-renewed fear.
A menial servant is bound with iron chains; a prince with gold.
A warrior feels the sword, suspicion gives us wounds
That barely can be healed. We float on the sea,
Yet when the angry tide hurls a small boat first to the heights   30
And then into the depths, and moves it safely into port,
A mighty ship is crashed to pieces on the craggy cliff.

During simultaneous string music and singing, Leo falls asleep while sitting in his chair.

Violas

Chorus:

   1. The quiet pleasure of the pleasant night,
   The time of rest that paints everything black
   Now crowns your head with shimmering splendor: 35
   The pale moon escapes the image of the sun.

   2. Earth congeals. Lazy Morpheus empties out
   His moist horn on thousands of limbs
   And covers with sleep what pain and daytime burden.
   The host of dreams creeps into cottage and house.   40

   3. The little world, great Byzantium, lies
   In proud repose, while its emperor remains awake.
   The mighty prince, who fights and conquers for us
   And totally crushes the power of the ruthless Persians.

   4. He lies awake for us! That the Pontus flows more calmly,   45
   That the Nile serves and the Ister [*Danube*] respects you,
   And that the Bosphorus doesn't inundate the land
   Happens because not a soul ever hears him snore.

5. He keeps watch for us, and He who watches over him,
Places the thrones of princes on solid diamond,   50
And bids the bivouacs of princes be drawn from metals,
And wounds their enemies with swift lightning.

6. God restrains those, whom He Himself calls gods,
Even if the wily band of giants gets excited
And no longer knows itself in its delusion and raging   55
And places mountain upon mountain and crag upon cliff.

7. If Atlas were standing right now on the Haemus [*Balkan*] mountains
And Athos [*Greek mountain*] reached up to the starry palace;
Even if the gate into heaven were found,
If Rhetus [*centaur*] were still so strong and so large;   60

8. Yet it would still be so, it would remain attempted in vain,
What they had wished! In one stroke
The prolonged effort would disappear. Whosoever meets God in battle
Turns to ashes and dust and mist and smoke and wind.

Violas

*During concurrent playing of the violins, a mournful trumpet sounds from afar
that can be heard ever more clearly until Tarasius appears, around whom several
lighted candles without candleholders appear on the bare ground; afterwards they
disappear together with him.*

Scene 2

The Ghost of Tarasius, the Ghost of Michael, Leo, the Trabant Guards.

Tarasius: Arise, sovereign! Fallen sovereign! Up! Up!
                              How can you sleep?   65
Because God's revenge awakens! Up! Drive out the lazy resting
From your mind and limbs: your scepter is being broken!
Swift Death has pronounced a swift sentence for you.

You untruthful man, the one whom you chased from the throne,

Who moans with burning tears about your guilt 70

And, always lamenting, strongly entreats impartial justice:

The church, which trembles before you, unfortunate man:

Your own arrogance; the one, who sits in the cliffs

Chased away by your command, who sweats in chains,

And from the center of the earth through the heavens 75

With a sigh-filled "Alas!" and whimpering uproar

Presses against God's heart: the never-silent blood

Eternally calling out "Murder!" that you deemed equal

To the brackish tide of Amphitrite[47] and spilled without guilt;

Those whom your heated vindictiveness had locked up in the cloister, 80

Whom you have tonsured, and the castrated man

Theophilactus [*Rhangabe*], and whoever else calls you tyrant,

Even without a tongue, hands over to disobeyed revenge

The sword of murder: Up, emperor, get up and watch out!

Insofar as you can keep watch – yet no! Your end is here! 85

No castle, no shield, no sword, no temple, no altar

Protects if God wants to strike with lightning! I see your angel yield,

You without head and hand; and your dismembered body

Creep through the city. Your hereditary line must perish,

Castrated and despised. Why do you want to persist any longer? 90

Stab him, Michael! Stab him!

[*Ghosts vanish*]

Leo: Murder! Murder! Traitors!

Sword, Shield! Murder! Guards! Murder! Help me slay the enemy!

Thou heaven! What is this? The dream has frightened us!

We behold this wide awake! Is that which threatens my neck

Discovered through a ghost? Whom did you find here? 95

---

[47] In Greek mythology, Amphitrite, a sea-goddess, was the wife of Poseidon, God of the sea. Later she became a symbolic representation of the sea (salt water) itself.

Guard: Nobody at all! *Leo:* No one? What? *Guard:* An unexpected nap

    Held his majesty bound. At his word we pressed,

    Armed, into the chamber. He sat in this place

    And called out for help and swords. *Leo:* Otherwise you noticed nothing?

Guard: Nothing whatsoever. *Leo:* Saw no one come through

                         the guards and gates?   100

Guard: Not one. *Leo:* Did sleeping make you blind and deaf?

Guard: We'd wish ourselves dead if we weren't keeping watch!

Leo: Are the palace and gate armed with people, and appropriately?

    Is the port manned? *Guard:* My sovereign, it's taken care of.

    The troops are reinforced; the ramparts are stocked with weapons.   105

Leo: Go see where Nicander is, and wake up Exabolius.

    How much of the time of darkness has passed?

Guard: The castle trumpet is just now sounding the sixth hour.

Scene 3

Leo.

Leo: What do we imagine?

    Do an empty delusion, a false invention move us?   110

    Is this trembling caused by fantasy?

        Shall it be all in vain,

        What this terrifying vision

        Of grim high justice,

        Of demise, fall, death, and wounds   115

        Has imbedded in our soul?

        A cold sweat breaks out.

    Our tired body quakes, our heart, surrounded with anxiety,

    Beats languishing between fear and burning desire.

        Nothing sounds in our ear: 120

        Except the rumbling-harsh revenge

        Of the case called out by God,

        We see the ghost still standing before us

        Power and empire are going to die with us.

"Stab him, Michael! Stab him!"   125
Thus the deathly ghost cried out. "Your scepter is being broken!
Grim Death has pronounced a grim sentence for you:
      Up! Up from your resting!
      Up!" Has resting ever refreshed us
      While the crown pressed against our head?   130
      Has any pleasure we've found
      Not disappeared from us into airy nothingness?

      "Your scepter is split in two!"
Death pronounces this sentence to us; the mighty throne will collapse;
This punishment will avenge the man whom we drove out.   135
      Then does the murderer go free?
      Did we sharpen this sword
      That will wound our own breast?
      Does our time rest in the hands of him
      Who is supposed to end his time in fire?   140

      "No temple, no altar protects
If God wants to strike with lightning:" will God then not protect those
Whom He bids to sit on the judgment seat in his place?
      Does he shorten the years of a sovereign?
      Or does he instruct only through symbols   145
      How one is supposed to escape from the grave?
      Thus it is! For sure He's used to threatening us:
      Yet He's also used to regretting his anger.

      Then is Michael free?
The one who sits in shackles? What if the chains were broken   150
With gold, promises, and treachery? What hasn't been promised,
      However expensive it may be,
      If one wants to bribe their condemned body
      From death at the stake?
      There's no metal that doesn't yield to gifts!   155
      No agent that money does not reach.

"Up!" the ghost screamed at us!

"Up, emperor! Up! Wake up!" Fine! Let's go see for ourselves

How strong the prison is, to what extent the castle can be trusted,

    While it still can be done safely. 160

    Whoever knows how to anticipate a calamity

    Has taken the impact away from the calamity.

    They can hardly ever escape the fall,

    Who stand only on unfamiliar feet.

Scene 4

Exabolius, Nicander, the Trabant Guards, Leo.

Exabolius: Where's the sovereign keeping himself?

                       Guard: He spent this part of the night 165

Here, yet without rest, filled with worry.

Now he's suddenly rushing through the arched corridors

Nicander: Alone? *Guard:* We followed him with the armed multitude.[48]

He immediately sent us back and shouted: "Leave us alone!

Part of you keep the Great Hall safe, part of you the gate,

                 until Exabolius appears

And Nicander shows up! Tell them both to withdraw from here

Until we try to get back to this room again."

Well, it is what it is! He isn't acting normal:

Something weighs heavily on his breast; he only wishes for daylight 170

And flees his soft bed! Further, it's not clear to us

Why he commanded [us] to call you in the night.

Nicander: Unfortunately the emperor only holds the wolf [*Michael Balbus*]

                              by the ear.

This, this is what upsets him. I certainly noticed it before:

That one would tarry so long through an extended trial, 175

Until, Exabolius, misfortune would overtake us ourselves.

---

[48] Version C, 1663, adds four lines following line 168 before continuing with line 169, revised.

What can a person possibly think that he's dealing with this night?
What kind of means he's seeking, in what delusion he finds himself?
Won't someone in the city secretly take it upon themselves
To free him [*Michael Balbus*] through negotiation or force?   180
If he breaks loose this time, then it's over (you'll see!)
For the emperor's crown and body, for me, and for you.
Exabolius: The matter is certainly grave. But to want to blame
The fault on the trial doesn't work. This part is simple,
That he was tried at once. Accused by his own mouth,   185
Even convinced by himself that with good reason
He was unanimously condemned right away. A lot was in this error
That the sentence also did not occur with enough haste.
Nicander: Why was a delay placed in the way of revenge?
Exabolius: The emperor was moved to this by his wife,   190
    And she by the high celebration. *Nicander:* Say rather by the doctrine
Of the priests, whom she's used to listening to as gods.
Exabolius: Who doesn't know what a woman can get by asking?
Nicander: Yes, the princess asked, but another prompted her!
    Why, after all, does the flock sworn to the altar   195
    Always want to be in the council? They hear through your ears,
    They slip through your mouth, they trouble themselves about the fields,
    About the camps, the empire, and the ocean: yes, about the
                                              world at large,
    Only not about the church! Has then so much been disturbed
    When an affronted sovereign avenges himself legitimately?   200
    Doesn't God himself place the sword in the hands of princes
    For punishing outrageous guilt, for protecting their position?
    The time, to be sure, must be correctly discerned:
    But if the time itself can tolerate it, if necessity can tolerate it, too,
    Salve and bandages for wounds are often sought after at a celebration,   205
    And means are brought to extinguish a purposely ignited fire.
Exabolius: We must make an effort to change what is amiss:
    The best would be that he is not able to escape so easily.
    Unless. . . *Nicander:* Silence, the monarch. *Leo:* We're done for!

What can we hope, now that he is also rowing in the same boat   210
That we entrusted to the enemy? How should he not subdue us,
He, who rules in chains and (rules) those who can overpower us,
Among whom the guard is sitting?
                    Exabolius: What weighs on the monarch's mind?
Leo: Nothing, except that the indicator points out the new monarch to us.
Nicander: Do you mean the one who will barely survive two nights?   215
Leo: And nevertheless wields the scepter with his hands bound.
Exabolius: What puts the monarch's mind in such distress?
Leo: The prison, in which he's filled with tranquility and we're exhausted
                                                  with pain.

Exabolius: The prison? What? *Leo:* We've just come from the prison:
    Where we beheld upon inspection the highest guilt.   220
    The gates are guarded, the group of cheerful guards
    Manned the stairs and corridor as was commanded.
    We slipped into the cell in which the murderer lies
    Who's gaining time for his deed through our forbearance.
    What didn't we see? He slept in lordly repose,   225
    Completely confident, without fear. We stepped more closely to him,
    And bumped into his head. Yet he remained unmoved,
    And snored more than ever. *Exabolius:* As a downcast person
                                                  usually does,
    Who, out of mortal fear, falls into a deep paralysis:
Nicander: As one who considers himself released from anguish and chains.   230
Leo: Let this describe the resting place! In which nothing can be found
    Except purple and scarlet, draperies, tapestries, and cords
    Embroidered with rich gold; the ceiling is studded with stones
    In the most sublime artistry; purple shrouded him!
    And what the Chinese spin; candles mounted in golden sconces   235
    Illuminated the cause of our pains.
    The work of the fates has adorned the shoddy walls,
    The ground is embellished with the work of Moors.
    Finally! His prison is more than a royal room.
    And you think it's abnormal, that our mind is troubled?   240

Exabolius: God help us! What are we hearing? *Leo:* This we've seen ourselves.
Nicander: It seems strange to me. *Leo:* Hear what is even more disparaging:

    Papias, to whom we had assigned the murderer,

    Is also performing in this sorrowful place, and blatantly assists

    The arch-traitor! He was sleeping at his feet   245

    (Since, after all, the new prince must also have servants).

Exabolius: So he was lying on the ground. *Leo:* As is fitting for one to do

    Who honors the majesty of the emperor in his sleeping chamber.

    One dares to do this in the castle! In our presence!

    We're already assumed to be dead. *Exabolius:* The outrage is too harsh.   250

Leo: Thou impenetrable time! Thou eternally-bright candles

    That shine down upon our pains from the castle in the air!

    Thou loneliness of the night, Thou spirits of that world

    And what keeps that which rules below us in obedience:

    Be witnesses of this grim fierceness. And vouch for this costly oath: 255

    If we do not, before time counts the third day lost,

    Inflamed by holy revenge, transform the murderer and his people

    And followers and their lineage into dust and dismay:

    If we don't sharpen our sword on Papias so that

    Even the cliffs are horrified in the face of his punishment;   260

    Then we must wander about chased, scorned, spit upon, ridiculed,

    Without scepter, without comfort and hope, day and night,

    Because we exist. And among the feet of strangers,

    Yes, in barbaric servitude, we must close this hard life.

    But how can we think so far ahead? This is the final night   265

    That heaven grants us. *Exabolius:* Let the monarch strike

                                     from his attention

    What anger and suspicion dictate. We haven't come so far,

    Loyalty has not yet diminished so completely at the castle,

    If one or two are missing! There are many thousand there

    Who are loyal to their emperor, who most willingly

                             will risk themselves   270

    In danger for his deliverance, who will give their beholden life

    As booty for his crowned head.

Leo: It is still something more that gnaws at our soul and senses.

Exabolius: May the monarch forgive him, who asks about his concern!

Leo: Just a short time ago a dream or ghost burdened us.   275

Nicander: He who pays attention to dreams stirs up fear for himself.

Leo: Heaven has often revealed great things through dreams.

Exabolius: Illusion has often frightened a tired heart through dreams.

Leo: The dream of Phocas didn't lie to Mauritz.*

Exabolius: Whoever relies a great deal on dreams is deluded
much too much.   280

Nicander: Does a dream overwhelm the mind that neither the power
of enemies,

Nor any armed aggression ever caused to panic?

Does a dream overwhelm the mind before which the defiant droves

Of the fates are terrified, before which the Bulgarians flee?

Where are we, great monarch. . . *Leo:* Nicander, know for certain   285

That no flash of lightning, no formidable pestilence,

Has ever robbed our courage. We admit that this one thing

Was almost powerful enough to separate the soul from our breast.

Exabolius: Do let the monarch reveal to us the frightening vision.

Leo: Come, follow us.

Nicander: Whoever is in fear doesn't sleep without suspicion.   290

Scene 5

Michael, Papias, a Guard.

Papias: Get up, lord! What are we doing? Alas! We're in the jaws of Death!

Up, lord! Alas! Well can't he be awakened?

Get up! Get up! *Michael:* What's the matter with you? What's
the need to rush?

Why are you trembling? *Papias:* My lord, alive we're already dead!

Michael: What do I hear? Are you dreaming? *Papias:* Alas!

Michael: Speak up. *Papias:* I'm lost!   295

Michael: What's the matter? *Papias:* Poor me! Alas! Alas! If only I were
never born.

Michael: What's bothering you? *Papias:* Alas! *Michael:* But quickly...

          Papias: My tongue is frozen

Out of fear. *Michael:* And why? *Papias:* The emperor. . .

            Michael: Are you dizzy?

Papias: Was... *Michael:* What? *Papias:*...Standing with us just now.

         Michael: In the prison? *Papias:* Here.

Michael: Oh heaven! *Papias:* It's over. My executioner is at hand.   300

Michael: The emperor? Here with us? How can that be possible?

 How can he get through the door without you opening it?

Papias: He took control of the keys himself.

Michael: I feel that it has now reached the highest point for us!

 Did you see him yourself? *Papias:* I? For whom a deep repose   305

 Closed my tired eyes! *Michael:* Then who told you about it?

Papias: The guards at the door. *Michael:* They want to increase our fear.

 Call someone here to us. Come dreamer, let yourself be heard!

 What insanity infects you? *Guard:* My lord! It's no illusion!

 While I've been here I've never shut an eye.   310

 One half of this night had passed, it seems to me:

 When, unseen, the monarch passed among the armed troops

 Right into the prison. *Michael:* Has such a thing ever been heard of?

 Do you know him? *Guard:* As well as I know myself.

          Michael: A haze deluded you.

Guard: But why does my lord believe that I'm reporting something false? 315

Michael: The emperor? In the night? I think it's a fib.

Guard: My lord, would it bring me an advantage or harm?

Michael: Who unlocked the prison? *Guard:* He himself.

          Michael: Did he come alone?

Guard: The person, who usually follows him, was not with him.

Michael: It appears unbelievable: how was he outfitted?   320

Guard: In purple. And he wore shoes embroidered with gold.

Michael: Now I believe it. Didn't he say something to the guard?

Guard: Not a word. *Michael:* Did he stay with us for long in the room?

Guard: He spent just about as much time as I have here.

Michael: How did he comport himself when he turned his back to you? 325

Guard: He shook his head and made a quick gesture with his hand.
Michael: Enough. *Papias:* Who doubts now? *Michael:* Not me, who senses
    How fiercely he's riled up. He will bind up with chains the one
    Who, at the stake, will just about cool his heated fervor.
Papias: Not me, who is still free, yet already feels the tongs.   330
Michael: I know that now he will pursue new martyrdom for me.
Papias: That he will curse all kinds of fear and misery on my head.
Michael: Bloodthirsty tyrant! Does the wide world possibly have
    A wild tiger like you? Does the scorched field
    Of the Libyan Desert have such colossal lions?   335
    Can hell itself threaten us with more lust to kill?
    Cursed prince! I'm mistaken. Can he be a prince
    About whom there's nothing princely, not even the slightest appearance?
    Who only thinks about hot murder on cold nights,[49]
    Whom our death amuses, whom our life offends,
    Who morphs himself from emperor to prison master,
    Who, more annoying than a slave, keeps watch on my shackles,   340
    Whom ever-constant fear, whom his impaired conscience
    Engrave in diamonds even harder than I am myself!
    What does Papias think? *Papias:* Nothing better occurs to me
    Than a hasty flight. *Michael:* Where will you be safe?
    Flee to that place, where Amphitrite encircles the hot sand;   345
    Flee to that place, where the sun and days are missing from the earth;
    The prince will be behind you and chase after you as swiftly
    As the speedy falcon (chases) the dove at the stream.
    Don't you think that already he has reinforced the watch on you[50]
    And observes your every footstep in highest secrecy?
Papias: We are (I admit it) in the most fierce lion's hell.
Michael: The unforeseen event emboldens my soul
    And suggests a means to me! Alas! If only I could find someone
    Who, for the highest reward, would take so much upon himself;   350

---

[49] Version C, 1663, adds two lines following line 338.
[50] Version C, 1663, adds four lines following line 348.

That he, indeed at once, would take two words to the city.
There are still those alive who are concerned about my distress,
Who are anxious about my wellbeing; they would venture everything,
If only a true friend would take my note to them.
Papias: A friend, he's not far away: *Michael:* Who? *Papias:* Our Theoctist.   355
Michael: Right. *Papias:* But how do you open the gate to the castle?

                                            Michael: With cunning.
Give me some paper and ink. In matters like this
Fear must encourage us and danger make us prudent.
Papias: This is a short letter! *Michael:* Indeed I'm not writing much,
But he who's supposed to read it will understand right away what I want.   360
Now we need to cover the paper completely with wax.
Papias: So whoever is taking it can hide it in his mouth.
Michael: This is the prodigious night in which those who honor Jesus
Praise his birth in the manger, and holy joy intensifies
Through sin cast off because of priestly absolution.   365
The time is right for me and helps me discover a way
To pass through the guard and gate. Pretend that I've requested
What is never denied Christians, and is granted to the dying:
To reconcile my spirit with our God in devotion,
And to crown my condemned head with genuine repentance.   370
I'm also begging for a priest, through whose comforting death
Will no longer be deadly for me! In final agony,
So much cannot reasonably be denied me, the one who laments.
If exit is granted to Theoctist now,
Then give him what I wrote: he can safely knock at   375
The house of the Crambonite and deliver the letter to him,
However he can, without suspicion! If saved out of these chains,
Out of this pain that is driving me into the abyss,
Out of this flood that is rising up to my lips,
From this knife that presses against my throat,   380
From this storm that agitates around my little boat,
And thunder that strikes with flashing lightning around me,

I should leave this chasm of the prison:
Then my life is yours, then it will go well for both of us.
Then trust that your service will richly reward you   385
In a way you can't even desire, and only I can provide.
But then if the flame completely consumes me:
At least I will have tried what was possible and you
                                        (will have tried) much.
Now let come whatever can! Either you will stand
Through me and always beside me, or (you will) soon perish.   390

Chorus of Aristocrats

Strophe

        Do we agree with the opinion
That fate frightens us before our destiny?
That a ghost, a dream, a sign often may reveal
            What can be expected?
Or is it mere phantasy that troubles the tired spirit   395
That, as long as it's in the body, loves its own misery?

Antistrophe

        Is the soul itself also supposed to envision,
As soon as sweet slumber has overcome the body,
(In which, as is taught, it is likewise imprisoned)
            What's to be hoped, and what has taken place?   400
Those consumed by epidemic plague, whom near-death embraced,
Often, indeed, have prophesied what took place when they paled.

Epode

We, who endeavored to know everything
From the beginning of time,
Still cannot fathom   405
What we find right before us every day.
Those, whom heaven warns through omens,
Can barely, indeed, they cannot escape.
Many, too, while exerting an effort to evade death,
Are seen advancing toward death.   410

The Fourth Act

Scene 1

The II and III Conspirators.[51]

II: So you believe through this action, cursed by God and man,
    Contrary to honor and justice, you'll find what you seek?
    Think about it! Should a spirit, should a cheater, dictate
    What should be carried out? Is he supposed to answer what we ask
    Without deception? Whoever desires such advice   5
    Rushes into his own grave. *III*: This game is going so amiss
    That no right way will any longer lead us to a finish.
    We have our standing and property and life to lose.
    For atypical infections you grasp for atypical remedies.
II: Yes, remedies! If only somehow you can be helped by them!   10
    Unfortunately you'll get nothing here but such words as those for which
    The precise meaning is received differently according to each mind.
III: You can interpret it however you wish! Fine! If only it's in my favor!
II: You can interpret it however you wish! But what if it's against you?
III: If I've sacrificed my neck then I can embolden myself   15
    To sweeten my accelerated death with revenge.
    If the sentence turns out well: then I'll remain undaunted,
    Because a person doesn't venture into such an attempt in vain.
II: Much better to have died without guilt, in case it fails,
    And to have achieved victory without guilt, in case it succeeds.   20
III: I can no longer stand between fear and doubt.

---

[51] Throughout Acts 4 and 5, Gryphius interchangeably uses Roman and Arabic numerals, with or without the designation "Conspirator" (*Zusammengeschworne*), to identify speaking roles of the enumerated conspirators. I have followed his flexible method of identification, also abbreviating *Conspirator* (*Consp.*).

You can, if you prefer, go to the Crambonite's house.

I'll follow straight away. But keep this exploit hushed.

This is Iamblichus' house. *II:* The factory of crazy lies.

Scene 2

The III Conspirator, Iamblichus, a Boy (silent), the Hellish Ghost.

Iamblichus: Who knocks? *Consp.:* Open up. *Iamblichus:* Who is it?

Consp.: Your friend! *Iamblichus:* Who is it? *Consp.:* Pay attention!   25

Iamblichus: Hey, why so late? It's almost past midnight,

    Astraea[52] is rising. The Great Bear [*constellation*] has turned.

    I've been waiting for your arrival with vexation for a long time.

    The really convenient time is slipping through our hand,

    The spirits don't appear at just any hour.   30

Consp. To avoid suspicion, I couldn't leave my court

    Any sooner than before sleep had overtaken all of them.

    You know why I've come, I gave you the

    Schedule for the mission today—don't hold me up any longer.

Iamblichus: Not at all. Just stay courageous; little is attracted to the site   35

    By trembling: abstain from speaking,

    Don't step out of the circle. Loosen the knots

    And ungird your body; your left foot must be bare.

    My son [*to silent boy*], bring us the tools with which I generate lightning

    And awaken corpses and move Hecate.   40

    Loosen my aged hair and take this cap away,

    And this improper garment. You have to remove your shoe.

    Where's my white coat embroidered with symbols

    That was stitched by a chaste hand at the appointed time?

    The light made of finest wax and children's tallow?   45

---

[52] In Greek mythology, Astraea was the virgin goddess of innocence and purity, usually associated with Dike, the goddess of justice. In the Golden Age, she was the last of the immortals to live with humans. In the Iron Age, she fled the depravity of humanity and ascended to heaven to become the constellation Virgo.

The switch that I recently selected with great effort from hazel trees,

When there was same amount of sun between day and night?

Give me the yew. Give it to burn for incense.

Wind this band around my head three times,

Pour out the dead bones, ignite the shrunken hand;   50

As long as these luminous fingers burn here before us

No unknown person, no unknown eye, shall recognize us.

Let this be the first ring, let this be the last circle,

And here's where the skull belongs. Hand me the scarf

Moistened with sweat of the dying; the linked hearts,   55

And here the skin of the woman who was strangled in childbirth

By this hand, with some herbs mixed in,

That I trimmed off with some ore in the silent moonlight.

Pay attention to whether I have correctly taken note of the symbols:

That nothing that is essential has been left out.   60

Frightening king of powerful spirits. Prince of the heavens,

                      possessor of the world!

Ruler of omni-present dark nights, who envisions laws for death and hell,

Who sees what vanished before, eternal ages ago,

Who sees what future hours yet to come

Have staged for mortals, who sees what still is blooming now,   65

And what will be trampled, as if it were the present.

Let me, your ordained one, greet you: permit me to fathom

                      your intent.

Grant that in such an important matter I discover what

              needs to be done, and what should be left alone.

Let, as this blood gushes from the vein;

Let, as this smoke penetrates the air;   70

Let, if what happened in your service ever pleased you;

Let us see the desired result of this very difficult act.

Thou, who conceived all cunning,

Thou, who invented poison,

Whom the wise Brahmin[53] honors,   75
Whom the naked teacher * hears,
Whom the Indian crowns
And reconciles with human blood.
For whom Chartag killed her child,
For whom the Scythians slaughtered guests,   80
For whom, in the land of Jews,*
The first fruit of mothers is burned to death,
For whom the Celts hang up heads,
And grant prisoners their lives.
Wherefore you often reveal yourself in the form of snakes,   85
To one who bends his knee to you,
Wherefore you're fond of frightening us
In huge bushes with signs, with visions, with light!
Wherefore it's your pleasure to move the heavens
With lightning and thunderbolts;   90
Wherefore your power can be found in subterranean cliffs,
In the graves of cold corpses:
Wherefore hidden treasures
Are in your care;
Wherefore nothing that delights you   95
Surpasses human blood:
Wherefore you can ignite the senses with wild sexual desire:
And dissolve true love:
Wherefore you often disguise yourself as a nymph or mermaid:
And consort with women and men: 100
Wherefore you block the woman from the man, and vice versa,
So that they enjoy no wedlock:
Wherefore you have killed brothers with a brother's hand;
And reddened the unashamed son with his parents' blood.

---

[53] *Brahmin* is a caste in Hinduism that is known for its priests, teachers, and those who protect sacred learning.

Wherefore you have often predicted the future   105
In the entrails of a virgin,
Who, by the sword of her own father,
Was sacrificed on the desolate heath.
Wherefore through the hacked-off head of a boy*
What was not known was discovered by you.   110
Wherefore far away a child that was snatched from the breast
Was impaled for your usage,
Wherefore a pregnant body, still alive, was cut open
In order to satisfy you, in order to outbid you;
Wherefore a mother herself consumed what she had borne   115
When you turned to her with favor.
Wherefore I am your priest, who never refrained from
Honoring you with such sacrifices:
Wherefore I ripped women's hearts warm from their breasts,
Accordingly, let me mercifully hear a reply.   120
Wherefore I have always desecrated what is holy:
And always cursed what is blessed;
If I shall spill innocent blood for your tomorrow
Then let me clearly know an answer:
Wherefore the secret strength of the strange words and symbols,   125
That I initiate,
Has the power to appease you, supreme ruler,
So grant that I receive what I request:
    (*After this he makes some strange signs and mumbles quite a while*)
Very well! I've been heard, the stars' brilliance pales,
Heaven is upset; the Lion and the Bear [*constellations*] disappear,   130
The Virgin [*star*] is scared off, lightning flashes in the murky heavens,
Earth's solid ground quakes, the wax images drip,
How Hecate rages! Flames break forth,
Don't be afraid! See the ghost? Here an attentive ear is useful.
The Ghost: The emperor's throne collapses, yet more through
                                 cunning than strength.   135
In the place where no blood is spilled, the job is done with murder.

The prison is elevated, if you don't stir up conflict.

You: seek no reward. You will get what Leo bears. *

Iamblichus: Done! My son, toss behind you what I give to you.

Don't look back! Keep still until the ghost departs. 140

He flees. Put everything away; take the rods, the tools, and light

To the proper place. What? Is the answer of no use?

Why are you standing there so stunned? *Consp.:* I'm shaking all over!

I don't know who I am. *Iamblichus:* Is the result objectionable to you?

Consp.: No, truly, even if, indeed, it seems somewhat obscure: 145

I ask that you please explain to me what he meant by places

"Where no blood is spilled." *Iamblichus:* Those which are exempt by law,

Such as churches, such as altars, and other such consecrated places.

Consp.: But how should I interpret this? "You, seek no reward:

You'll get what Leo bears:" *Iamblichus:* What does he bear but the crown? 150

Consp.: Enough. You shall not find me unthankful, my friend:

The appointed time will quickly vanish, I think:

I'm leaving. *Iamblichus:* Indeed he's beginning the task fearlessly

And will complete it successfully, but from what I can guess,

With little or even no value. What the ghost explained to us 155

Appears ambiguous. You will be given as a reward

What Leo bears. Yes, indeed. What does he bear? The crown and death!

I fear that you will be forced into the same plight.

I deliberately kept the danger hidden from you:

But what evening doesn't reveal, morning will clarify. 160

Scene 3

The Crambonite, the Conspirators, a Servant of the Crambonite.

Crambonite: So it goes! When good fortune smiles at us with a sweet mouth,

Then we defy death and break down all the power

Of the mighty scepter. Then the earth's firm ground

Must tremble beneath us and nearly turn into ashes.

We rip the mountains apart and split open the cliffs. 165

We almost impede the richly swirling course of Pontus [*the sea*].

The Danube cannot flood onto our land.

Great Thetis [*granddaughter of Pontus*] herself learns to flow

more calmly before us.

We enter a conspiracy that has the power to force onto a yoke

Everything the world and the beclouded firmament   170

Hold within their bounds. Yet when the heavens warm up,

And the night of thick clouds wants to flash to give us light,

No one knows where we are. Our great courage vanishes

Like snow, when Titan [*the sun*] transits Aries [*March 15-May15*];

As quick as our mouths are, so slow are our hands.   175

The beginning burns and glows; the middle, with the end,

Transforms the severe cold into ice. *4. Consp.:* Does someone

accuse us of this?

Us? Whom dire necessity can't stop in our rapid rush

For revenge? Who nearly surround the blaze

In which Michael offers up, for our property and life,   180

His body, blood, and spirit. Us? Whom the bitter night

Has brought through in solidarity, without fear and suspicion?

Us, who until now have talked of nothing except how to storm his castle

And how to overthrow from his throne the one who overthrew him?

Crambonite: Then, when the lion threatened with blood,

and murder, and strangling   185

There was no emboldened hero who pounced against him.

4. Consp.: Whoever wounds a fierce animal when there is no advantage

Is like someone who baits a lion without an arrow and dogs.

Crambonite: A tyrant should be attacked wherever, whenever, and

however possible.

4. Consp.: He warns, who cannot attack and can kill at the same time.   190

Crambonite: A quick sword accomplishes far more than a long composition.

4. Consp.: A wise mind can deliver more than a thousand spears.

Crambonite: He who ponders everything puts no plot into action.

4. Consp.: Send fools to the fire and your whole house will burn down.

Crambonite: Well, can a bright mind extinguish the emperor's flames?   195

4. Consp.: Well, can a quick sword fight with so many troops?

Crambonite: Who doubts. *4. Consp.:* For sure not I, who detected your courage,
    Provided there was no enemy. *Crambonite:* Then just observe
                    whether my hand
    Is equal in strength to my courage. *I. Consp.:* What are you doing?
                4. Consp.: Let's test and see
    If he is as courageous to fight as he is to curse.   200

Crambonite: Let loose! Let loose! Well? *4. Consp.:* I implore you
                  not to grab me.

2. Consp.: But just keep in mind where we are! This mad raving will break apart
    Our firm bond, this squabble will reveal
    What we could barely conceal with so much cunning and oaths.
    Do you have a mind to fight? Thrust your valiant sword   205
    Into the breast of the tyrant who desires your death.
    Attack the Trabant guards who occupy the wall and gate,
    Who surround the prison. If we ourselves injure one another,
    Then a contract is out for you, Michael:
    Then we'll fall with you, then we'll take the same route   210
    To the open grave. Can Leo desire anything more
    Than that we turn our sword on our hearts?

4. Consp.: He's not the one who can defy me and everyone!

Crambonite: Nor is he the one who shall mock me and you:
                2. Consp.: But look at
    The fear that surrounds us so. Those who run amok on the waves   215
    When the raging North wind blows in all the sails,
    When the beleaguered ship dashes from cliff to cliff,
    And breaks up in pieces and wreckage, now here, now there,
    [They're] unworthy that anyone should lament their severe distress.
    Heed my advice, and at the first light of day extinguish   220
    The scorching flames with the blood of our enemy.
    Courage, boldness, body, and fame and our salvation and home
    Demand this of you. May he be hailed as the strongest
    Who will drive his sword through the emperor's throat.
    The silent phase of dark night doesn't allow more.   225

Go and rest until the dawn calls us again.

Crambonite: Who's there? *Servant:* My lord! *Crambonite:* What is it?

         Servant: A stranger's at the door.

Do you want me to lead him into this room right now?

6. Consp.: We're betrayed! *Crambonite:* Ask him what he wants then.

I. Consp.: Oh, disaster! *II. Consp.:* Arm yourselves!   230

Crambonite: Whom does he have at his side? *Servant:* My lord, he is alone.

Crambonite: Armed? *Servant:* No. *Crambonite:* Say what you think.

        6. Consp.: I think

That our meeting has been exposed by a false friend!

And squads are hidden around the court, people around the square:

That they're planning to furtively press in on us: 235

Since the emperor has called for them to raid us in the night.

I. Consp.: In vain! As long as I can still move my fingers!

Ye heroes without fear! It's a challenge for all of us:

Much better to have suppressed your enemy with your own corpse

Than to suffocate in the hangman's noose, without resistance. 240

Crambonite: Still, who knows if that's true: I'll go out to the entryway

And find out who it might be. *II. Consp.:* We want to back you up:

Because our hearts are beating fast. *Crambonite:* You stay hidden here

Until you hear me call: who knows if our worries

Are not in vain. *2. Consp.:* Act as if you've just awakened.   245

Crambonite: Sure. *2. Consp.:* Loosen up your clothes. Oh, troublesome night!

III. *Consp.:* Out of trouble, tranquility is born; out of displeasure, pleasure.

Those who swore allegiance to the common good,

They are cheered up by work. *II. Consp.:* Work doesn't frighten me.

Whoever is horrified in the face of adversity, given that

            fear enters in   250

And the ambitious goal is overturned, must perish;

The sigh spurs me on! Just like the power of flames,

That one wants to conceal, crackles in its restriction,

And lives because of the crackling. *I. Consp.:* Fine, heroes:

            hold your words 255

And seize your weapons. We stand on this place

On which we must conquer. *2. Consp.:* If Leo succumbs,

    Then, if I fall right on his body, I have prevailed.

I. Consp.: Right: he is praiseworthy, who, if he must attack,

    Can bring to the ground, together with himself,

                    whatever wants to overpower him.   260

Scene 4

The Crambonite, the Conspirators.

Crambonite: Take courage! The fear that overwhelmed us is unfounded.

    You all know Theoctist. *I. Consp.:* What kind of a game is this?

Crambonite: Through him Michael is letting us know his intention.

2. Consp.: What? By word of mouth? *Crambonite:* No, in writing.

I. Consp.:   Let's open the letter.

Crambonite: It's a small piece of paper completely covered with wax.   265

3. Consp.: Done! It's already coming unfastened. The message is hidden here.

4. Consp.: Is this his seal? *Crambonite:* Yes:

               6. Consp.: But what could be bothering him?

Crambonite: Is that worth asking? *6. Consp.:* Come on, read us his request.

Crambonite: "I've come through you, and you through me, into the

                            greatest plight:

    If the morning sees me here, you will be looking at pain and death."   270

I. Consp.: I see no way to save him yet tonight;

    The castle is heavily manned; the gates are secured with soldiers

    All around, the strength of the iron latch

    Closes off every entry. *3. Consp.:* If he made it possible

    For Theoctist to find the way through the gate and the castle,   275

    Then why do we doubt? We? We who are not bound up.

I. Consp.: One person exits the court more easily than many can go up into it.

Crambonite: Can a single individual accomplish more than a whole group?

I. Consp.: Yes, for sure, if you have to camouflage yourself in fox fur.

Crambonite: The lion's skin is at stake. *I. Consp.:*

                         Time won't allow for this.   280

Crambonite: In the event that what he threatens overcomes us in the morning,

Then we'll depart from the world by torture, dishonored and for nothing.

2. Consp.: Lest we've been revealed to the emperor;

Lest Michael is just scaring us with his message,

I would advise this: don't hesitate any longer. This, what we together   285

Have resolved, believe me, can't be kept silent

By keeping still a while longer. *5. Consp.:* Can anyone be found here

Who truthfully could be associated with betrayal?

2. Consp.: Don't fool yourself. Dead marble hears

Whatever is thought about princes. This statue, that pillar tells   290

What has been reported against them, and can speak of rubbish.

I. Consp.: There's more than enough rubbish. Let's inquire about some advice.

Crambonite: Start an uproar in the city. *I. Consp.:* How? When? In an instant?

2. Consp.: Break into the castle with gold.

                         I. Consp.: Who'll give it to the guard?

Who'll supply us with the money? Can such coarse minds   295

And so many desperate heads be won in an hour?

5. Consp.: Listen to my proposal: When the fourth part

Of the night is sounded, in quick haste

The procession of priests, to whom the palace church is commended,

Must find itself up in the castle. Hidden among them, we can   300

Penetrate through the guard. With most magnificent splendor

The high holy celebration of the joyous night,

In which the Virgin gave birth to the Son of the Highest,

In whose presence and to whom we have sworn ourselves,

Will be celebrated, as usual: So rise and dress yourselves   305

As priests! Toss off your helmet and anything that can hinder us!

Hide your sword in hollowed-out candles,

And take over the temple until the wellspring of pains,

The monstrous animal, unaware of his plight,

Unaware of this power, comes to give himself up   310

To his death, deserved long ago! *I. Consp.:* Here we've got to consider,

My brother, what should we do if someone recognizes us on the way,

Yes, even in the temple, dressed in garb

That doesn't suit us? *2. Consp.:* If the sentry attacks us—

5. Consp.: Dismiss all concern; darkness covers the narrow streets.   315
    Priests are usually admitted immediately, without asking.
    The extensive space in the temple assures safety from danger
    Until the monarch arrives. Then throw him on the bier!
3. Consp.: One more thing: we all have to pounce on him at the same time,
    So wait until you hear him sing with the priests.   320
5. Consp.: Let this be the signal: when you hear the second refrain,
    Strike up, then go and tear away the dead member
    Of the great empire. *3. Consp:* We have time to scurry:
    Tell us where you have in mind to stay in the interim.
Crambonite: Why? What are you talking about? *3. Consp.:* I want to get   325
    Myself a robe. *Crambonite:* No need. Everything we need,
    All just alike, will be delivered to my house.
    I ask of you: let's not separate from each other any more
    Until the deed is done. *I. Consp.:* Dire necessity unites
    Us all: if you now feel the inner strength;   330
    And your blazing courage scorns the invisible arrows
    Of dark trepidation; if you conquer without any fear the thunderbolts,
    The storms of cruel fortune, like cliffs in the sea; and if the horrific height
    Of the cliff on which we stand do not hurl you into a swoon: 335
    Then we have reduced the power of tyranny.
    If the grim glance of death makes you fainthearted;
    Then believe that our fall is certain after this night.
    It's much better to have sacrificed one's blood
                      and courage and goods and life
    For the common good, than dishonorably.   340
    In brief: here is fame, if honor attaches to you:
    Here is despair, should despair inspire feeble courage.
Crambonite: Let this sword, that I now touch with this hand,
    Bear witness to who I am. If I don't plunge this steel
    Into the breast of the lion: so may it pass through my heart.   345
    I beg of you! If I don't thrust because intense pain
    Won't let me move my arm, then strike me, myself, to the ground.

I. Consp.: This is also my resolution. I speak it with my mouth,
   I swear it with my fist. The deed shall be the guarantor
   That I am the enemy of tyrants. That no fear of pain   350
   Will challenge my spirit. The hour shall make clear
   If my courage is too slight to annihilate the throne.
3. Consp.: Assure yourselves firmly of this: that each of us goes willingly
   Wherever this task call us; sooner will the blaze turn itself into snow,
   The tree trunks into glassy ice, the sea into grass,   355
   Before I stand aghast to carry out the attack.
Crambonite: Gold is strengthened by fire, a hero through fear and shock.
   Whoever is fearful: live in despair. Whoever courageous:
                                             draw your sword.
   Forward then, follow! I myself will lead you into the room
   In which it will be easy for you to garb yourself like clerics.   360

Chorus of Priests and Virgins

First Strophe

Virgins: Joyous night
         In which the true light autonomously appeared to us,
         In which He, Whom earth and sea and sky serve,
               Before Whom hell breaks,
         Through Whom all that draws breath must live,   365
         Entered into the vale of tears;
         In which God came from the canopy of clouds;
         Precious night refreshes the great world.

First Antistrophe

Priests: Ever-brilliant radiance
   That darkness shrouds, that obscurity has hidden,   370
   Now rends the cover asunder. The sun, that before morning,
     Before the starry galaxy
   Adorned heaven's vast firmament,
   Before eternity itself glanced forward,
   Beamed forth in gleaming bright splendor;   375
   Suddenly rises in black midnight.

First Epode

Virgins and Priests:
   Let earth stand firm, the sky breaks,
   Yet not split by hot thunderbolts;
   Behold the host of angels hastening toward us
     Because the creator speaks to us.   380
   Yet no longer encircled with mighty storms, with wrathful passion:
   Ah! His gentle whimpering is heard, while His lofty host sings.

Second Strophe

Priests: We erred without light,
   Exiled in black night by God's solemn curse:
   Therefore the blessed Savior will seek us in the darkness.   385
     Don't you hear His calling?
   You, who have lost the image of the Highest,
   Behold the image born unto you.
   Ask not "Why does it enter in a stable?"
   He seeks us, who are more bestial than a beast.   390

Second Antistrophe

Virgins: The shadow reaches an end,
The ancient prophecy is fulfilled by this child:
By His tears the fire of hell is extinguished:
He offers us mouth and hands.
If you couldn't recognize our followers 395
We now may call God Brother!
He is no more a fire that consumes;
The Lord has transfigured Himself into a servant.

Second Epode

Priests and Virgins:
Glory be to God on high,
Who honors our flesh beyond merit, 400
Who has extended His grace without end.
May His steadfast peace remain
Longer than the sun shines upon us: May this child grant us all
To will His will, so that we shall always well please Him.

The Fifth Act

Scene 1

Theodosia, Phronesis, the Highest Priest, a Messenger.
Theodosia is sleeping on a couch. Her mother's ghost stands before her
(as described in lines 12-36), and disappears when she awakens.

Theodosia: Alas! Night of horrors! Ha! Terrorizing time!
    Dismal darkness! Must the fierce pain
    Of worry deny even the repose of weary sleep?
    Does nothing encircle thrones but harsh animosity?
Phronesis: Does Her Majesty lament? What is it that bothers her?   5
Theodosia: A bitter dream prevented our brief rest.
    My cold breast freezes, yet all my limbs sweat
    And my whole body shakes: we sat down,
    Dressed as if we were at a celebration: as my soul remembered
    And contemplated that year, a slumber overcame us.   10
    The earth, as it seemed to us, began to split in two;
    We saw our mother come forth from her grave:
    Not blithe, as she was when she lived,
    Not as her father adorned her with luxurious gold.
    The purple was asunder, her gown lay torn to shreds,   15
    Her breast and arms were bare; she stood on bare feet,
    No diamonds, no ruby adorned her lovely hair,
    That, sadly, was all tousled and wet with tears.
    We kissed her face, and called, "Oh, welcome!
    Welcome, worthy lady. Now nothing has been taken from us,   20
    Since the Lord of Lords, whom you loved so devoutly,
    Lifts you from your grave and gives you to your child.
    Lay aside your mourning garb, and sing praises to Him who

Smiles in the manger. The desolate cliffs listen
To the angels rejoicing! The narrow sea resounds   25
While joy-filled Byzantium offers thanksgiving upon thanksgiving."
"Alas!" she spoke, "alas, my child!" and wrung her pale hands.
"It is not time to rejoice! Your rule is coming to an end.
Arise, if it is not too late (if one can still rescue,
Once death already grasps) and save your son and husband.   30
The holy night shrouds the greatest atrocities;
The safe church, murder! Alas! You cannot be warned—"
She wanted to say something more, when a torrent of tears
Streamed down both cheeks and her voice broke.
A bloody sweat appeared on each of her limbs,   35
The drops clung like corals to her hair.
When (before we expected) she vanished in a gentle breeze,
Our purple gown was transformed into a sack.*
We wandered, lost, all alone in unfamiliar deserts,
In which ferocious bears and fierce tigers dwell,   40
Until an enraged beast flung his claws at us
And tore off both our breasts and ripped our heart out.
Then anxiety rubbed the sleep from our tear-stained cheeks.
What can the omniscient Being have ordained for us?
Omnipresent Eternity! Let the power of your lightning,   45
The glow of your grave thunder, and what the solemn night
Threatens your poor maid, vanish in profound favor.
And yet, if we ask in vain, then let this head feel
What your judgment declares. Accept us as a sacrifice
For him, without whom this country cannot live in peace.   50
Phronesis: Where there are worries, there are dreams.
     A troubled conscience is terrified even at that which we need not fear.
Theodosia: Where there is a scepter, there is fear!
Phronesis: Fear is but a game and a joke
          Where there is nothing to fear.

Theodosia: Oh, would, would but God!
    Where is the Prince?

Phronesis: Gone to the divine service.

Theodosia: We tarry   55
    Here really too long! Come, ladies, let us hasten.

 Priest: Murder! Murder!

Phronesis: God help us! What is it?

Priest: Murder, murder.

Phronesis: Where?

Priest: At the altar!

Theodosia: Oh, Heaven. Our dream is sadly much too true.

Phronesis: Princess! She's dying! Behold her cheeks and lips pale,
    Her pupils congeal, as in deceased corpses: 60
    Bring balsam, ointment, and wine. Princess? She's dying.
    Princess!

Theodosia: Alas! Were we elevated to this fall?
    From where does this misfortune come?

Priest: I cannot know the reason.

Theodosia: Where is the prince?

Priest: He was still there when I ran away.

Theodosia: He stayed, of course he stayed, the one who can't escape.   65

Phronesis: Has someone been attacked?

Priest: Look at my wounds.

Theodosia: Tell us how this tragedy began:

Priest: The third part of darkness had passed,
    When the chorus of priests entered God's church;
    The songs began, the sound of the sweet chords   70
    Resounded more pleasant in the stillness:
    Each person was reminded to honor the great night,
    In which the One who is equal to God in power and being
    Came from his glory, the realm of the highest Father,
    Into flesh. Devotion could be felt   75
    With holy fervent passion, and it ignited heart and soul
    With a chaste flame. Sighs advanced

And rose high above before the vapors of incense.

The prince himself began to sing of Christ's army, *

That neither tyrant, nor death, nor henchman can defeat.   80

Meanwhile an unknown mob emerges,

Unseen, from every corner, and tears up the barriers

That separate the priests from the congregation, choir, and temple.

In a flash swords are drawn from sheaths,

From candles, canes, and robes. The gleaming weaponry   85

Shines more frightening in light, and flashes

Its quick reflection back and forth; everyone gapes and falters

And doesn't know what they're doing and asks the one who asks them,

Like when quick lightning strikes the tall fir trees

And turns branches, trunk, and stump into a glowing fire;   90

A tired wanderer, in such a swift cracking,

Thinks nothing else except that he's already in the jaws of death.

The wrath finally breaks out; the daggers strike at me;

Before I realized the danger, I received this wound.

I cried: "Ye heroes, spare, spare my venerable hair,   95

Think of the holy time: you're strangling by the altar

The one who never harmed you." They backed off when I hollered,

And attacked others. This one wept, that one ran,

The next fell down—I escaped from the storm, I know not how.

Theodosia: Doubt not: body and realm have been taken from the prince.   100

The storm lashes out at him! What am I saying? Alas, he lies fallen!

The treachery of our crazed enemies has conquered us.

Did our tolerance kindle the hot flame

In which everything we possessed, envisioned, or wished for perished?

Phronesis: It's still not clear.

Theodosia: What? Can anything be more clear?   105

Phronesis: Princess! She absorbs herself, prematurely, in pain!

Theodosia: Princess without a prince! Princess without a crown!

Princess without a country! Pushed by this blow from the golden throne

Into the abyss.

Messenger:					Cursed cruelty!
   Wrath unheard of before, unexpected sorrow-					110
   Has the Christians' enemy, the Bulgarian, ever perpetrated this?
   Has the heated Persian? Or the one who loves only deathblows,
   The depraved Scythian, ever tried such a deed?
Theodosia:					We know what he laments,
   His pains affect us! Ask! No, don't ask! Yes, ask!
   Let him tell what he knows! Bid him to hide nothing;					115
   We imagine even more than he can reveal to us.
Messenger: The church is desecrated. At the altar the prince is
   Stabbed to death; your crown and life are in danger.
Theodosia: Can the one who no longer rules hope for anything but the bier?
   Come tell us which sword will pierce through this heart;					120
   She pleads, she commands. Just show us the hand
   That will release our soul.
Messenger:					What the bond of blood,
   What friendship, long favor, what political ambition and promise
   Bind to Michael, has, to end his distress, snatched up
   The bare sword; and into the holy place					125
   It has ventured, unrecognized. Much has tainted the prince's fame
   With crazed envy. Many who hope to make themselves great
   When change occurs and the demise of others takes place
   Support this gang of murderers! The raging was aflame,
   And someone yelled: "Attack! Attack!" And the armed hand					130
   Struck out for the priest's head, in error, not in revenge.
   Then our prince, filled with courage in such a confused event,
   Ripped the sword from both fists of someone, I know not whom;
   And he smote the breast and the skull of the one who struck at him,
   Until the sword shattered like ice on the enemy's steel blade.					135
   He saw himself surrounded! His guards were pushed far back:
   His friends without direction: yet he stood undaunted,
   Like a riled-up lion, who, when the close chase
   Cuts off all escapes for him, with wide-open jaws
   Scares the hound, then the hunter, and tries to free himself.					140

In vain: since he was pressed upon from all sides,

He, whose warm blood now flowed from limbs and veins.

He felt that his strength was gradually leaving him

When he gripped the cross, on which He had hung,

Who dying, saved us: the tree on which the world   145

Was freed from fear: so that death was felled,

Before whom hell recoils in fear. "Think," he called, "of the life

That gave itself for your soul on this burden.

But don't contaminate the blood of the Lord, that stains this trunk,

With sinner's blood. If I have committed so many sins,   150

Then for fear of Him who carried this staff

Refrain from banging your angry fist on the altar of Jesus the Son."

They stopped still at these words, like in an avalanche

When the frustrated creek halts its proud course,

And the flood then rises upwards, the foaming waves rage,   155

Until, with a formidable roaring, the tenth stroke surges

Over the barrier and rips everything along with it,

And hurls the mossy stones into the deep valleys.

The hardened Crambonite only then really began to rage;

He shrieked: "Now, tyrant! Now is not the time to plead!"   160

And thrust up his murderous sword that came down on the prince

And with one stroke took from him both his arms and the cross.

As he fell, they stabbed him twice through his breast.

I, myself, saw how he kissed the cross

Onto which his body sank, and departed with that kiss: 165

As his corpse was mutilated, as the dull dagger

Was forced through his every limb, as the final gifts of Jesus,

His precious flesh and blood that sooth weary souls,

That refresh a languishing heart in its final anxiety,

Were mixed, oh horror! with imperial blood.   170

Theodosia: Thou sulfurous glowing heat of thunder-strong flames,

Attack! Ravage them! Ravage us together!

Break, abyss, break asunder, and, if you can,

Thou cleft of eternity, devour us and the murderers!

We err! No, not them! Only us, only us alone,   175
Them, too! Yet far from us, let weep whoever wants to weep.
The eye's spring congeals; what's happening? Is our heart
Transformed into hard steel? Does the bitter pain separate
Feeling from our breast? Is our body becoming a corpse?
Come, where the stroke of lightning doesn't want to reach your head: 180
Where, distant, the earth is deaf: come, thou desired death!
Thou end of dark anxiety! Thou port of desolate despair!
We call in vain to him, who avoids the melancholy,
And only attacks the spirit who suffers no affliction.
Come! Come, assassins! And cool the burning courage,   185
The hell-inflamed revenge, in the blood of these veins.
The prince is not yet gone. While our limbs still move
He lives in this breast. Approach, and thrust the dagger
Through this, which beats in me. A quick demise
Is a certain comfort, when one can no longer stand.   190
Priest: Princess! The One who created you hath predestined this death.
Theodosia: And He predestined that we long for our grave.
Priest: He biddeth us to deal patiently with whatever oppresses us.
Theodosia: Then why did He not send patience with the cross?
Priest: Can there be such an evil, that no solace could reach it?   195
Theodosia: Can there be such an evil, that it can be compared to ours?
Priest: God doth not burden us with more than we can bear:
Theodosia: On one day He taketh throne, crown, realm, and husband.
Priest: He taketh, Princess, that which He previously hath given.
Theodosia: One thing alone He doth not take, that which isn't wanted: life.   200
Priest: He doth test with heated anguish, like gold, those whom He doth love.
Theodosia: Those, whom He doth hate, go free while He doth afflict us.
Priest: He who causeth your wounds can heal all wounds.
Theodosia: The stroke is noxious that can sever hearts.
Priest: What isn't severed by time? Death ends everything.   205
Theodosia: The prince must enter his troubled grave before his time.
Priest: He doesn't die before his time, who ends his own epoch.
Theodosia: With blood that was spilled in the church on God's table.

Priest: One doesn't die as one would wish, but only as the Highest willeth!

Theodosia: Then doth the Highest will murder and such tragedy?   210

Priest: Can he, who is mortal, comprehend His judgment?

Theodosia: Speak thus! And teach the masses to topple princes

from their thrones!

> Restrain your comforting! The pains are too severe,
>
> The wounds are too fresh, the clanging weapon
>
> Trembles before the door: arise, spirit, the murderers are coming!   215
>
> Well! Let us, comforted, follow after him, whom they took from us.
>
> Arise, my spirit. She pays little heed to the enemy,
>
> She, who lives imperially and wants to die royally,
>
> Farewell! Don't weep for me! Open up! Bolting is useless here—
>
> Open up! One must greet death when it arrives.   220

Scene 2

The First Group of Conspirators, Theodosia.

I. Consp.: The diamond-firm yoke of dreadful tyranny,

> The cliff-heavy burden of harsh torturing,
>
> The scepter of metal, the throne established on blood,
>
> The all-consuming anxiety that lays waste to cities and fields,
>
> And whatever else a ferocious prince puts into action,   225
>
> Is, although belatedly, finally abolished by us.
>
> Your reign is now over. The unbridled raging,
>
> The arm striking everything is atomized into the air:
>
> Learn now to obey those whom you ruled; and understand,
>
> How often there is only one night between falling and the height.   230

2. Consp.: The heavily oppressed country that is relived of its weighty burden

> Now inhales fresh air, and rejoices that your grandeur
>
> Declines in such disdain: yet everyone laments
>
> That tyrants can't be punished according to what they deserve.
>
> He offers but one corpse for thousands of misdeeds;   235
>
> When a commoner offends, no pardon spares him.
>
> A simple offense receives wheel, pillory, noose, and sword,

Oil, seething lead and pitch, a horse of glowing iron;
He [*tyrant*] becomes great through evil and blooms when those wither
Who stand with heart and hand for honesty.   240
I. Consp.: In the end, what can a person do? Whoever grasps what
                                            he [*tyrant*] does
Is pressed by him [*tyrant*] until at last the overwhelming burden
Crushes his neck and spine. If one should refuse him,
To carry more than is indeed possible (however great his courage!),
Him he besmears with rebellion! Whoever has incited the populace,   245
Impugned the prince, or insulted majesty,
He must clear out! If he himself doesn't want to venture against you!
Tyrants! Whoever doesn't strike you down is struck down by you!
Theodosia: So have you, as you boast, murdered tyrants?
I. Consp.: Who doubts?
Theodosia: Listen to us! Who places you in power?   250
Who entrusts you with this sword? Who so endowed you,
That you, who were nothing before, now have more than everything:
Who? The one you now inveigh against. When he, with utmost splendor,
Elevated you next to himself and turned you virtually into gods,
Who was he? A tyrant? You sang with different tongues.   255
Now, since you've succeeded with your prank, your murder,
He is called: I know not what. As long as a prince awards
And loves as well-deserving those who are unworthy,
And seeks to satisfy their greed with gold and honors,
His praise must fill the realm, his fame the world.   260
As soon as he no longer gives, indeed no longer can give,
As soon as he punishes insurrection, disloyalty infects you.
As soon as the disease arouses you and rogues join together
The desire for new power and political might is easily kindled;
Then he is called a tyrant: the one who lies dead is slandered.   265
Thus a dead lion is often attacked by a mouse.
2. Consp.: The lion, whose life was cut off by this sword!
Theodosia: Fame worthy deed! You have toppled from his throne
Whom? One person! So many of you! You have, in the black of night,

Betrayers, murdered more through deceit than wounds, 270

The one, to whom previously you often swore oaths:

What weapons did you not employ against him,

Who went unarmed? May this atrocity

Be compared to anything? You've desecrated the glorious moment

In which GOD gave Himself to us, with regicide: 275

And in this holy place, that releases sinners,

You've spilled innocent blood: who can henceforth doubt

If you're still Christians; behold in the temple

The mutilated corpse that lies on the cross

Upon which JESUS conquered hell: 280

The true flesh of the LORD: that you splattered with blood,

His blood, that you have mixed with the emperor's blood.

2. Consp.: It's not a matter of how, when, or where evil ones are disrupted.

Theodosia: A human differentiates, but not you, you monsters!

I. Consp.: Guilt is punished with justice.

Theodosia: Who gives to you this power? 285

     A prince serves Him alone, who keeps watch in the clouds:

     He who places us on the throne can ban us from the throne.

2. Consp.: The lowliest of the populace is master of the tyrant.

I. Consp.: The Highest executes His justice with the arms of men.

2. Consp.: And with men He topples tyrants and their house. 290

Theodosia: Thus without effort one can disguise a dastardly deed.

I. Consp.: Does one call what a thousand souls are praising a dastardly deed?

Theodosia: And ten times one thousand disdain!

                2 Consp.: Do you know to whom you say this?

Theodosia: To you, who stand charged with this murder before

                             the court of God.

I. Consp.: Your life, blood, and death rest in these hands. 295

Theodosia: Therefore hasten to end the tragedy with our death.

2 Consp.: Courage that is mighty strong before one senses earnestness

     Collapses when distress breaks in.

Theodosia: Strike! My breast is bare!

     Do you think that Leo is dead? He lives in this heart

And calls "Revenge!" out of us. Through his pains,   300
Through his wounds, we are dead. It is his spirit that moves us,
That draws breath in us, that moves this hand,
That beats in these veins: come, open the door for him,
Open the prison, this flesh, so that he might lead us with him.
Yet use the same sword that went through his heart,   305
When his hacked-up arm embraced cruel death.
There's nothing more beautiful than when two so firmly bound souls
Withdraw from the caves of the body at one time and place.

I. Consp: After the heroic hand has executed the lion
Before whom the world trembled, no attention is paid to the dogs.   310
Nor ought a woman's blood stain the glorious steel,
That the holy night bid be thrust into the tyrant's breast.

2 Consp.: Let someone else kill you; it's more than enough for us
That your fallen spirit doesn't want to see the light of day.
It's more than enough for us that we can kill you   315
And yet spare your life, which you yourself don't spare.

Theodosia: Compassionate cruelty! Disguised tyranny!
Poison concealed with gold! Gentle barbarism!

I. Consp.: Follow us.

Theodosia: Where are we going? What misery is at hand?
What is intended for us? Will my fragile limbs be locked up   320
With chains and bonds? Will my neck be displayed
To the raging mob of riffraff as a sacrifice?
Come, fear, however great you are, and hasten to abort this suffering,
The misery-filled remnant of life.
Farewell, ruled realm! Farewell, possessed throne!   325
Farewell, lost court! Farewell, stolen crown!
Farewell, thou splendor of the world! Farewell, confused life!
The sugar-coated poison, encircled with a pearl-studded cross,
Palaces full of anxiety, your scepter, heavy with woe,
Thou purple, red from blood: we pass away, farewell.   330

Scene 3

Michael, the Second and First Groups of Conspirators, Theodosia, the corpse of Leo.

Michael: You now give to me light, freedom, soul, and life!

     You give to me myself: what will I give in return,

     I, who, saved from death and tomb and ignited conflagration,

     And, what is even more terrifying, from the tyrant's hand,

     Through your loyalty now mount the great throne: 335

     And I show the shaken world, with my example,

     That friendship goes beyond crown, and love beyond scepter,

     That a hated prince stands on shifting sand.

     There he lies, who lowered me. I rule in these chains,

     In which I plan to mount the throne,   340

     From which the lion was toppled. How will I reward this courage,

     That risked intrepid blood for me in greatest peril?

     Will I ever find anything

     That has the power to bind you and me more powerfully together?

     Yet if my arm is too weak; believe, that the great world,   345

     That you led out of dark anxiety to golden freedom;

     Believe, that the wide realm that you, in a few hours,

     Yet not with slight strength, bound to yourselves for eternity;

     Believe, that whoever here and there, up until the noble night,

     Languished in prison, in chains, in dungeons;   350

     Believe, that whoever shall be born into light after us,

     Will praise you heroes. Yes, when the earth's orbit

     Vanishes in flames, your excellence,

     Crowned in perpetual honor, will deride death and time.

Theodosia: Alas, wellspring of our anguish!

Michael: Ha! Widow of the tyrant!   355

     Your cruelest- raw power, your burning and banishing,

     Now banishes you yourself!

Theodosia: This is still unheard of,

     That one, who is so exalted and honored,

     That one, for whom so often such enormous guilt has been forgiven,

Whom we kept alive, thus causing our own death,   360
Should call us cruel! And yet we've proven
So much, who alone it is that may rightly call us cruel;
In that we gave you such full rein,
And tore you from the flame that you deserved!
Did our enraged fist whet the sharp sword   365
That your bloodthirsty arm holds at our throat?
He is indisputably the cruelest on earth,
Who, through pity, must become his own executioner.

Michael: Thus he who digs trenches for others falls in himself.

Theodosia: Thus one gets mockery for gratitude, for charity,
                                                                anguish, and pain.   370

Michael: One gets what one deserves: grievous anguish for grievous sins.

Theodosia: Fine! Thus in time revenge will find you, too.

Michael: Whoever commits no crime does not fear revenge.

Theodosia: Is it just that the oath and princes' necks are broken?

Michael: If princes themselves first break the solemn oath.   375

Theodosia: Did the emperor ever go back on his solemnly sworn promise?

Michael: His life and his terrible end demonstrate that.

Theodosia: Terrible not according to justice, but only through the
                                                         hands of murderers.

Michael: Justice is for the populace: on princes swords are sharpened.

Theodosia: They will, in the end, also pass sentence on you.   380
With this wish mount the oft-sought throne;
Take the crown, which you won through treachery, blood, and murder:
We know the court and the injustice of palaces:
The jealousy, false fidelity, and those cursed guests
Of princes, trouble and fear. Elevate yourself, defy and bedevil,   385
Slash, rage, kill, and stab, until your hour strikes.
Elevate those beside you, stained with our blood,
Who inherit greater honor and fortune through our fall.
Elevate what has loved perjury more than integrity,
What has trained itself so masterfully in regicide,   390
What has power to destroy church and court and prison.

And sharpen a sword that yet will pierce your breast.

Michael: You see what the future holds, not your present plight.

Theodosia: That prophesies your misery.

Michael: You're struggling toward your death,

 That waits outside the doors.

Theodosia: We ask for the life   395

 That you owe to us: bid sword, bid dagger to be given

 And end our torture: insure your power,

 Prove what you can: grant that the night

 Might cover my eternal sorrow with constant darkness:

 Grant that they be placed in one grave,   400

 Whom one love, one marriage, one throne, one realm, one station,

 One heart, one spirit, one fall, one demise, united.

Michael: Of what use is your death?

Theodosia: Your death (if I live) shall come from me.

Michael: The viper threatens in vain, whose head and poison

         have been removed!

 Depart! I'm not the one who is thinking of killing the one   405

 Who, as she boasts, gave me my life.

Theodosia: This evil is now impossible to endure;

 That after so much anxiety, death will be denied to us.

 What in the world can she hope, she who cannot have this,

 Which is granted to enemies? You people, behold us: 410

 You spirits, listen to us: she, who when daylight paled,

 Who, before midnight had crept upon the earth,

 Was accustomed to ruling the great world like a goddess;

 She finds herself, before time lets the sun greet

 The now approaching day, disdained, scorned, reproached,   415

 Discarded, deposed, crowned with woe and anxiety.

 She learns how close together the heights and falling stand;

 How little time passes between throne and prison.

 She who ruled everyone, she asks but in vain

 For the end, not of the burden, but only of her toppled life.   420

(Leo's corpse is brought in)

Whom does the grim mob drag along? Oh, agony! Is it the one
Who rules this realm? What abyss, what sea
Of pain swallows us up? What can we recognize
That isn't battered? Can a single limb be named
That the sword hasn't mangled? Where is his lovely hair   425
That previously was encircled with bejeweled gold?
Where is the strong hand that bore sword and scepter?
The breast that shining steel, as well as royal purple, embellished?
Woe unto us! Where is he himself? Behold! His innocent blood,
Aroused by our anxiety, surges and spurts anew   430
From all his wounds! His blood calls eagerly for revenge
Even if his lips are silent! His blood exposes the injustice
Of your cause, bloodthirsty ones!
Michael: Take the tyrant away!
Theodosia: Take us with him! His corpse and chain are my prizes!
Strike with pike and sword! Use flames and cruel weapons!   435
We wish (leave us here) we wish to fall asleep
On his paled mouth, on his beloved breast.
Michael: Tear the corpse away from her.
Theodosia: Where are we? What kind of pleasure
Do we now experience? The prince has not faded away:
Oh, joy! He lives! He lives! Now this sorrow is vanquished.   440
He wipes away our tears himself, with a gentle hand.
Here he stands! He angers and brandishes sword and fire
Upon the betrayers' heads.
I. Consp.:   The pain has overcome her!
She rages in dire distress.
Theodosia: My light! We have succeeded!
The murderers are strangled! He offers us his kiss: 445
Oh, unexpected bliss! Oh, soul-refreshing greeting!
Welcome, worthy prince! Ruler of our senses!
Comrades, mourn no longer: he lives!

Michael: Take her away!

 We'll hasten to the church: announce to the whole state

 The fall of tyranny: call the great council. 450

 I want the great patriarch to crown me now, here,

 In the presence of my sons and in your presence.

 You, keep watch on the castle! You others tell the troops!

 You; secure anything that can still hinder us.

 I am the one who will suppress those hostile to us

          and elevate our friends: 455

 Be firmly assured of this.

All of the Conspirators: Long rule and live the emperor!

Notes Appended by Gryphius to *Leo Armenius*

Explanation of Several Obscure References

The first Scene. The division of tragedies and comedies into specific parts or *Scenes* was completely unknown to the ancients, as can be observed from manuscripts and to some extent from printed books. Nevertheless we have retained them more to please the reader than because we greatly endorse them.

[*Note*:[54] Gryphius "retained" the concept of *Scenes* from the tragedy *Leo Armenus seu Impiietas punita* by the 17th Century English Jesuit Joseph Simon, which he most likely saw staged while in Rome (1644). *Leo Armenius* is the only drama in which Gryphius numbered the scenes and gave them the title *Eingang*, or scene.]

I.53 (See p. 33, above): "The trusted Michael." *Michael Curopalates* with the surname *Rangabe*. Emperor Leo's predecessor. See *Cedrenus* and *Zonarus*.

[*Note*: Michael I. Rangabe (c.770-844) became a monk (under the name of Athanasios) after abdicating in favor of the general Leo the Armenian. He died a peaceful death on January 11, 844.]

I.64 (See p. 33, above): "His son Theophylact." [Son of Michael Rangabe] whom *Leo Armenius* had castrated.

[*Note: Leo V the Armenian* had all three sons of *Michael I Rangabe* (c. 770 – 844) castrated and consigned to monasteries. The eldest, Theophylact (c.793-849), served as co-emperor with his father (812-813) and had once been considered

---

[54] This and following *Notes* (in brackets) offer additional comments on the *Explanation of Several Obscure References* provided by Gryphius.

for marriage to a daughter of Charlemagne. The second son, Niketas, became Patriarch Ignatius of Constantinople (847-858; 867-877) and is venerated in the Roman Catholic and Eastern Orthodox churches as Saint Ignatius, with a feast day on October 23. A third son, Staurakios, was also castrated, a process that eliminated any possibility of succession to the throne.]

I.73 (See p. 33, above): "Let him suffer what he did!"

Michael banished Leo's sons Symbatios, Basil, Gregory, and Theodosios from the court and had them castrated and deported to the island of Prote. *Zonaras.*

[*Note*: Renamed *Constantine*, Leo's eldest son, Symbatios, had served as co-Emperor with Leo V. the Armenian (814-820). Theodosios, the youngest, died from castration in 820.]

II.471 (See p. 68, above): "You can move a snake itself with kindness."

Casaubon speaks extensively about tame snakes in the words of *Suetonius* in the Seventy-first [sic] Chapter of his *Tiberius: Erat ei in oblectamentis Serpens Draco,* and even today these same things are not strange to the *Africans.*

[*Note*: The full Latin passage cited by Gryphius from Chapter Seventy-two of *Tiberius* by Suetonius reads: "He (Tiberius) had among his pets a serpent, and when he was going to feed it from his own hand, as his custom was, and discovered that it had been devoured by ants, he was warned to beware of the power of the multitude." Gryphius here refers to the published commentary on Suetonius (1595) by the renowned classical scholar Isaac Casaubon (1559–1614).]

II.495 (See p. 69, above): "Consider the dream."

It appeared to Leo's mother in a dream as if she were in the Church of the Mother of God at Blachern and saw there a woman whom several boys, dressed in white, accompanied. She also saw that the floor of the church was overflowing with blood. One of the boys instructed the aforementioned woman to fill a cup with blood and present it to the emperor's mother, which, horrified, she rejected. The aforementioned noble woman spoke: "But your son is accustomed to filling those who honor me with blood and doesn't understand that he moves God and my son to anger." *Zonaras.*

II.552 (See p. 71, above): "How quickly our glory."

Jacobus de Beaune, former advisor to various kings in France: when, in the sixtieth year of his life, he had to die by the executioner's hand, ended his life with the words: "What's happening to me is indeed just, because for so many long years I have only served men. I don't doubt at all that I would have received far more if I had served but for a single year the Lord of Heaven."

[*Note:* Gryphius added this explanatory note to Version C, 1663.]

III.279 (See p. 85, above): "The Dream of Phocas."

 It seemed to Emperor Maurice as if a great crowd of people was standing around the image of our Savior, which was above the holy gate, and crying out to the emperor: also the image emitted a voice that bid Maurice to appear: and soon after his appearance, it asked him if he wanted to atone for the crime committed against the imprisoned in this life or in a future life; who then clarified himself with the words: In this life, most gracious Lord: and thereafter he also heard a different voice, which commanded to deliver him with his entire family to Phocas. *Cedrenus* in *Mauritius. Zonaras* in *Mauritius. Theophylact Simocatta* in the *Life of Mauritius,* and others.

[*Note: Emperor Maurice I* (Byzantine Emperor 582-602) dreamed that he would be turned over to a soldier named Phocas, a general who later killed the emperor and his six sons. Phocas then served as Byzantine emperor 602-610, until he was overthrown by Heraclius, Byzantine emperor 610-641. *Theophylact Simocatta,* an early seventh-century Byzantine historian writing in the time of Heraclius (c.630), was best known for his eight books on the reign of Emperor Maurice and widely regarded as the leading historian of the period.]

IV.76 (See p. 94, above): "Naked Teachers."

Otherwise *Gymnosophists*, mentioned by *Pliny* in Chapter Two of Book Seven, by *Cicero* in Book Five of his *Tusculan Disputations*, by *Philostratus* in his works every now and then, by *Augustine* in Book 15 of *The City of God*, and many others.

[*Note: Pliny the Elder* (23-79 AD), in Book 7, Chapter 2 of his *Natural History*, describes various unusual people observed in India, including: "Their philosophers, who are called *Gymnosophists*, remain in one posture, with their eyes immovably fixed upon the sun, from its rising to its setting, and, during the whole of the day, they are accustomed to stand in the burning sands on one foot, first one and then the other."

Cicero (106–43 BC) writes in his *Tusculan Disputations*, Book V ("Whether Virtue Alone be Sufficient for a Happy Life"): "Is any country of barbarians more uncivilized or desolate than India? Yet they have among them some that are held for wise men, who never wear any clothes all their life long, and who bear the snow of Caucasus, and the piercing cold of winter, without any pain; and who, if they come in contact with fire, endure being burned without a groan."

Philostratus or *Lucius Flavius Philostratus* (c.172-250) was a Greek sophist of the Roman imperial period who authored at least five works.

Augustine of Hippo, known as *St. Augustine* (354-430), presents an analysis of the events in Genesis, between the time of Cain and Abel, to the time of the flood, in Book 15 of *The City of God*. He refers to the *Gymnosophists* in Book 15, Chapter 20:

> But it is regeneration that takes the City of God from the pilgrimage of this world, and places it in the other, where the sons neither may nor are married. Thus, then, generation is common to both the cities here on earth: though the City of God have many thousands that abstain from generation, and the other hath some citizens that do imitate these, and yet go astray: for unto this city do the authors of all heresies belong, as livers according

to the world, not after God's prescription. The Gymnosophists of India, living naked in the deserts, are of this society also: and yet abstain from generation. For this abstinence is not good, unless it be in the faith of God, that great good.]

IV.81 (See p. 94, above): "For whom in the land of the Jews." Various authors have written extensively about the forbidden sacrifices of the Jews. For the purpose of better information, I will here include just one place from the Book of Yalkut by which the words of the seventh chapter of Jeremiah are explained: Molech was an image with the face of calf and the outstretched hands of a human, who opens his hands in order to receive something, with a hollow interior. Herein seven chapels were set up, before which the aforementioned image was set: whoever sacrificed a bird or young doves went into the first chapel; whoever a lamb or sheep into the second; whoever a ram, into the third. Whoever [sacrificed] a calf [went] into the fourth; whoever a young ox, into the fifth. Whoever an ox, into the sixth. Whoever ultimately sacrificed his own son earned the seventh: this one kissed the Molech (image) as it is written there.

וקשי מילגע םדא יחבז םירמא םה םהל Hosea 13

The son was placed before Molech. Molech was heated with fire built below until he was as radiant as a light; then the priests took the child and laid it in Molech's glowing hands and in order for the parents not to hear the whimpering and wailing of the child, they beat on drums: for this reason the place is called תפת {Topheth} taken from םיפת which means "to drum." {*toph* = drum and *taph/ toph* = to burn in Hebrew}: The valley, however, was called םנה {Hinnom} because the boy's voice was םהב or screaming, or also because the priest standing there used to say הנהי דל It would be useful to you. *Kircherus* expounds upon this image of Molech extensively in his *Oedipus Volume I, Syntagma IV* entitled *Pantheon Hebraeorum* [on the Hebrew gods] where on page 334 he provides a sketch of this image and instead of the seven chapels he places seven windows right on the chest of this image: let us consider, however, if it would have been possible to conveniently mount such a lofty and glowing hot image. And I don't

mean to say to shove in a child or a calf, but an entire ox, conveniently and without great danger. How huge these windows would have had to be; what kind of
a partitioning of the entire image, what a (huge) fire would have been required
to heat up such an edifice; what a broad and lengthy stairway to mount such
an edifice with a whole ox. Re: Molech carefully observe the greatly renowned
Seldenus: *De Diis Syris* (*On the Syrian Gods*).

[*Note:* The *Yalkut Shimoni* (Hebrew: **ינועמש טוקלי**), or simply *Yalkut,* is a
compilation of various interpretations of books of the Hebrew Bible. The author
collected numerous interpretations and explanations of Biblical passages and arranged these according to the sequence of those portions of the Bible to which
they referred.

From Jeremiah 7: 31- 32: "And they have built the high places of Topheth, which
is in the valley of the son of Hinnom, to burn their sons and their daughters in
the fire; which I commanded not, neither came it into my mind. / Therefore,
behold, the days come, saith the LORD, that it shall no more be called Topheth,
nor The valley of the son of Hinnom, but The valley of Slaughter; for they shall
bury in Topheth, till there be no place *to bury.*"

Hosea 13:1-2 "When Ephraim spoke, there was trembling; he exalted himself in
Israel: but when he offended in Baal he died. / And now they sin more and more,
and have made them molten images of their silver, even idols according to their
own understanding, all of them the work of the craftsmen: they say of them, Let
the men that sacrifice kiss the calves."

Athanasius Kircher (1602-1680), known personally by Gryphius, was a German
Jesuit scholar and polymath whose vast scholarship included a three volume
work of Egyptology (*Oedipus Aegyptiacus*; Rome, 1652-54). Therein, his *Syntagma IV* entitled *Pantheon Hebraeorum* (on the Hebrew gods), Chapter XV (pp.
328-337) on "Moloch Idolum Ammonitarum," contains (on p. 334!) the illustration of Molech that is cited by Gryphius. (See Fig. 1, next page.)

CAP.XV 334 OEDIPI ÆGYPTIACI TEMPLVM ISIACVM

Atque hæc eſt figura Molochi, quam nobis ſatis conuenientem Mythriacis,& Ægyptiacis ſacris deſcripſit Radak; eſt autem adeò ſimilis furno laterum, vt illud Sophoniæ c. 1. v. 5. iurant per Regem ſuum, id eſt
Hebraicè במלכם per Malcam; Maſorethæ מלכו id eſt, furnum laterum;
ideò interpretati ſint, eâ voce Molochi figuram, quæ ſpeciem furni ad
conficiendos lateres inſtructi præſeſerebat, inſinuantes.

His itaque ſic ritè demonſtratis, nunc ſupereſt, vt, qui principalis fi
Origo ſacri nis noſter eſt, vndè funeſta hæc ſacrificandi ratio originem duxerit, oſten
ficiorum Mo damus. Sunt, qui ab Abrahamo, cum iuſſu Dei filium ſacrificare conſti
loch. tuiſſet, huius funeſti ſacrificij deriuent originem; alij à Iephte filiam ſacrificante; Priores, rationem aſſertionis ſuæ deſumunt è Porphyrio apud
Saturnus Euſebium præparat. Euangel. 1. & 4. Saturnum enim, quem Phœnices
Phœniciæ Iſraël nuncupabant, Regem Phœniciæ vetuſtiſſimum, vt regnum ſuum à
Rex filium ſummo imminentis belli periculo liberaret, ſuperoſque propitios habe
immolat. ret; vnicum μονογενῆ, quem ex Anobreta ſuſceperat, filium, regio ornatum faſtu, conſtructam ſuper aram immolaſſe; quod exemplum poſteritas poſteà ſecuta ſit; quod autem Porphyrius hic de Abrahamo loquatur,
Porphyriaſ. inde patet; quod μονογενῆς, id eſt, vnicus filius ille appellatur à Porphyrio,
& à Philone, Icoud; & in Geneſ: 22. Iſaac dicitur: בנך את יחידך ſcilicet
filius tuus vnicus, vbi in Iehid ipſum Iehoud ferè integrum legimus. Veriſimile itaque eſt, Gentiles inde, ſi non omnia, aliquam ſaltem ſuperſtitionum ſuarum partem traxiſſe. Etſi, vt in pleriſque profanorum Scri
Gentiles ſcri ptorum monumentis videre eſt, ſacram hiſtoriam falſis ſuis narrationibus
Pturæ ſanctæ miſerandum in modum corrumperent, acdeſœdarent. Moſem enim, vti
hiſtoriæ miris Deum, & Patriarchas errore inextricabili conſundebāt; verba & res ſacras
contamina ad impias Magorum operas arripiebant, & ex rebus diuinitus geſtis, & ad
bant fabulis. tabulas ſanctas relatis, profana Numina formabant; nouos, ridiculos, &
neſna

Fig. 1. Moloch, illustration from Athanasius Kircher, *Oedipus Aegyptiacus*
(Rome, 1652-54) 334.

John Selden (*Seldenus*), 1584-1654, English jurist, scholar, and politician, published a study of Phoenician and Syrian mythology in *De Diis Syris Syntagmata (On the Syrian Gods)*, London, 1617. His description of Moloch appears in *Syntagma* I, Chapter 6, pp. 169-170.]

IV.109 (See p. 95, above): "the hacked-off head of a boy"

Observe what *Seldenus, Kircherus,* and the *Commentators* inform us about the *Teraphim*: actually, according to their opinion, I should have written "twisted off or pinched off" head. But here I have chiefly looked at that cut off head that, in *Bodin's Daemonomania*, is screaming *Vim patior* (I suffer violence) on the consecrated host. Because this book is in everyone's hands, I will omit including such a horrible tale here. What was further sought in past times through such sacrifices, as also what is to be thought of appearances and prophesies like that, many have tried to explain. We will express our opinion more extensively in our thoughts about ghosts: which we intend to publish, God willing, as soon as possible.

[*Note*: Gryphius added this explanatory note to Version C, 1663.

John Selden (see above *Note* to IV.81) writes on *Teraphim* in *De Diis Syrii, Syntagma I* Chapter 2 (*De Teraphim*) pp. 96-123.

Athanasius Kircher (see above *Note* to IV.81) writes on Teraphim in *Oedipus Aegyptiacus*, Vol I, Syntagma IV, Chapter II: "De Teraphim primis Hebraeorum Idolis" pp. 254-256.

The *Commentatores* are possibly the seventy "interpretes" listed by Kircher in the index to his sources. Early rabbinical commentators on *Teraphim* include: the *Targumin* of pseudo-Jonathan (re: Genesis 31:19), the *Pirke* (Chapters) of Rabbi Eliezer or PRE (80-118 A.D.), Ibu Ezra (1089-1167), and Nahmanides (1194-1270).

Jean Bodin (1530-1596), a French jurist and political philosopher, was a member of the Parliament of Paris and professor of law in Toulouse. Although best known for his theory of sovereignty, his work on demonology cited by Gryphius was first published in 1580: *De la démonomanie des sorciers* (*The Demon-mania of the Sorcerers*). By 1604, ten editions of this work had been published, along with a Latin translation in 1581 by François Du Jon (*De magorum daemonomania libri IV*) and a German translation by Johann Fischart (*Vom außgelaßnen Wütigen Teuffels heer Allerhand Zauberern/ Hexen und Hexenmeistern/ Unholden/ Teuffelsbeschwerern/ Warsagern*: Strasbourg, 1581, 1586, and 1591). This prolific publication history clarifies Gryphius' comment: "Because this book is in everyone's hands I will omit including such a horrible tale here." Translated from the French, Bodin's "horrible tale" that Gryphius omitted from his explanatory note to IV.109, reads:

"I heard from the Sieur de Nouailles Abbé de l'Isle, now ambassador in Constantinople, and from a certain Polish gentleman named Pruinski, who was ambassador to France, that one of the chief monarchs of Christendom desired to know the future of his country. He called for a Jacobin [*Dominican friar*] Necromancer, who first said mass, and having consecrated the host, cut off the head of a first-born son of ten years, and placed it upon the host. Speaking certain words, and deploying symbols that it is not necessary to know, he asked it what it wanted. But the head said only: '*Vim patior*' [*I suffer violence*]. And at once the king fell into a frenzy, relentlessly shrieking that the head should be removed, and so he died insane.

This story is held to be true and beyond doubt by everyone in the kingdom in which it took place, notwithstanding that only five people were present at the event."

(For information re: my Bodin translation see *Select Annotated Bibliography* below, p. 280.)

Gryphius' "promised" work on Ghosts: No extant copy of this work (*De spectris*) has ever been found. If published, it undoubtedly would have contained information on dreams, magic, ghosts, etc. from Selden, Kircher, Bodin and other collections known to the poet. So much more could be written here, but like the venerable Silesian poet, I will express my opinion more extensively in my thoughts about Gryphius and ghosts, which we intend to publish, God willing, as soon as possible.]

IV. 138 (See p. 96, above): "You'll get what Leo bears."

When *Theophilos* (*Michael's* son) came to the regiment, he let himself be charged with nothing more than to punish with their lives those who had been helpful to his father in achieving emperorship and who had murdered Leo. And so that none of this same group would remain concealed, he announced to the entire council, called together in the court. that he intended to carry out his father's command. According to which he had desired to reward those who had served him in attaining supremacy, according to merit, but the lack of time to carry out his intention stood in the way; because first war, then illness, and finally death prevented him. Therefore he [*Theophilos*] ordered himself to willingly and generously repay such a debt. That is why he enjoined the same (individuals), who had assisted his father in the removal of *Leo*, to separate themselves from the others. Those (!) who did not understand this cunning stepped to one side and openly announced that they were the ones who had helped his father. However, he soon put aside the mask of his sham and spoke: "Why did you lay your hands on the Anointed of the LORD? And not only have (you) become murderers, but also patricides, of your emperor." Then he turned directly to the chief captain and commanded that they be led away and punished according to what they deserved. *Zonaras* in Part III. of the regime of *Theophilos*.

[*Note*: Theophilos (813-842) was the only son of Byzantine Emperor Michael II (Balbus, or "the stutterer") and the godson of Leo V Armenius. Two years after his own accession in 820, Michael II crowned young Theophilos co-emperor (aged 9). Immediately after his own accession as emperor following his father's death in 829, Theophilos executed his father's co-conspirators against Leo V Armenius.]

V.38 (See p. 107, above): "Our purple gown was transformed."

Michael had Theodosia banished to a cloister.

[*Note*: Michael II exiled Theodosia and the four sons of Leo V to the island of Prote. The sons were castrated, and the youngest died soon thereafter. Zonaras records that the sons were not required to take monastic vows, but instead were allowed to inherit part of the personal property of Leo V and the associated revenue, and to have their own attendants. Theodore the Studite (759 -826) sent a letter to the deposed Empress Theodosia sometime between 821 and his own death in 826.]

V.79 (See p. 109, above): "The Prince himself began to sing"

Zonaras and Cedrenus speak rather sarcastically about this singing by the emperor: the beginning of the song, with which the tumult rose, is supposedly this:

ΤΩ ΠΑΝΤΑΝΑΚΤΟΣ ΔΙΕΦΑΥΛΙΣΑΝ ΠΟΘΩ

They distained all splendor
Of the great world.
Out of love / to please only the highest.

CATHARINE OF GEORGIA
o r
PROVEN CONSTANCY

Introduction to *Catharine of Georgia or Proven Constancy*

Although most of our contemporary world pays little heed to the heart-rend-
ing fate of Queen Catharine of Georgia (1560-1624), her martyrdom is still honored today in Georgia, a post-Soviet country with a population of 3.75 million
inhabitants set between the Caucasus and the Black Sea. Every year on September 26 Georgians celebrate the Feast of Saint Queen Ketevan of Kakheti in her
honor. Not long after her death, Queen Catharine (Ketevan) was canonized in
the Georgian Orthodox Church by Patriarch Zachary of Georgia (1613-1640)
with commemoration set for September 13, the day after her death on September 12, 1624. This date was later moved to September 26 in accordance with the
Gregorian calendar.

In 2016, exactly 400 years after the birth of Andreas Gryphius, his dramatic female protagonist made headlines in India and Georgia when the *MINT
SUNDAY* published a lead story entitled "The Travelling Hand: A 17th Century
Royal Martyr, Portuguese Friars, a Ruined Augustine Church and a Search that
Stretched on for over 25 years!"[55] Mystery and intrigue still surround the shrouded legends of how Queen Catharine's charred remains were taken on an extensive and circuitous journey in 1624 by attendant Portuguese Augustinian friars
from her place of execution in Shiraz, Persia. Eventually, if only partially, they
reached her son King Teimuraz (Tamaras), in Georgia, for burial at the Alaverdi

---

[55] Srinath Perur, "Hunting for a Georgian Queen in Goa - The Travelling Hand: A 17th
Century Royal Martyr, Portuguese Friars, a Ruined Augustine Church and a Search that
Stretched on for over 25 years!" *The Mint on Sunday,* Updated 11 April 2016, p. 1.

Cathedral near the village of Alaverdi in the Alazani River Valley of Georgia. In 1628 the holy relics of Queen Catharine / St. Martyr Queen of Kakheti were interred beneath the communion table in the Alaverdi Cathedral. Previously, the Augustinian friars had moved her remains, for security reasons, first to Isfahan and from there to Goa, India, where they buried them in the Augustinian complex there. In 2016, after a quarter-century of cooperative efforts that had been underway since the 1980's, "two governments [*Georgia* and *Goa*], priests, archaeologists, historians, and genomics researchers"[56] were able to locate and positively identify the part of her remains that for so long had been lost in the ruins of the former Augustinian church in old Goa!

Over the centuries, many other accounts of Queen Catharine's martyrdom have surfaced with varying degrees of authenticity. Prior to Gryphius, literary efforts to immortalize her sacrifice include the poem *The Book and Passion of Queen Ketevan* (წიგნი და წამება ქეთევან დედოფლისა, *ts'igni da ts'ameba ketevan dedoplisa*) written by Catharine's son Teimuraz (Tamaras) in 1625, and a near-contemporary account written by the Georgian monk Grigol Dodorkeli-Vakhvakhishvili of the extant sixth-century David Gareja cave monastery in Kakheti, Georgia. Among the sonnets written by Pietro della Valle during his June-August 1622 stay in Shiraz, one was on "the sad fate of the Queen of Georgia," with whom he exchanged gifts, although he never met the Queen personally.[57] Much later than Gryphius, the Scottish poet William Forsyth (1818-1879) composed *The Martyrdom of Ketavane* in 1861. Forsyth's poem was inspired by Jean Chardin's (1643-1713) account of Queen Catharine's martyrdom in *The Travels of Sir John Chardin*, 1686-1711.

Every eyewitness and contemporary record of Queen Catharine cites the Portuguese Augustinian missionary Brother Ambrose as the friar directly responsible for her religious care during her long imprisonment, final attendance at her death, and the disposition of her remains. Gryphius' dramatic character *Ambrosius the Priest* is based on the actual role played by this friar. Soon after her martyrdom in 1624, Augustinian missionaries present in Shiraz at the

---

[56] Perur.

[57] See footnote 61, below.

time dispatched a full report to the Vatican.[58] Their description of the Georgian queen's execution differs from that presented in the drama by Gryphius,
for although it also depicts her torture with "red-hot pincers," her state of dress
and final death by strangulation with a bowstring do not coincide with the final
scenes of the drama or its primary source (see discussion of Claude Malingre's
Histoire, below). The missionaries reported that officials had already lit a great
fire in a brazier and inserted iron pincers into it, which were now as hot as the
fire itself. They then stripped the queen from her neck to her waist, and taking
the red-hot pincers, proceeded to tear away the flesh from her delicate body with
great cruelty, until at last the queen fell half dead to the ground. However, she
continued to invoke her Lord God with the greatest courage and fortitude. When
she had fallen to the ground, they picked up the whole brazier and threw it on
her body. She was finally put to death by strangulation with a bowstring. Queen
Catharine's final humiliation and degree of suffering are significantly heightened
in Gryphius' drama: closely following his primary source text, there is no mercy
shown through the hastening of the queen's death by strangulation.

The early report of Brother Ambrose and the Portuguese Augustinian missionaries in Georgia is now housed at the National Library in Lisbon. Even today,
a large tile fresco at the Convento da Graça in Lisbon, Portugal, commemorates
the execution of Queen Catharine as it was described by the eyewitness Brother
Ambrose and the Portuguese Augustinian friars in their report submitted to the
Vatican. As reported by Flannery, the scene depicting the execution of Queen
Catharine is but one panel of an extensive series of tiled panels dating from the
early part of the eighteenth century. The complete series illustrates significant
events in the order as recorded by the order's chroniclers. The portrayal of the
Queen's torture includes her prayer on a banner issuing from her mouth that
reads: "Adjuva me Deus in tortua mamilearum mearum." (See Figs. 2. and 3.,
next page.)

---

[58] Basing his narrative on the Augustinians' report, John M. Flannery provides detailed
information on the imprisonment, execution, and subsequent fate of Queen Catharine's
remains in Chapter Nine ("The Martyrdom of Queen Ketevan and the Augustinian Mission
to Georgia," pp. 197-238) in *The Mission of the Portuguese Augustinians to Persia and
Beyond (1602-1747)* (Leiden and Boston: Brill, 2013).

Figs. 2 and 3. Fresco Detail and Detail Enlargement at Convento da Graça, Lisbon, Portugal[59]

Let us consider the later portrayal of the Queen's sacrifice in 1624 by the German dramatist Andreas Gryphius in his *Catharine* tragedy. How and when did Gryphius become acquainted with the event of her execution in 1624? What led him to select her story for his second tragedy? We know from Gryphius himself that in 1646 his work on the tragedy was already underway in Strassburg. Indeed, he refers to it in the *Dear Reader* preface to his *Leo Armenius* (see above, p. 27). His stay of almost a year (1646-1647) in Strassburg directly followed his time in Rome (1646), where his friendship with the German Jesuit polymath Athanasius Kircher (1602-1680) could very well have led to his acquaintance with Kircher's close friend, the well-traveled author and collector Pietro della Valle (1586-1652). Given his stated interest in reports of contemporary travel in Persia (see his note re: *Catharine*, II.380) and familiarity with the works of eclectic scholars then active in Rome, it is most likely that the Silesian poet was familiar with della Valle's *Delle conditioni di Abbàs Rè di Persia* (Venice: F. Baba, 1628).[60] Della Valle's detailed account of his experiences in Persia fully reports

---

[59] Photos of the "Martyrdom of Georgian Queen Ketevan. Convento da Graça, Lisbon" are available online. In 2015 an exact copy of this Portuguese tile panel was installed at the Chateau Makhrani, the historic winery in Eastern Georgia, not far from Tbilisi. (Banner translation: "Help me, God, as my breasts are tortured.")

[60] Like Gryphius, the German poet Johann Wolfgang von Goethe (1749-1832) was also familiar with della Valle's experiences in Persia. Eighteen of the fifty-four letters in della Valle's *Travels* (*Viaggi di Pietro Della Valle, il Pellegrino*) are written from Persia. Goethe testifies to the seminal influence of della Valle on his own *Divan* poetry 200 years later in his c.1815 report "Pietro della Valle," included in his notes to the *West-Östlicher Divan*. Goethe's *Werke*, Ed. Erich Trunz, (Hamburg: Wegner, 1965), vol. II, 228-42.

the imprisonment[61] and death of the Christian Queen Catharine. Like Gryphius, della Valle was in Rome in 1646. Della Valle's five years in Persia (1618-1623) had included close association with Shah Abbas I, whom he met through his Nestorian Christian wife (they met and married in Bagdad in 1618). Thus positioned, della Valle was able to observe Shah Abbas from a Roman Catholic perspective while at the court in Isfahan as well as during his three years of service in the Shah's army (1618-1620). He was plagued by failing health for the next three years. After the tragic death of his young wife on December 30, 1621 and a series of misadventures that restrained his further travel, della Valle left Shiraz in August, 1623 for India, where he remained until November, 1624. While in India, he was directly involved in advising various Catholic orders in Goa that competed to return Queen Catharine's remains from Goa back to Georgia for the purpose of gaining favor with Teimuraz (Tamaras) and thus receiving a welcome from the Georgian king to establish a mission in Georgia. Della Valle also played a role in supporting Queen Catharine as a candidate for sainthood in the Catholic Church. The wealthy Italian adventurer returned to Rome in late March, 1626, where he was appointed by Pope Urban VIII as a gentleman of the chamber. Flannery describes della Valle's continued involvement in Rome with actions related to Queen Catharine's martyrdom: "The Augustinian prior at Goa also wrote in October of 1627 to Pietro della Valle, reminding him of the case of the queen . . . and asking his support for the Order with the Holy Father. There is no doubt that della Valle shared the opinion that the Georgian queen was a true martyr. In his *Informatione della Georgia,* sent to Urban VIII in 1627, he refers only briefly to the martyrdom, but in his work of the following year, *Delle con-*

---

[61] Wilfrid Blunt recounts pertinent notes in della Valle's *Viaggi* (*Travels*) re: Queen Catharine's imprisonment in Shiraz that were not yet published when Gryphius wrote *Catharine.* These notes describe "the hostage in Shiraz" as an "accomplished woman (who) possessed everything but her freedom: a fine house with a private oratory in which candles burned day and night, books and icons, and a staff of twenty Georgian servants." (p. 226). Blunt notes that while in Shiraz from June-August, 1622, della Valle established contact with the imprisoned queen via a chance meeting with her chaplain and later exchanged gifts with her, adding that before leaving Shiraz for India, della Valle wrote a sonnet on "the sad fate of the Queen of Georgia" (pp. 227). *Pietro's Pilgrimage: A Journey to India and Back at the Beginning of the Seventeenth Century.* (London: J. Barrie, 1953).

ditioni di Abbàs Rè di Persia, he lends his full support to her cause."[62] This later report of his experiences in Persia offered a full account of the imprisonment and death of the Christian Queen Catharine: *Delle conditioni di Abbàs Rè di Persia* (Venice: F. Baba, 1628). Even after della Valle was back in Rome, however, it was not until November of 1626 that Augustinian authorities in Goa approved Brother Ambrose's return of the Queen's remains to Georgia following a route from Goa through Persia. On May 11, 1628, Brother Ambrose arrived at the encampment of King Teimuraz (Tamaras) and his court in Georgia. An overjoyed Tamaras received the remains of his mother's body, which were then interred in the Alaverdi Cathedral. Della Valle's evaluation of Queen Catharine's death as the means by which she received "the martyr's crown and the glory of heaven"[63] anticipates the proclamation set forth by the German playwright Gryphius with such detail and passion in his dramatic portrayal of this event.

But was Pietro della Valle's narrative possibly Gryphius' *second* encounter with the story of Queen Catharine? It is highly probable that his *first* encounter occurred in Paris two years prior to his visit in Rome. It is certain that he relied on the sixteenth narrative ("Histoire de Catherine Reyne de Georgie et des Princes Georgiques mis à Mort par commandement de Cha-Abas Roy de Perse") in a collection of short biographies by C.M. Sieur de St. Lazare (Claude Malingre, 1580-1653) entitled *Histoires tragiques de notre temps* (Paris, 1635). It is also very probable that Gryphius first read this story of the Georgian queen in the extensive library of Cardinal Richelieu (1585 -1642)[64] while in Paris in

---

[62] Flannery, 219.

[63] Della Valle, *Delle conditioni,* p. 93.

[64] See report of Gryphius' first biographer Balthasar Sigismund von Stosch (1635-1677) that for Gryphius in Paris "it was not so much the city hall or the armory, the palaces, or the royal gardens or other rarities that enthralled him as much as the library of the Lord Cardinal (Richelieu), which was splendid and decorated beyond belief, and was open afternoons, as he himself mentions in his diary." Stosch, *Last-und Ehren- auch Daher immerbleibende Danck- und Dencksäule* (Glogau: n.p., 1665 and Leipzig: Schlovien., 1683*),* 34. (Also noted by Willi Flemming, *Monographie,* 4 and Julius Tittmann, *Dramatische Dichtungen von Andreas Gryphius,* [Leipzig: Brockhaus, 1870] xxi.) Richelieu had specified in his will that left the library, fully funded, to his great nephew, that it should serve not only his family, but be open at fixed hours to scholars. By the time Gryphius was reading in Paris, *three* editions of

1644. This source provides a detailed political background that explains precisely how Queen Catharine became the prisoner and ultimately the victim of Shah Abbas of Persia. Gryphius' conviction that a complete and accurate presentation of historical reality within the dramatic text (*pictura*) is a necessary prerequisite to proclaim a higher truth (*subscriptio*) is underscored by his use of many reference notes to authenticate specific historical facts.[65] Such notes are appended to each of his historical tragedies, and *Catharine* is certainly no exception. However, although the polyhistorian-dramatist supplies the reader of *Catharine* with supplemental information to clarify many specific historical details included in the play, it is his only historical drama that does not include reference to his primary source. Gryphius so closely follows this source with its many obscure details concerning historical events, regional geography, and complex political intrigues, that it is clear he had access to it while writing his own *Catharine* tragedy in Strassburg. Indeed, the meticulousness of Malingre's detailed report would have inspired the German dramatist-poet to seize this story as a perfect vehicle to proclaim his positions on regicide, the futility of worldly *vanitas,* the virtue of constancy, the glory of Christian martyrdom, and the certainty of divine justice and revenge, all within a single drama.

The Presentation of History and Geography in *Catharine of Georgia*

Aesthetic problems inevitably arise when Gryphius extends several of his lengthy dramatic monologues by inserting Malingre's minutely detailed summaries of historical-political background information. When Gryphius repeats this comprehensive information in the dramatic monologs of Demetrius and Catharine (Act I, 410-725 and Act III, 63-392, respectively), he either assumes that the audience (reader) is already familiar with the complexities of Georgian-Persian-Russian politics prior to 1624 or that his presentation of this background

---

Malingre's *Histoires tragiques* would have been available for his consideration (1st and 2nd eds., Paris: Claude Collet, 1635; 3rd ed., Rouen: Thomas Davé and David Ferrand, 1641).
[65] See my clarification of emblem terms in "Gryphius' Emblematic Technique of Constructing Historical Tragedies," p. 10, above.

material within his drama will inform them sufficiently. However realistic either assumption might have been in the seventeenth century, the modern reader can be overwhelmed by the confusing muddle of assassinations, unfamiliar geographical terminology, and complex international political intrigues that can surface precisely when, or even because, the dramatist seeks to *clarify* the historical facts that underlie his dramatic plot. In order to appreciate his attempt to accurately reiterate historical facts by including these complicated recapitulations in the dramatic monologs, it will be useful to briefly review the historical-political background of Queen Catharine's life and death as presented by the poet's own source.

The Historical Source

The following summary of excerpts from Malingre's complete historical narrative is intended to provide the reader of *Catharine* with an overview of the *geographical terminology* and an identification of the *historical figures* that Gryphius borrowed directly from his source. This summary does not examine the accuracy of Malingre's (or Gryphius') report in view of modern historical scholarship, nor does it include Malingre's detailed description of the attempted rescue and execution of the imprisoned Queen Catharine. It should be noted that Gryphius divides the historical-political background information he presents in monolog reports into two sections: events that occurred *prior* to Catharine's imprisonment are related by the queen to the Russian ambassador in Act III, 63-392, while events that occurred *subsequent* to her imprisonment are related to her by Demetrius, an ambassador from Georgia, in Act I, 410-721. After an introduction that compares the "improper and cruel passion" of Shah Abbas for Queen Catharine to such famed and fated lovers as Semiramis, Paris, Tarquin, and Theodoric, Malingre launches his narrative with a review of the geographical situation. In his account, *Georgia* consists of four kingdoms. However, only two of these kingdoms, Tiflis and Yuerie (the latter is also called Gurgistan and is referred to at times simply as *Georgia* by both Malingre and Gryphius), form the geographical setting of events mentioned in Malingre's account. Yuerie/Gurgistan/Georgia all refer to the old Kingdom of Kakheti, now a region in Georgia. It should be noted that Tiflis was actually not a kingdom, but the capital city of the Kingdom of Kartli. Called *Tbilisi* since 1936, this city is the present-day capital of Georgia. Malingre notes that due to their respective locations, Tiflis is dominated by nearby Turkey, while Yuerie (Gurgistan/Georgia) falls mainly under the Persian sphere of influence. In Malingre's account, as repeated in Gryphius' drama, the relentless struggle between the smaller Christian kingdoms and their powerful Muslim neighbors provides the regional political backdrop of Catharine's difficult life. Although Malingre, and therefore Gryphius, refers at times to the leaders of these Christian kingdoms as *dukes*, they were actually heads of state that held the rank of *king*. In the source and in the drama, Tamaras, the son of Queen Catharine, rules over Georgia. Historically, he was known as King Teimuraz (1589 -1663), the King of Kakheti. Similarly, both Gryphius and his source refer to Prince Alovassa as the ruler of neighboring Kartli, a kingdom that they both identify with the name of its capital city Tiflis (modern Tbilisi). Historically, Kartli was ruled from 1606 until 1615 by King Luarsab II (1592-1622), who appears as *Prince Alovassa* in *Catharine*. After his capture and seven years of imprisonment in Persia, King Luarsab II was executed by Shah Abbas I in Shiraz. For his martyrdom he later received sainthood in the Georgian Orthodox Church.

It is remarkable how Gryphius' geographic references to *Iberia*, from the Greek Ιβηρία, have been misunderstood by critics and scholars of his *Catharine* drama. His use of the term, prevalent in cartography of the seventeenth century, refers to the larger region of Georgia that included both Kakheti and Kartli. A closer observation of early regional maps, such as Homann's *Map of the Persian Empire* (c. 1724) indicates that IBERIA at one time identified the region that included GEORGIA, GURGISTAN, and Tiflis, terms that are also inscribed on

Fig. 4. *Map of the Persian Empire and all of its provinces* by Johann Baptist Homann, Nürem-
berg, c. 1724.

Homann's map. [66]

When Gryphius' dramatic character Demetrius, one of two ambassadors
from Georgia, lauds Queen Catharine as "the sun of Iberia" (I.191) or describes
the uprising led by Meurab against invading Persian troops ("The boiling anger
of revenge, like a flame, swept the weeds from all Iberia" (I, 648); or when the
Russian ambassador refers to Queen Catharine as "A woman who once wore the
crown of Iberia and now grieves in captivity" (II, 162), Gryphius is referring to
the land area that once was the early Georgian state of Iberia. In the period of
600-150 BC, the states of Iberia and Colchis (located along the coast line of the

---

[66] See Fig. 4., above: *Map of the Persian Empire and all of its provinces (Imperii Persici
in omnes suas provincias nova tabula geographica)* by Johann Baptist Homann, Nürem-
berg, c. 1724. (For complete map see U.S. Library of Congress https://www.loc.gov/
item/2004629239/.)

Black Sea) contained most of the land that constitutes modern Georgia. Later, the region of Iberia referred primarily to the Kingdom of Kartli, in which the city of Tiflis is located.

Since antiquity, *Iberia* has been the term used for the region of Georgia. The *Iberian Peninsula*, consisting of Spain, Portugal, Andorra, and Gibraltar, was a term used to identify the eastern and southern coasts of the Iberian peninsula by the 6th century BC. It appears in early Greek and Roman sources, including the texts of Hecataeus of Miletus, Avienus, Herodutus, and Strabo. The region was called *Hispania* at the time of the Roman conquest (220-19 BC), although the Greek historian Herodotus (fifth century BC) wrote of the sea captain Kolaios, the first Greek to visit Iberia, which the Greeks then called the peninsula. It is important to distinguish between *Caucasian Iberia* and the *Iberian Peninsula* when reading Gryphius' tragedy about the Georgian Queen Catharine!

The following excerpts summarize the source text used by Gryphius when he created his second historical tragedy, *Catharine of Georgia or Proven Constancy*:

Summary of Excerpts from Claude Malingre's Text: *The Story of Catharine, Queen of Georgia, and the Georgian Princes, Put to Death by the Command of Shah Abbas, King of Persia*

When Achmet, father of Sultan Ossman, was the Turkish emperor and Abbas I was Shah of Persia, Duke Simon, father of Prince Alovassa, ruled *Tiflis*. Duke Alexander, father of Prince Constantine and Prince David, ruled *Yuerie*. Duke Simon, refusing to follow a Turkish demand, was defeated by invading Turks, taken to Constantinople as a prisoner together with his son Alovassa, and was then poisoned by Achmet. Since Alovassa was then too young to rule, the Turkish sultan sent him back to Tiflis accompanied by Meurab. (Following Malingre, Gryphius refers to the ruler [*Mouravi*] of Tiflis as *Meurab*, although modern histories identify this ruler by name as *Giorgi Saakadze*.) As regent of Tiflis, Meurab earned praise for his wise and gentle rule. Shah Abbas followed the

Turkish action by insisting that Yuerie place itself under Persian protection in the belief that the small kingdom might otherwise, like Tiflis, enter an alliance with Turkey. To avoid the fate of Duke Simon, Duke Alexander agreed to join Abbas and was then required to send his son Constantine as a hostage to Persia. In Persia, Constantine converted to Islam and was consequently disinherited by his father, Duke Alexander, enabling Constantine's brother David to become successor to the throne of Yuerie. David married Princess Catharine and their son Tamaras, although sent to Persia as a hostage at the command of Shah Abbas, nevertheless remained Christian in faith. Abbas then suggested to Constantine that he could regain his rightful power if he would invite his father Alexander and brother David to Persia, murder both of them, return home with an army, and then marry his brother's widow Catharine after reconquering his land. Constantine agreed and carried out the double murder of his father and brother, after which Shah Abbas had to appease the angry Georgian soldiers who had accompanied Alexander and David to Persia. The shah accomplished this by blaming the family quarrel on the effects of too much wine. Constantine then left to invade Yuerie with not only the same four thousand Georgian soldiers who had accompanied his father and brother to Persia, but with an additional fifteen thousand Persian soldiers as well. Catharine, informed in advance of this imminent invasion, raised an army of ten to twelve thousand men. She positioned her army in a narrow pass, knowing that Constantine would have to proceed through this pass in order to enter Yuerie. When she personally met him in the pass, she first expressed her amazement that he would try to forcefully acquire a land already rightfully his own and then hinted that she might become his wife. Just as the satisfied Constantine was returning to his troops he was shot in the back by Catharine's men. A fierce battle between the Persians and the reunited Georgian troops ensued, resulting in the near annihilation of the Persians. Shah Abbas concealed his rage at this event and even returned Prince Tamaras to rule Yuerie with the suggestion that Catharine find a wife for her son as soon as possible. Believing Abbas' statement that she had rightfully avenged the murders of her husband and father-in-law and that Yuerie could now peacefully coexist with Persia, Catharine turned her attentions to a search for the bride. A princess from Tiflis was chosen, and although the young girl agreed to marry Tamaras, an unfortunate quarrel arose when Alovassa, ruler of Tiflis, decided that he would like to marry the same princess. The princess, wanting to marry Tamaras but also under obligation to Alovassa as his subject, took refuge in a fortress after declaring that she would marry whichever prince might win her in combat. Abbas took advantage of this dilemma by secretly offering his encouragement and full support to both princes. On the day of battle Alovassa sent a message to Tamaras in which he expressed his regret that their unfortunate quarrel would weaken the Christian kingdoms to the advantage of their powerful Muslim neighbors. He explained that he was engaging in the battle at the personal request of Shah Abbas and not just for love of the princess. Since Tamaras had also received the Shah's support in this controversy, Tamaras correctly suspected Abbas' treachery, and the two princes were thus able to avert confrontation and settle the matter peacefully. Tamaras married the princess, and both princes then established closer alliances with Turkey. In an effort to embarrass Shah Abbas, the sultan of Turkey sent an ambassador to Persia to inquire of the shah whether the Georgian kingdoms favored Persia or Turkey. Completely unaware of the newly established Turkish-Georgian alliances, Abbas requested both Christian princes to send troops to Persia as a demonstration of their good faith. The princes' refusal, which clarified their position, humiliated the shah and he decided to invade Georgia immediately. Duke Alovard and Courchi Bachi (Gryphius transcribes the latter as *Curtzi Bassi),* the two advisors who attempted to dissuade the shah from participating personally in this invasion, were severely punished: the enraged Persian ruler poisoned the former and not only had the latter whipped, but also bit off the fingers of his wife! Abbas then marched on Yuerie, where he was met by Catharine in the same pass in which Constantine had been slain. In the meantime, Tamaras and his wife were able to escape to Tiflis. On seeing Catharine, Abbas concealed his anger by feigning amorous passion for the queen, assuring her that Georgia was not in danger and requesting that fifty Georgian nobles appear to establish officially a peace agreement. The nobles arrived, were promptly assassinated at a banquet, and Catharine herself was taken prisoner. Abbas' search for Tamaras led him to neighboring Tiflis. When Alovassa and Meurab came forth to meet him, they were both seized as prisoners. Abbas appointed an elderly descendant of the royal house of Georgia, who had converted to Islam, as the new ruler in Georgia. Alovassa and Meurab, together with Meurab's wife, son, and daughter, were taken to Persia. There Abbas poisoned Alovas-sa[67] and, with vast promises, persuaded Meurab to convert to Islam, whereupon he molested Meurab's wife and children in Meurab's presence. When Meurab had been a convert to Islam for a considerable time, and Abbas believed that he could trust him completely, the Persian ruler offered him command of a great army that was to enter Georgia for the dual purpose of 1) accompanying the shah's daughter to her marriage with the puppet ruler there and of 2) seizing all Christians, who, to avenge Georgian offenses, were to be led naked and in chains to Persia, where they would be offered the choice of converting to Islam or death. Unaware that Abbas had also ordered his assassination, Meurab led the army to Georgia, where he was remembered for the goodness of his former rule there and was openly welcomed. Because he had promised the Georgians that they would not be harmed, Meurab was infuriated when one of the Persian dukes assassinated several Georgian nobles. Discovering that the Persian duke had act-ed according to secret orders from the shah, Meurab realized that he himself was the probable victim of another double-cross by Abbas. He therefore revealed his own orders from Shah Abbas concerning the Christians to a group of Georgian leaders and together they devised a plan to annihilate the Persians who had ac-companied him to Georgia. The plan succeeded and Meurab then wrote to Ab-bas, charging the shah for his many traitorous deeds and proclaiming his own destiny as the instrument of God's justice sent to punish him for his immoral acts. Abbas was completely outraged by this turn of events, but Meurab's message carried such force that he abandoned plans to oppress Georgian Christians and decided to leave Georgia in peace. In Georgia, Meurab had the heads of the mur-dered Persian dukes bound to poles and presented to him at a banquet, where he offered a toast to each head, reproaching the dukes severely for their wicked deeds. Meurab sent for Tamaras to return and rule Georgia, but only when he was thoroughly convinced that Meurab's offer was sincere did the exiled prince return. Joined by Tamaras, Meurab then went to Constantinople to seek an alli-ance with the Turkish sultan. Meurab remained in Turkey, where he aided the Turks against Persia. Malingre completes his narrative with a comprehensive ac-

---

[67] Historically, the execution of Alovassa occurred in 1622 after seven years of imprison-ment in Persia (see p. 143, above).

count of how Prince Tamaras attempted to secure his mother's release from imprisonment in Persia, the fatal attempt of the Russian ambassador to assist in this effort, and the brave suffering of the martyred Queen Catharine as she is pursued, tortured, and executed by Shah Abbas.

As previously noted, details of almost every specific incident in St. Lazare's historical account as paraphrased above appear either in the dramatic text itself or in the appended notes to *Catharine*. The dramatist's concern for historical accuracy demonstrates his indisputable conviction that real historical events (*pictura*) provide a valid demonstration of theological principles and metaphysical truths (*subscriptio*). The ultimate message that Gryphius drew from the specific events related to the life and death of Queen Catharine inspired and directed his creation of the dramatic work.

Artistic Dramatization and the Proclamation of Metaphysical Truth

Gryphius begins the introduction to his first drama *Leo Armenius* with the following statement of purpose:

> Since our whole nation is now burying itself in its own ashes and evolving into a theater of vanity, I feel bound to present to you the transience of human affairs in this and several tragedies to follow. Certainly not because there isn't anything else available to me that might be more pleasant for you, but because once again it pleases me as little as I am permitted to present anything else.[68]

It is therefore not surprising that *Catharine of Georgia* opens with the figure of Eternity descending from heaven onto the stage of mortals (*Theatrum Mundi*) to declare her message of *Vanitas Mundi*, thereby proclaiming the metaphysical truth to be drawn by the audience from the subsequent dramatization of Cath-

---

[68] *Werke*, V, 3. See Gryphius' *Dear Reader* letter preceding *Leo Armenius*, above, p. 26

arine's martyrdom. Eternity admonishes the audience to eschew earthly vanity by laying bare the illusion of possible greatness on earth, epitomizing the vain dream of human grandeur by any means or in any form with the image of Icarus. Both the heroine Catharine and the tyrant Shah Abbas suffer reversals of power in Gryphius' drama, but it is the poet's religious-political interpretation of historical events that determines his ultimate casting of their representative roles. Catharine gives up her throne, country, and life for her religious and political convictions, but by demonstrating this Luther-like Christian freedom she is elevated to the status of martyr. Abbas, whose fiery passion and lack of principled self-discipline exemplify uncontrolled, tyrannical power on earth, demonstrates the inherent vanity of any human action that ignores or transgresses the law of God and man, for he exits as the suffering object of both divine revenge and human repulsion. As Eternity rises from the transitory world and returns to her permanent domain in heaven, she summarizes the exemplary struggle and triumph of Queen Catharine, who, by heroically overcoming the trials imposed upon her during life on earth, achieved eternal glory:

> Theater of mortality, farewell! I am borne away on my throne.
> The worthy princess follows me; she already perceives a higher realm
> Who, free while in fetters, not bound to earthly things while on earth,
> Struggled and suffered for church, throne, and subjects.
> You who hold a high ideal according to the same honor:
> Scorn with her that which transpires on earth.
> Give as did she your valiant blood as a pledge
> And live and die in solace for God, Honor, and Fatherland.
>
> (*Catharine* I, 81-88)

The contrary fate of the tyrannical Shah Abbas warns the audience of the lasting consequences suffered by those who act in defiance of moral law, religious tolerance, or political freedom, for he is condemned by both man and God. An appeal to God for divine justice and revenge against Abbas is first voiced by the Chorus of Princes murdered by the Shah:

Oh Judge of this world! Counsel of princes!
How long willst Thou look on?
Does the bloodhound, in spite of time! In spite of justice and God!
Still enjoy peace on his throne?
Willst Thou, Lord of the world, not awaken
And make an end to this cruel raging?
Willst Thou not avenge our death?
Willst Thou no longer pass judgment?
Do not so many thousand sufferings
Affect your heart any longer, great Judge?
Willst Thou allow that at the beckoning of one man
Entire kingdoms drown in blood?
Solemn Judge! Take vengeance!
Wake up! Great God awaken!
Wake up! Wake up! Wake up! Wake up!
Revenge! Revenge! Revenge! Revenge!

(Catharine II, 401-416)

The drama's final scene exposes the wretched terror in Abbas' distraught mind following the execution of Catharine in what is perhaps the most poignant and convincingly realistic portrayal of emotion in all of Gryphius' original (i.e., not adapted from historical source material) dramatic writing. The shah's suffering conscience and unrequited passion for the dead queen call forth the apparition of her ghost, which condemns him with the prophecy of his forthcoming misery on earth and eternal damnation after death:

Tyrant! It's heaven that seeks your ruin.
God doesn't let innocent blood cry out to no avail.
Your laurel wreath withers! Your conquering is finished.
Your lofty fame vanishes! Death already reaches out
For your condemned head. Yet before you perish,

You will have to behold your Persia standing amid the flames of war,[69]
Your house infested with the dark poison of discord,
Until, stained by infanticide and incest,
Unbearable to foe, friends, and yourself, you will hand over your life,
After the gruesome horror of pestilence, to the Judge.

(*Catharine* V, 431-40)

Gryphius' artistic portrayal of Malingre's historical narrative evolves from his identification of a moral imperative in the historical events chronicled by the French author, for he views them in terms of a diametric opposition between Catharine's glorious martyrdom and Shah Abbas' eternal damnation. His proclamation of this moral imperative in *Catharine of Georgia* warns spectators to contemplate their own life *sub specie aeternitatis*. In order to present this exhortation convincingly, he employs such creative variations of language, imagery, staging techniques, and innovative dramatic forms that the resultant drama takes its place, together with his other original tragedies, as an outstanding seventeenth-century German literary achievement. Today we view this drama as a perhaps curious but nonetheless revealing compendium of seventeenth-century literary forms, in which we can examine attitudes, ideas, and beliefs concerning history, geopolitics, religion, and social/moral issues in a Germany torn and disillusioned by the Thirty Years' War. Gryphius' contemporaries, however, most likely granted full attention to the higher message intended by its author.

From the comments Gryphius offers in his introduction to *Leo Armenius*,

---

[69] The ghost of Catharine's warning that not only Abbas, but all of Persia, will be affected by her sacrifice, appears conceptually again in Gryphius' poem "About the Martyr *Catharine* Queen of Georgia," included as verse LVI in his *First Book of Epigrams or Addenda* (Breslau: Veit Jacob Dreschern, 1663). The poem begins:

Oh, most beautiful miracle! Oh, great power of the senses!
Oh, highest queen of women ever crowned!
Spirit that can face pincers and fire without fear,
That can scorn the highest favor and most severe ferocity of *Abas*!
All of *Persia* stands aghast and beholds the qualities
That his raging mind rejects. All of *Persia* stands and is fearful,
While, undaunted, you are tortured by a slow death,
Which, indeed, can tear your flesh into pieces, but not you. (*Werke,* II, 179)

we know that he had already begun *Catharine of Georgia* during his year in Strassburg, 1646-1647. Following a brief interruption to fulfill his promise to friends in Amsterdam that he would write *Cardenio and Celinde*, he completed his *Catharine* drama in the autumn of 1647 while visiting his friend Wilhelm Schlegel at the Schlegel family estate near Stettin.

Although the first published edition of the tragedy does not appear until 1657, repeated productions of the play prior to 1657 attest to its early popularity. The first public presentation was staged in Cologne (1651) by the traveling theatrical company of Joris Jollifous (George Jolly, fl. 1640-1673), and it was repeated by this troupe in Frankfurt one year later. In 1655 the tragedy was performed at the court of Duke Christian von Wohlau (1618-1672) in his newly renovated castle. A commemorative edition of eight engraved illustrations that depict various scenes of the drama was dedicated to Duke Christian's wife, Princess Louise of Anhalt-Dessau (1630-1680).[70] Gryphius intended his play to be performed by the schools of his native Silesia, and we know that *Catharine* was performed in the Elisabeth *Gymnasium* of Breslau before 1659, since the poet mentions this production in the Latin dedication to his drama *Papinianus* published that year. The centennial anniversary of the *Gymnasium* in Halle was celebrated with a production of *Catharine* in 1665, just one year after the poet's death. Records do not provide information regarding subsequent performances of the play, but a testament to my esteemed mentor and colleague Professor Willi Flemming's undaunted enthusiasm for *Catharine* can be found not only in his critical editions of the *Trauerspiel* (1st ed., Halle/S: Niemeyer, 1928; 4th ed., Tübingen: Niemeyer, 1968) but also in his staging and direction of a student production of the play in the *Aula* at Gutenberg University in Mainz c. 1960!

May this enthusiasm accompany your reading as the curtain now rises for the
Second Historical Tragedy by Andreas Gryphius:
Catharine of Georgia or Proven Constancy!

---

[70] The eight illustrations printed for the Wohlau production of 1655 appear below, pp. 265-272.

Dear Reader: Introductory letter Gryphius included prior to the text of *Catharine*

Dear Reader

The *Catharine* I treasure now appears on the stage of our fatherland, and presents to you in her body and her suffering an example of inexpressible constancy scarcely heard of before this time: the crown of Persia, the honor of the most victorious and famous king, the bloom of youth, the inexpressible passions, freedom that is to be treasured more than life, the horrible martyrdom, the force of the fates, the manner of death even more horrible than death itself, the tears of the ladies-in-waiting captured with her, longing for her throne, her child, and her kingdom – all besiege a tender woman and must lie, overcome, at her feet. In brief: honor, death, and love struggle in her heart for the prize that love (indeed not the earthly and worthless kind, but the holy eternal kind) receives, although death delivers and secures it. It (death) is so powerful in the weakest instrument, whose honor this queen strikes out with her blood, that I only lament this one thing; that my pen is too feeble to worthily describe such extreme patience, such vigorous constancy, such a ready decision to prefer the eternal over the transitory. Indeed the first draft about this queen has been kept concealed by me almost longer than she herself languished imprisoned by the Persian king. Not to mention that a friend (in this case not too trustworthy) tried to abduct it (the drama) from its prison (uncharitably and while it was still flawed with the detritus of its birth). It is better than that they could spit any defamations at it; (as indeed, while it was still hidden with me, someone, I don't know how, wanted to dishonor her, the very one who honored the divinity of Christ with her death). I, however, am more reasonable than to believe that everyone can be pleased, indeed even those who only commit blasphemy so that someone will still be pleased in that one (i.e., the playwright) will acknowledge his imperfection. Pardon me, Dear Reader, for detaining you so long, and with me turn your face away from that which is transitory to ever-reigning ETERNITY.

Content of the Tragedy

CATHARINE, Queen of Georgia in Armenia, after most praiseworthily protecting her kingdom on different occasions against the great king in Persia, avenging the deaths of her father-in-law and husband, and finally ambushed by the king from Persia with insurmountable power, betook herself in person to the enemy camp in order to plead for peace: there she was straightaway placed in custody and taken as a prisoner to Shiraz, the Persian court, where she was kept under lock and key by the enamored king. In this place, after considerable time, when she refused marriage to the king, who was inflamed with unchaste love, and persisted in her commitment to Christ, she (irrespective of the strenuous efforts undertaken by the ambassador of the Russian grand duke on behalf of her freedom) steadfastly suffered the horrible martyrdom of glowing tongs and filled with joyful patience ended her wretched life by burning at the stake. She herself relates the entire course of her life in detail in the third act: supplemental information is given by the Armenian ambassador in the sixth scene of the first act.

Content of the Acts

I.

Eternity repudiates the vanity of the world and indicates the means by which everlasting honor can be attained. Demetrius and Procopius, who have a secret arrangement with the queen's lady-in-waiting, are led by her to the queen, going past the guards who have been put to sleep by specially prepared wine. They make Georgia's current status known to the queen, and assure her of her certain release. Such conversation is interrupted by the unexpected arrival of the Persian king, who unsuccessfully pressures the queen's chastity. The imprisoned maidens conclude (the Act) and bewail the fall of their fatherland with a song of mourning.

II.

Shah Abbas complains that his love is fruitless. He is requested to attend the farewell audience of the Russian ambassador, who in person requests from the king
the release of Catharine, which is promised to him. But soon after the ambassador's departure, Shah Abbas laments that, ill advised, he agreed to her freedom.
The Act closes with the choruses of the princes murdered by Shah Abbas.

III.

The Russian ambassador visits the captured queen, assures her of her freedom,
and listens to the entire course of her life. Meanwhile, the shah, driven by love,
jealousy, and honor, decides to offer the queen his marital bed and the crown
of Persia or the most ferocious death. The choruses of the imprisoned maidens,
who are preparing for the supposed homeward journey, close the act.

IV.

The queen prepares herself for the supposed departure, but when an unexpected sadness overcomes her, she suspects a new misfortune is at hand. Imanculi
informs her of the king's final decision. Catharine chooses death, prepares herself for the final battle, blesses her deeply grieved ladies-in-waiting, and is led
away by the executioner. In the chorus the Virtues admonish humanity to true
constancy, and they conclude the argument between Death and Love, who each
emphasize their power.

V.

Serena, who has fallen into a faint during the martyrdom of the queen, is carried
by the eunuchs into the ladies' chamber, where she is revived. She tells the other
virgins of the suffering and the constancy of the queen. The virgins hurry to
fetch the queen's corpse, but find that she is already at the stake, upon which she
ends her long suffering most valiantly. Shah Abbas, who regrets his haste, gives
a command to arrest Imanculi and save the queen, but it is too late. The Russian

ambassador receives news of the queen's demise and condemns such ferocity to Seinelcan, while, too late, Shah Abbas mourns the queen's death.

Characters in the Tragedy

Catharine	Queen of Georgia
Salome Serena Cassandra	The Queen's Ladies-in-Waiting
Ladies of the Court	Four Attendants to the Queen (See Act IV, 397-99.)
Procopius Demetrius	Ambassadors from Georgia
Ambrosius	The Priest
Shah Abbas	King of the Persians
Seinelcan Imanculi[71]	Privy Councilors to the King
The Ambassador from Russia	
A Servant	
The Chief Executioner	
Eternity	

---

[71] The similarity of the name *Imanculi* with that of *Imam-Quli Khan* (Persian امامقلی خان, Emāmqolī Khan) raises the interesting possibility that Gryphius named his character after the famed Persian military and political leader who was a favorite of Shah Abbas I. As second in command of the military, Imam-Quli Khan served as viceroy and was governor of Fars, Lar, and Bahrain until he and his family were put to death in 1632 by Shah Ṣafī, the successor of Abbas I.

Silent Characters

Courtiers of the King of Persia; Two Enuchs; Courtiers of the Russian Ambassador, Executioners (listed only in the first printed edition, 1657)

The Choruses

Acts I and III: The Imprisoned Maidens; Act II: The Ghosts of Princes Murdered by Shah Abbas; Act IV: The Virtues, Death, and Love

The tragedy begins before sunrise and closes at day's end. The scene is the royal household at Shiraz in Persia. The action portrays the last day in the life of Queen Catharine.

The First Act

The stage is strewn with corpses, crowns, scepters, swords, and other insignia of earthly vanity. Heaven is revealed above the stage; hell, below. Eternity descends from heaven and comes to rest on the stage.

Eternity

Oh dwellers in this troubled world	1
Circumscribed by woe and sorrow and the arid bones of the dead;	
You seek me, where everything topples and tumbles down,	
Where your every entity disintegrates to naught, and your joy	
to bitter tears!	
You blind ones! Alas! Where do you think you will find me?	5
You, who must collapse and perish before me,	
You, who capture nothing but false dreams for truth,	
And who refresh yourselves at mud holes, not clear springs!	
A will-o'-the-wisp leads you astray, oh mortals!	
A foolish raging that distorts your minds.	10
Could anyone desire eternal life, when the brief span,	
The handful of years granted him by heaven,	
This age, that withers even as it blooms,	
Is parceled out in hostility and transience?	
Thrones crumble if He withdraws his firm support;*72	15
He, who by a single word moves hell and earth.	
Often a crowned king, who has seized the power of other ruled lands,	
Has suddenly trembled before a foreign throne in iron chains:	
More than once have anointed heads been severed	

---

72 An asterisk indicates that Gryphius appended an explanatory note to the annotated line: see *Brief Notes of ANDREAS GRYPHIUS about Several Obscure References in his CATHA-RINE*, below, p. 255 ff. Note: Brackets [ ] are used to enclose clarifications provided by the translator.

By sword, by axe, or cleaver.   20
The sacred blood of princes has spilled by the cursed executioner's hand
Into sand stained darkly by the atrocious deed.
The victor, too, how often his laurel wreath has been
Transformed into cypress twigs:
He entered his joyous celebration   25
With the pomp of triumph, only to attend the dance of death.
What one man builds, another will destroy tomorrow.
Where palaces now stand,
Someday will be just grass and fields,
On which a shepherd's child will tend the flock.   30
And you, for whom great palaces are yet too small,
When soon you will have to pass from here,
A narrow house, a slender coffin, will enclose you.
A coffin! How truly it reveals the dwarfed stature of man.*
But whither and for what do you struggle—   35
You, who believe that the power of your pen
Has harnessed both death and time?
Believe, for sure, eternity does not exist on paper.
Even as you strange ones seek to avoid doom,
You fail to notice how our days are fleeing.   40
You hasten (in spite of the lights of heaven!) as you keep watch
Into the night of your grave.
How many climb toward greater honor, blinded
By the smoke of false glory, and plunge into deepest disgrace
When their waxed wings, swung far too near the sun, melt--   45
And they are scorned by the entire world!
Oh foolish ones! He, who prostrates himself before you on both knees,
Often wishes to see you where there is nothing but death and trouble.
You, who fall in love with gold,
And race through South and East to enrich others;   50
Where will you be when everything is surrendered?
When a given hour hastens the reckoning of all things?
Does the one who counts the years ever think of me?

Does the one defrauded by a charming form
Or the one deceived by the blush of his cheeks --   55
Oh, Lord! Oh Lord of Heaven, does he perhaps consider himself more
                                        beautiful than Thou?
Raise monuments! Sail far on the vast sea!
Discover a virgin land and bestow names upon its snow!*
Name shores and name mountains after your famous men,
Yes, inscribe your name and your friend's on the rim and
                                        core of the moon!*   60
But in so doing, remember this:
That even that which you possess is still not really known to you;
That here you have not yet found what is eternal;
That only vanity and illusion are attached to you.
Behold, you poor ones! Behold, what is this vale of sorrow?   65
A torture chamber, where noose and pillory
And death are used for pranks. Prince and crown lie before me,
I trample on scepter and mace and rely on Father and the Son.
Jewels, images, gold, and scholarly documents
Are nothing but chaff and worthless dust before me.   70
Here above you is the joy of eternal bliss;
There below you, that which eternally burns and roars.
Here is my realm. Choose which you wish to possess.
Whosoever errs in this can be helped by nothing on earth.
Behold the bliss of heaven! Here there is only comfort and delight!   75
Behold the dungeon of corruption! There, nothing exists but
                                        distress and woe.
Behold the ancestral palace of sublime joy: here there is only
                                        happiness and sunshine!
Behold the pit of black spirits: there, nothing exists but darkness and misery.
Which do you choose?
Your choice can eternally reward or punish you.   80
Theater of mortality, farewell! I am borne away on my throne.
The worthy princess follows me; she already perceives a higher realm
Who, free while in fetters, not bound to earthly things while on earth,

Struggled and suffered for church, throne, and country.

You, who hold a high ideal according to the same honor;   85

Scorn with her that which transpires on earth.

Give, as did she, your valiant blood as a pledge

And live and die in solace for God, Honor, and Fatherland.

Demetrius. Procopius. The scene changes to a pleasure garden.

Demetrius: This is the mighty fortress that has confined our treasure!

    The jewel that we cherished so briefly, yet so much.   90

    The sunlight of Iberia [*Georgia*], who descended so bloodstained

    Just as her glow had begun to radiate through the mist,

    Is shrouded by these stone walls. She who rules over us

    Was driven as a slave into bondage for us.

    With her our fame and freedom and advantage   95

    And sovereign power traversed into unknown misery.

    Who, until now, has not grieved and mourned for you

    With inexhaustible longing, with sighs of lament,

    And unfeigned tears? Who wouldn't face

    Death with great consolation, if dire need   100

    Should require such a sacrifice for you, oh queen of women?

    Queen, who ever-crowned could behold the world!

    Who has protected fatherland and realm with might and right!

    Who has held back the stream of tyranny with force and courage,

    Who has avenged the murder of her prince by the death of him   105

    Who broke his oath to God, his pledge to us, and all justice

    That binds the nations; of him, who stabbed his brother's heart*

    Through the heart of his father. Woman! Hope of your time!

    Who comforted Tiflis, invigorated Georgia,

    Who terrified the Persians and set free beleaguered Gurgistan,   110

    When the furious power of the cruel multitude joined

    To extinguish our people with saber, arrow, and fire.

    Who, when there was nothing left to venture for the salvation of all,

    Valiantly wanted to risk her own life.

Is there, Honored Queen, is there hope that rescued   115
From your heavy burden, from your yoke unbreakable as diamonds,
We shall yet salute you? Will heaven allow
That after so much anxiety we will be able to honor you?
Returned to your castle, placed upon your throne,
Praised by your people, and kissed by your son?   120
Will my grey head experience the glorious day
That will overturn our long suffering with joy?

Procopius: Henceforth I have no doubt. God places in our hands
The keys to these chains. He tears the mighty bond
Asunder with His strong hand. He opens the doors for us,   125
And shows us the means to lead away the pearl.
You've heard it yourself (trust, I beseech you, your own ear!)
How the ambassador took an oath to Tamaras,*
How sincerely he promised not to think of returning to Moscow
Before trying to persuade Abbas with every means possible.   130
You saw how splendidly the great court honored him,
With what amicability the Persian leader heard him!
How favorably he accomplished the reason for his mission,
As he, according to the utmost hope, completed his whole charge.
The favor has not yet been granted, which, on this day   135
That he plans to depart, he might easily receive.
Should the one for whom, up to now, so much has not been refused,
Be denied an imprisoned woman by Shah Abbas?

Demetrius: A woman, however, who has ruled, and has troubled
                                          his entire realm.

Procopius: To whom, in heated anger, he granted life.   140

Demetrius: So that, through long suffering, she might fade away in
                                          greatest anxiety –

Procopius: Much more so that she might find her happiness in the prison –

Demetrius: Her happiness in this court? In this place, where only
                                          murder and death –

Procopius: The greatest relief has often been found in the greatest distress.

Demetrius: How long has Tamaras sought after her, only in vain?   145

Procopius: Whom he [*Abbas*] has declared his enemy so many times.
Demetrius: He knows that this request comes from her son.
Procopius: Who expresses his plea by means of a greater crown.
Demetrius: But is Russia really so concerned about our welfare?
Procopius: What can't be achieved by bribing princes with gifts?   150
Demetrius: Favor bought with gifts is felled by other gifts.
Procopius: Let it fall! If only we can keep the gain!
Demetrius: Keep the gain from Persia? Is Abbas so unknown to you?
        The bloodhound! *Procopius:* Do you doubt the ambassador's sincerity?
Demetrius: Not at all his sincerity, but I greatly doubt his power.   155
Procopius: Shah knows the Russians' strength in case their anger awakens.
Demetrius: Shah knows that Russia will not go to battle over a woman.
Procopius: Someone who fears a conflagration must also put out sparks.
        Someone who curses war doesn't give his enemy a ready cause.
Demetrius: Someone who wants security firmly holds on to his pawn.   160
        One doesn't recklessly let lions spring from their cages.
Procopius: Let it happen as it may, this new day will bring it to pass.
Demetrius: Surely there isn't a wretched pain where there is not
                                        the greatest joy.
        I feel – I don't know how – something weighs heavy in my heart.
        I languish between fear, longing, terror, and hope –   165
        Where is Salome, anyway? *Procopius:* Stop! The door is open!
        She told me to come to the covered passage
        When I bribed Persian steel with Greek gold.

        Salome. Procopius. Demetrius.

Salome: The brown night fades. Diana will soon pale,
        The wagon of Phoebus turns, the host of stars grows dim   170
        The sky is tinged with color, the rosy dawn laughs,
        The great light of the world, the noble sun, awakens.
        A pleasant breeze moves through the green forests,
        Pearls of dew refresh the parched fields,
        The world appears renewed. But we, we alone   175

Perish in anxiety. The darkness of anguish,
The cruel despair of the dungeon, and the fetters that bind us
In foreign tyranny are to be found here forever.
We wish: without counsel! We hope: without reason!
We plead: without solace! The exploding abyss   180
Of hell roars back at us and heaven empties bolts
Of thunder upon us. Brimstone arrows –
Oh grieving queen! (I lament not for myself)
Oh grieving queen – forever wound you.
Thou Prince of Princes! How long willst Thou rage?   185
Can Thy gracious heart be implored no further?
Shall she who trusts in Thee forever see the people
So defiant towards her, they who desecrate Thy name?
Who interpret our bitter despair as Thy disgrace,
Who oppose a lone woman with power and intrigue?   190
My Jesus! Behold us! Tear asunder this cloud
That hides Thy countenance, and free the soul
That is entangled in the snare. Who so excites my heart?
My cold spirit ignites. Dost Thou hear my plea,
Omniscient Being? How? Or does my heart   195
Feel the foreboding of new anxiety? Can yet another pain
Still await us? How can it be that I've not seen
The ones who've come to visit us from Gurgistan?
Could they have forgotten the time and place
That we chose yesterday in such great haste?   200
Alas! Have I come here too late?
Alas! Has the guard's fury perhaps already bound them?
Shall I withdraw? I'll try! No! Your life is in danger!
Whither would you be running, poor creature? Where?
                                        To the funeral bier.
Shall I trouble the queen in vain after all the anxiety,   205
Shall I withhold from her the only means
That heaven shows us? No, indeed! Salome!
Risk everything you can; if you can do no more, then perish.

There, I see them both. No! But yes! Oh praiseworthy are they,
Who alone prove themselves true to us in our distress.   210
Who, now that lightning's fury has triumphed over us,
Still seek their lady, who lies in fetters.
What leads you to this court? *Demetrius:* The will to set you free.
Salome: You seek to free a lamb from the jaws of a wolf.
Procopius: The Russian Ambassador himself is concerned with
                                        this matter   215
And advances the effort. Whoever sees us in Persia
Considers us to be his colleagues. *Salome:* Oh! May it please God!
Demetrius: Prince Tamaras himself has written to the queen.
Salome: Do you have the prince's letter?
Demetrius: Is there then no way
To kiss her hand? To see her face?   220
Salome: Are you tired of living?
Demetrius: Ha! Could I die in any better way
Than in her glorious service?
Salome: You seek to ruin us
And struggle towards your own grave. But what am I thinking?
The door is without guard. Quickly, follow me inside.
If heaven is with us, it will know how to guide you.   225
If not, then at least loyalty will embellish our tomb.

Catharine.

The scene changes to the Queen's chamber.

Catharine: Lord of this world, who counteth our days,
Who, before heaven and earth were formed, choseth those
Who are tested by scorn and pain; how long shall I suffer?
When willst Thou call my soul to depart from my body?   230
My soul, which constant sorrow burdens with fierce pain,
Which thousand-fold despair consumes with lasting torment.
What melancholy have I not experienced since my childhood?
What fresh wounds has this heart not always felt?

Hasn't my purple garb been painted over with blood   235
As long as murky daylight has shone upon my face?
You, who deem your princes high and more than blessed,
Behold how much despair the sword has honed on me:
I won't mention my parents, whom already I had lost
When Alexander chose me for his daughter-in-law.   240
Who didn't wish me happiness, when upon my hair
The crown of Gurgistan was placed? When still of tender age
The prince of Georgia placed me at his side,
And his golden scepter was placed in my right hand;
Who didn't rejoice when I gave birth to Tamaras,   245
Who seemed to be chosen as the shield and hope of the realm?
You poor ones! Behold us! What heaven gives to us
Is the means by which He, as soon as He get angry, saddens us.
How often I sat in tears as my husband's father lamented
And summoned his rebellious blood before God's justice!   250
When he tore the white hair from his scalp
And burst out with sighs, curses, and woe upon his son!
When he cursed the very light that shone on Constantine,
Who trusted the Persian court more than God's covenant;
When with tear-stained cheeks he kissed his last child,
                                        my worthy husband,   255
As salve to a bitter wound and comfort for inflamed torment.
Alas! This is beyond all comprehension
Amid this host of miseries that wound my spirit!
This was a thunderbolt that pierced my soul
And encompassed my scathed heart with a burning glow,   260
When I had to send my tender child to Abbas,
He, who still knew little or nothing of God or of his parents.
Soon the storm gathered fury and with swift power
Crashed upon the heads of my husband and his father.
My husband's father fell from wounds inflicted by his son,   265
My king found death at the hand of his brother.
Cruel Constantine (Oh mad raging audacity!)

Used his brother's corpse and his aged father's blood
To defile the banquet set for his guests. Can anyone possibly grasp
With what feeling and heart and bitter shedding of tears   270
I received both coffins? How my spirit was terrified,
When this raging tiger who had wounded me so deeply,
Offered me his bed and marriage? Adulterer! I had to hear
How you thought to dishonor the wife of your brother,
Still warm from his murder! As this grief passed,   275
I saw the new storm that hung in the air,
And that was powerful enough to hurl all of Georgia, by civil wars,
Into flames, smoke, and rubble,
And atrocious conquests. Until the tyrant came
And took me from my throne into the dungeon.   280
What haven't I seen! What haven't I suffered!
What haven't I lamented! How haven't I been opposed!
What haven't I experienced! And what must I yet endure!
Savior! How long must I struggle in this yoke?
How far from my court! And stolen crown!   285
And subverted kingdom! And banished son!
My child! My Tamaras! Has the sword of Persia,
Has the wrathful conflagration of Armenia consumed you?
Is there a single stone-pile left in Gurgistan?
Is there anyone, whom Abbas hasn't driven into misery?   290
Is there someone in the world who laments my plight?
Someone, who asks if I'm alive or dead?
I don't even know that myself. My life is over;
Yet I gasp in terror. My blood has not been spilled;
Yet I am more than dead. The earth doesn't cover me;   295
Yet the dungeon's vault hides my melancholy face.

Salome. Catharine.

Salome: How can I best tell her such joyful tidings?
Catharine: From whence do you come with these roses, Salome?

Salome: I wandered in error through the courtyard, as Her Majesty
    Was offering her fervent prayer to our Lord,   300
    And there, by chance, I found these signs of summer.
Catharine: Oh flowers, to which in truth we can be compared!
    It barely opens its bud and appears in full splendor,
    Pearled with fresh dew. It casts its withered garb,
    The pale petals, aside. The noble roses live*   305
    Such a brief time and yet still are covered with thorns.
    As soon as the sun rises, it embellishes the garden's canopy;
    And then is turned to naught, as soon as the sun descends.
    And thus we greet the day, dampened with our own tears,
    And perish, when we first really yearn to live.   310
    Behold how the crimson pales: thus we shall fade away.
    Thus flees all worldly joy, thus breaks the golden throne.
    Nothing remains in our grasp except the worthless twigs,
    The thorns, this cross, the terror, the soul's pestilence,
    The dreadful anxiety, and overwhelming sorrow,   315
    And only the memory of vanished loveliness.
    Thus, like the rose, my scepter also had to break.
    I still feel the thorns that relentlessly pierce.
Salome: Yet just like now, when winter's raging has calmed down,
    The prickly thorn bush bears new roses;   320
    Thus, if now this storm of agony will vanish,
    Your Majesty likewise will find desired comfort.
Catharine: Our winter is, indeed, at hand. This rose twig reminds me
    Of images that a dream, before night passed,
    Impressed upon my mind. The palaces we owned   325
    Appeared before us. Gurgistan's defiant citadel
    Was most magnificently adorned with crafted gold,
    And we (just as before!) were led to the throne.
Salome: This is a sign of something joyous!
Catharine: As I ascended the throne,
    I saw the entire splendor vanish in an instant,   330
    The gleam of diamonds sparkling on my gown

Morphed into pearls. And (so it seemed to me) I felt*
How the bejeweled crown that formerly adorned me,
Pressed my beleaguered brow with more than usual force,
Until clear blood streamed down from both my temples   335
And I grasped only rose twigs instead of the crown.
Dried out rose twigs that were woven as a wreath
Pressed tightly round my brow and lay upon my hair.
The purple tore apart, the scepter broke like glass,
As I myself, alas, was sitting on the very sharpest thorns.   340
Many tried to help me, but in vain:
Yet even more, in opposition, tried to torture me most brutally,
Until a strange man rushed at me, and not without pain,
More than somewhat roughly grabbed both of my breasts.
I fainted away completely. Yet when the fear had passed   345
Oh! Salome! I found myself surrounded with such joy!
Far more beautiful than when I was most magnificently adorned,
Far greater than when I received the crown of Gurgistan.
I beheld my white gown sparkle with diamonds.
Shah Abbas trembled at my feet in fear.   350
Everyone called out: "All Hail! To her who has been raised so high!"
Until all the uproar took the sleep from our eyes.
Salome: If one thoughtfully considers the misery
    That Your Majesty has borne along with the crown,
    That has tested her until now, then the dream is only too real.   355
    Yet this vision makes the relief obvious to her.
    Freedom calls us home! Can Salome restrain herself
    Not to rush to tell of such unexpected joy?
    Prince Tamaras— *Catharine*: What is it? *Salome*: has—
Catharine: What? *Salome*: conquered— *Cath.*: Pray tell! *Salome*: his kingdom—
Catharine: Tamaras? *Salome*: and is trying as hard as he can—
                                        Cath.: My child?   360
Salome: To break this firm bondage that imprisons us.
Catharine: My Tamaras! *Salome*: Oh God! She cannot speak for joy!
    She trembles! She faints! Princess! *Catharine*: Oh, my son!

Salome: Up! My Queen! This is the splendid crown

    That the night revealed to you. *Catharine*: Now I shall heed no pain,   365

    The storm of terror subsides! The burden of my heart

    Vanishes at this hour! Oh! Chains, despair, and stone

    Are but child's play to me, if you alone, my son,

    Have not been struck by lightning! My son, since you've escaped,

    My son! Since you rule, I am no longer captive!   370

    Oh, vacillating joy! I believe what I wish.

    And yet, unfortunately, without reason.

Salome: There are more than many reasons.

    A prince of Gurgistan, recently arrived from Russia,

    Has told me this himself. *Catharine*: What he perhaps assumed

    From uncertain rumor. *Salome*: I have an absolute guarantee   375

    That authenticates this story. *Catharine.*: And what is it?

                            Salome: The prince's own note.

    Would Your Majesty believe what Tamaras has written?

Catharine: When? How? By whom? To us? *Salome*: What should

                                be dearer to him

    Than his mother's well-being? *Catharine*: Oh heaven, can it be true?

Salome: Does Your Majesty wish to see envoys from him?   380

Catharine: Envoys? *Salome*: Whom I hid earlier, when the morning

                         was not yet bright,

    In a secret place here in the fortress.

Catharine: How did you recognize them? How did they contact you?

Salome: At night I opened the back garden gate.

    It's been two days since they happened to see me.   385

    Now I've been informed why they were sent.

Catharine: Then they can't have been discovered? *Salome*: They

                         live unrecognized

    With the one whom the Czar of Russia recently sent.

Catharine: Oh unexpected event! Oh strange course of things!

Salome: Does Your Majesty want me to bring them before her?   390

Catharine: If it can be done in secret. *Salome*: The guard is unconscious,

Sedated by strong wine that I poured over herbs
The envoys gave me for this purpose.
Catharine: Go there. Oh highest Prince! Thou doth give and heal
                                                 our wounds!
Thou doth lower us in pain, yet offer us Thy hand,   395
When all human hope and counsel have vanished.
Well then! I will bear the yoke of misery,
That Thou hath placed upon my neck,
With defiant courage,
Because my weeping has moved Thee.   400
Thou hath, while I am here imprisoned,
Looked upon my kingdom and my child.
I regret not that which I have lost,
For Thou hath sustained this pledge.
I feel as if I am born anew,   405
I feel no burden of grief.
I willingly give this life of sorrow to Thee,
For my kingdom and my son.

Catharine. Demetrius. Procopius.

Demetrius: Most Royal Highness ever to honor the face of the earth,
Whosoever previously heard with dismay of your bravery,   410
Of your patience and virtue, is now appalled,
As the barbarous enemy offends us with your despair.
Forgive Georgia, who greets you so belatedly
And seeks to moisten your bonds with tears;
Forgive your son, who grieves incessantly   415
And considers the burdens you bear as his own.
Forgive us, Queen, that after such a long time
We have arrived only now to lead you to the throne,
Which you, for our sake, exchanged for a bier
That carried you, in great pain, further than the grave   420
To a multitude worse than the dead. With you, oh longed-for sunshine

Of our storm-beaten kingdom, all bliss and joy was lost!
How long the night of servitude has frightened us!
How often our land was stained with its own blood
After your downfall! How often did their own fruit fall   425
Upon the corpses of mothers? Sisters had to die
In the cold arms of their brothers. The stream flowed, darkly stained
By nobles, whom the Persians' sword had destroyed.
Yet once again we hope, since the rosy dawn,
Your Tamaras, is with us; that also Death might kill himself,   430
And your return might dispel all our sorrow.
Armenia wishes this, and yearns for the time
That will give you back to us. For so long already
We have yearned to see you; heaven has prevented it.
The enemy refused everything. Persia's defiant power   435
Scorned with proud boldness whatever Gurgistan asked.
Yet now Russia herself offers Georgia her hand
And seeks an end to the prolonged misery in Abbas' court.
Meanwhile, Queen, accept this note,
This pledge of unfeigned loyalty that could only be sent   440
By your crowned son and Meurab, who broke
That which forced Tiflis* and who avenged his own humiliation;
Who placed your Tamaras on the throne,
Upon which, without you, he does not yet consider himself king.
Catharine: The meaning that our kingdom has held for us until now   445
Lightens this cross placed upon us
By Him who giveth and taketh away all crowns. We have accomplished
What a princess should; what a woman has in strength
And a mother in loyalty, we are ready to risk;
(If it might help you) our life and limb,   450
The soul, that still stirs in these breasts,
The blood, that surges in us and pulsates through our veins.
The freedom, that you have come forth to give us,
Is indeed the joy and uttermost yearning of mankind
And it is sought by us; yet only if it pleases Him,   455

Who placeth us in bondage to strengthen us.

If the Prince of Princes doth wish to release us,

We shall embrace His salvation. If Death should find us here,

Death, which plagues us hourly with extended martyrdom

And aggrieves us before we die, then here we are, His handmaiden.   460

It is quite enough for us that we have learned from you

That our kingdom is at peace and he to whom we gave birth

Rules the kingdom. We would wish him understanding

And better fortune than ours and prosperity for our fatherland.

Demetrius: He, Who restoreth Gurgistan so well after so much terror,   465

Will not allow the priceless pledge, for whom we've been sent out,

To remain in foreign tyranny forever.

Catharine: May this what He willeth come to pass! How was Gurgistan set free

And Tamaras redeemed?

Demetrius: When God's wrath seeks to punish

He employs strange means and unexpected weapons.   470

To whom (Oh misery!) is the bitter time unknown,

When Abbas, aflame in a mad rage against us,

So forcefully took to the battlefield? When he, after false oaths,

Had Your Majesty led into this prison?

How he pursued Tamaras on his flight   475

And, after much plunder and murder, sought him near

Alovassa. [i.e., *in Tiflis*]

Catharine: Sadly enough, we know it only too well!

Demetrius: Yet when he [*Tamaras*] wasn't to be found

He [*Abbas*], in a burning rage, ordered Prince Alovassa bound

And Meurab's lofty spirit, the right hand of the prince,

Was exiled with his wife and children to Shiraz.   480

Catharine: Woe unto me! There Alovassa perished by dark poison!

There Meurab converted to the Persian's false belief!

There Meurab's wife in Meurab's presence was so

Flagrantly violated by the shah! Oh, heaven does not flash with lightning!

There Meurab's young son and daughter suffered that   485

Which innate justice and even dumb animals forbid!

And Meurab saw it happen!

Demetrius: And waited for the time

That, before his remaining years plunged into mortality,

Would offer him, after defiant terror, the sword of revenge,

Which also didn't fail to appear. After extensive raging,   490

The shah was so rocked to sleep by Meurab's steady service

That the saddened man gained an opportunity for revenge

Even before he or anyone imagined. When the tyrant decided

To hold by force that which the mighty power of bare swords

Had won, he spoke to Meurab in this way: 495

"Now you may hope from us what anyone would wish!

We have decided to raise your standing.

Now we will announce our decision. The time has come

That shall indeed demonstrate to the dismayed world

How fortunate is he, who stands and builds on Abbas' counsel.   500

Five hundred princes have appeared at our command,

Ready to serve us with sword and folk and life.

The camps are filled with heroes, horses, and cattle.

Be commander-in-chief for us and captain of them all!

Whoever lifts a hand against your command–   505

Punish him without mercy or regard for his life.

In short: take the staff, the kingdom will be under you,

And you are only under us."

Catharine: God help us! What do we hear?

Demetrius: "You will," he continued, "be bound ever closer to us,

If we now find you willing to carry out a certain task;   510

The one, to whom we entrusted the crown of Georgia,

Is also entitled to our child as his long-promised bride."

Catharine: Whom had the tyrant placed upon our throne?

Procopius: A man more degenerate than of royal blood:

A distant relative of Alovassa received both kingdoms.   515

Demetrius: "Go then," spoke Abbas, "and attend with power equal to our own,

The marriage of our daughter. Thereafter, command

That all Christians still found in Gurgistan be bound –

Woman, virgin, man and child, mother and son,
Naked to their feet. And lead this naked band to us   520
In all its humiliation. When this is done,
Those who deny the true God (Allah) and still believe in Christ
Shall be brought in similar splendor
To our palace, for we have decided
To end the abomination and break the defiance   525
That blooms in such profusion. Revenge shall be spoken of
As long as our name lives. Whoever doesn't renounce the cross
Will be transformed by flame to corpse and dust."
Catharine: Did Meurab pledge to complete this task?
Demetrius: Right away the king found him more than ready.   530
    The host of princes swore allegiance to him, he was armed
                                with the staff,
    And, with great ceremony, was declared highest commander.
    But Abbas sent along two more men, whom secretly he had ordered
    To assassinate Meurab, unaware.
Catharine: That's how the shah honors those true to him!
Demetrius: When rumor informed us   535
    Of Meurab's return, everyone was frightened
    By such amassed power. Yet no one revealed
    The inner terror of his heart. Many found in those deeds,
    That Meurab formerly had carried out among us with the highest glory,
    Some hope amid their fear. Yet others no longer trusted   540
    Him, who had become unfaithful to God. As soon as he was met
    By us, who received him in full strength at the border,
    He renewed the favor that previously he had won,
    Before his glowing reputation died in scornful disloyalty.
    He loudly promised, by is soul and under oath,   545
    That he wanted to break the yoke from us and his country
    And protect morality and justice. He swore to us, that his
    Army had arrived for the bride's honor and the kingdom's benefit;
    That perpetual prosperity would issue from this marriage
    And ever sweet joy and a more secure peace would be generated.   550

Thus he promised one and all, as he should,
That he would die, duty bound to their ever-constant favor.
These were Meurab's words. But alas! His princes
Proved all too soon how those whom Abbas ever raised
Thirst for blood. In a short time   555
The finest flower of the nobility fell by strange tragedy.
Nothing was seen but murder, but distress, pain, and tears,
But corpses, prisons, axes, but totally stunned aching:
Despair rose higher than ever before.
In short: our country was almost on the bier!   560
When Meurab saw our agony and deep sorrow
The prince, who set the naked sword at our heart and throat,
Was finally sent for at his command.
"What raging," he cried, "Has incited you against the people of this land?
Why are you always seen spilling innocent blood?   565
Are my high office and authority to be trampled by your feet?
Is this what you swore to me? What the king bid you,
When he put the entire army in my hands?
Is my power so underestimated? Do you listen with deaf ears?
Have you, perhaps, not I, been chosen to be leader?   570
Do I carry the staff in vain? No indeed! It shall be seen
Who Meurab is and who you are." "If I have done anything—"
The murderer interrupted him—"then the shah
                                        has commanded it of me
And it is not a crime." "I'll find out the facts," spoke Meurab.
"If the shah commanded you to commit the cruel deed,   575
Then you are only doing what you should; if he didn't, then you are dead!"
Meanwhile, anger and suspicion aroused his temper:
His keen intellect sensed a false benevolence
That Abbas was showing him; he, too, had felt
How the tyrant played with cunning and incessant perjury.*   580
His heart revealed to him the two messages of the betrayer,
The means by which he so dishonorably wanted to kill
                                        one prince by the other.

He wisely investigated, until he discovered
That the bow was already drawn on his breast.
As soon as he'd pondered how the danger was to be averted,   585
He sent quick messages throughout the entire land
And called us in a group, as if he wanted to deal with
The people's wages and the tax and the invested gold
Of the king. But when we appeared,
He quickly chose those qualified to serve him—   590
Whom blood ties, favor, and honor can bind,
And courageously appealed to them with these words:
"You, who together with me see our land totally devastated;
You, who mourn with fear and distress and sorrowful tears
Altar and home; and inexpressibly lament,   595
Due to the compounded burden that gnaws at your souls:
Have faith that I don't observe your torment unmoved.
That I despise, with you, the yoke under which you strain.
The whip that stings your limbs lashes me, too.
What clutches your heart is the same thing that chews away at mine.   600
Consider me your foe! You may indeed call me enemy
Because I light the flame in which you must perish,
Because the tyrant honors me. Though my robes look Persian,
(In spite of power, force, and deceit!) I am a Christian in my heart.
This land nourished me, like you, in its womb.   605
Here I spent my time when I was free.
Here I want (heaven help!) to freely, not in servitude,
Entrust my now grey hair to the open funeral-bier.
If you still have enough courage to draw a sword with me,
Then let us take back this land from the shah's hands!   610
But if long servitude totally has made womenfolk of you,
Then leave me here alone. I'll say farewell to you.
Tears are of no use. If you deplore the ones
Who recently slaughtered my people, then believe what he tells you,
He, who seeks freedom or death, salvation or the end: 615
They didn't know what terror is! Cursed be the hour

In which the tyrant expressly commanded
To fetch you with your wives and children to Isfahan,
Bound in pairs, naked and miserable, dragged through the land,
Spit upon and scorned. Then he declared he'd kill   620
By means of stake and fire, those whom even this threat does not force
To deny Christ. The army that occupies
Your streets with sword and shield has been chosen for this task.
Yet may He, Who counteth every hair upon our heads,
Direct his lightning-wrath on Meurab's weak limbs   625
If he can treat his fatherland and you, beloved brothers,
With such horror. Your prosperity and life blossom
Wherever someone strives to offer him his hand."

Catharine: In what frame of mind did he find you?

Demetrius: Astounded.—Yet daring to risk with him
Our possessions, our life, and blood. We asked that he propose   630
What he thought advisable. "No extensive advice is useful here,"
Spoke Meurab. "The completed deed will praise what we do.
The princes will gather at a banquet
Before the sun sets! When they have succumbed to drink
This dagger will be sharp and ready to stab their breast.   635
Keep separated, however you like, yet on the bridge.
As soon as I give this signal to you through a window,
Attack the patrol. We want to eradicate trunk and branch
And root, so that barely a memory of tyranny
Will be found here anymore.   640
The army that is scattered through the city and the kingdom
Is, when its heads are missing, a dragon that still threatens
When its head has been snapped off, but that a weak man easily
Can tear into pieces or a child can trample with its feet."

Catharine: How did the assault work out?

Demetrius: According to wish and beyond expectation.   645
That which spilled our blood was drowned itself in blood.
The boiling anger of revenge, like a flame,
Swept the weeds out of all Iberia [*Georgia*].

Prince Meurab, blind with hate and defiant from so much suffering,
Had the pale heads of the dead cut off,   650
And when the row of heads of those who had wounded him so deeply
Was set upon his table for a mock tribunal
He took the chalice that was offered to him, completely delirious,
And cried: "This is the cup that I wrested from my avengers.
No longer as a slave! Oh, my tortured wife!   655
Oh! My humiliated child! Ye, whom the long torture has drenched
With tears; Ye, who perish in terror
And rot in the earth! Ye, whom the open grave
Did not deem worthy – My King Alovassa!
Imprisoned Queen! Exiled Tamaras!   660
My fatherland: a toast! Repose and joy must now refresh you
After such extreme suffering! How the pain oppresses me
That you have felt and feel. If God still sits in judgment,
      Meurab here turns his attention to the row of heads
            and addresses them in lines 664-670.
Then let death, which is much too easy, be for you
 Just the beginning of new pain and the origin of
                              constant torment,   665
To which revenge and woe summon you condemned ghosts
                              before judgement,
You pestilence of these times, you, whom the day curses!
You, upon whom the world spits! You, whom punishment seeks,
Even now when you're without spirit! As I, with this wine,
Drink to your shame and derision. Appear, Justice! Appear!   670
And transform, even as you ought, the tyrant's house
And lineage and crown to dust, to smoke, to ashes, and to rubble."
Catharine: Have the Persians thus completely perished under
                              Meurab's sword?
Demetrius: Except for those who took flight with the greatest haste.
      Meurab sent two courageous men, who were captured in Gurgistan, 675
      Back home with a letter to Abbas

In which he [*Abbas*] could behold a portrait of his own deeds:

The faithlessness with which he paid for true service;

Treachery, cruelty, betrayal, deception, perjury, defiance, and poison.

The murders, committed and conceived by him: 680

The unjust justice, the double false tongues:

The ideas that were wrought for self-benefit alone.

The outrages with which he saddened his [*Meurab's*] wife and child

As he perpetrated before the father's own eyes

What cannot be said aloud. "My Christ will ruin you,"   685

(So he wrote) "and your realm! And will shorten your days!

He who fears no king, through me does He carry out His justice

And your punishment. Through me who used to be your servant,

And now is your scourge, and who must forever torture you

Because of your blood shedding. The distant future shall conclude,   690

Taught by your fall, that (even if it happens belatedly!)

God never tolerates tyrants!"

Catharine: Didn't the violent prince find out who wrote such a

brutal message?

Demetrius: Until now his anger had not broken out against us,

Even though the loss of the people deeply moved him;   695

Because Meurab had more planned for him.

As soon as the land was freed from the tyranny of foreign masters,

He had sent to Tamaras by rapid post

What Tamaras needed to know, and he summoned him from exile

Back to his kingdom. To be sure in vain, at first;   700

For the exiled prince was terrified of deceit

And warned with much anxiety, he couldn't deem too safe

That which barely seemed believable to us. Yet called home several times,

He returned and sought free air

In his fatherland, where he was received   705

With jubilant rejoicing after most ardent longing.

There Meurab and his people honored him on the throne

That belongs to him, after you, by nature and by law.

Soon he [*Tamaras*] wanted to proceed with Meurab to Byzantium

Since Osman [*Turkish ruler*] himself promised to give him

strong protection   710

And he [*Osman*] took Meurab, who knew Persia well,

Into his service and named him supreme commander

Of the now victorious power, that rules to the shore of the Tigris

[*Persian border*]

With a bare sword and attends with blood and burning alone

To its swift expeditions. Meanwhile, Gurgistan blossoms   715

And sees its Tamaras, who hourly sighs for you,

In highest majesty. In vain! The shah refuses gifts

And the most urgent requests! The shah denies what we have

Sought so hard, so often! Yet Russia comes to our aid

And wants on this day to see you free from long suffering   720

And no longer imprisoned.

Salome. Catharine. Demetrius. Procopius.

Salome: Oh heaven! Leave at once!

    Hide! Do you hesitate? Run! Flee! Escape with me!

Catharine: What calamity strikes us?

Salome: The king is coming.

Catharine: The enemy of my honor and executioner in my bondage –

    Oh witnesses of our struggle, hide behind the tapestry.   725

    Oh thunder! That breaks loose upon us after such brief happiness!

Shah Abbas. Catharine.

Shah Abbas: Here we find the sun, even if the sky may be resplendent

    With the radiance of its flames! How? With tearstained cheeks?

    What gloomy haze clouds this dear face?

    What does the sigh's wind threaten? This day must seem,   730

    Princess, to her and to us, as pleasant

    As this heart wishes! Let her cease her bitter crying

    And enduring lament, and give her attention to the one

Who, for so many years, has sought the grandeur of her honor.

Catharine: Most omnipotent monarch, he must himself be met   735

    With what is great and splendid!

Shah Abbas: She alone can bless us.

    What can delight us resides only in her power.

Catharine: Powerless is the power that languishes in the dungeon.

 Shah Abbas: She rules in our castle; the dungeon is open for her.

    She herself has ensnared us. The freedom that we hope   740

    Offers her a scepter and all a prince might want,

    Who counts more owned lands than lived days.

    Does she want to see all of Persia bowing at her feet?

    Does she want to see Isfahan* greet her as her subject?

Catharine: We don't consider ourselves worthy of this honor.   745

Shah Abbas: Oh word! That consumes our spirit unto death!

    Why has nature, who has not forgotten to give her anything,

    Who dealt her grace and beauty without measure,

    And embellished her beauty with reason, her reason with fame,

    Not impressed the capacity for pity into her heart?   750

    And yet it is just this, Princess, that binds us.

    A treasure to which one finds access without toil

    Can never be so splendid! Oh! But she who denies too much

    Reveals that she wants nothing human

    And is herself becoming inhuman. For what reason is this given   755

    That time allots to us, if we, while alive,

    Don't make use of it as we should?

Catharine: We know not this reputation

    Of beauty in us. The flower of tender youth

    Has sadly perished in the heat of furious terror.

    At high noon, night and darkness have found us.   760

Shah Abbas: Call it a misty cloud, in which she seems even more pleasing!

    Often a storm guides (us) into port sooner than we expect –

Catharine: And dashes the fragile barge on formidable cliffs.

Shah Abbas: People have swum to shore even though water already

                           touched their lips.

Catharine: This ship is wrecked by the storm on the rising tide.   765
Shah Abbas: The skipper takes courage, even if the mast just has split.
Catharine: Death will soon show us the port as we wish.
Shah Abbas: She shall mount the Persian throne, as we have wished.
Catharine: We'll let, as fortune will, another heart have our place.
Shah Abbas: Fortune can raise no one equal to her as she deserves.   770
Catharine: This far-reaching kingdom offers him many
                                        more beautiful faces.
Shah Abbas: She, our sun, makes the stars fade away.
Catharine: Then does Your Majesty love only physical attractiveness?
Shah Abbas: Even more the noble rearing that makes her immortal.
Catharine: Then does he want that we should lose this that he so loves?   775
Shah Abbas: We seek to embellish even more this that so attracts us.
Catharine: Alas! It is not embellishment when virginal chastity is violated.
Shah Abbas: Isn't it believed that chastity is strengthened in chaste marriage?
Catharine: Isn't Your Majesty married to others?
Shah Abbas: Whom we selected for your maids, oh goddess!   780
Catharine: The Christian law binds only two with this bond.
Shah Abbas: The Persian law supersedes. We're in their country.
Catharine: Even more the law of the Highest! We stand upon His ground!
Shah Abbas: Whatever Abbas commands must be the law, even if it's wrong.
Catharine: He cannot command love who acknowledges no master.   785
Shah Abbas: We give to her complete control over us.
Catharine: She lets herself be led on the right paths by reason.
Shah Abbas: She rules in the one who in no way seeks to offend her.

    Love ignites this heart with scorching flames—
    The feeble spirit languishes! Who can rescue us   790
    If she doesn't provide the means? One tries to win her over
    With what one has and as one can. That which one can offer her
    She refuses with pride, and she listens with a deaf ear
    To these long sighs. The tears burst forth—
    She doesn't, even just once, condescend to observe this misery   795
    That she arouses in us. We let it happen!
    And only through time and self-control and patience seek

To find this treasure of genuine grace,
Since we are more than free to wrest from her by force
That which she completely refuses. She knows we could force her!   800
Yet no! We don't want to, unless her obstinate spirit
And our inflamed passion finally drag us
Where we prefer to go calmly.
Catharine: We simply can't believe
That he would want us disarmed of what the sword allowed
                                             to be abducted.
Should Abbas commit such a deed against the one
                             whom he holds imprisoned,   805
Who sighs in the dungeon, who falls at his feet?
And of the one who cannot defend herself,
Except with a sorrowful moan and tears of grief
After the loss of her kingdom, also despoil her honor?
No! Surely not! Abbas loves his lofty praise too much.   810
We know where we are! We are . . . we are captive!
And yet our spirit remains free: the years have passed
In which we ruled, yet our virtue stands firm
And lets no heavy yoke of oppression bend it.
We serve; undefiled! We suffer; without shame!   815
We endure, without disgrace! Our chastity scorns the bonds.
Allow us, since everything now is lost, this one possession:
Unbroken courage and immaculate reputation.
Shah Abbas: Don't force us to do what love charges us to do.
Catharine: He is the greatest prince who transcends himself.   820
Shah Abbas: Fine. Transcend yourself and the imagined illusion.
Catharine: Against which desire and force concurrently have
                                        battled in vain.
Shah Abbas: The Shah will go to battle armed with desire and force.
Catharine: Death offers us his hand if we cannot escape.
Shah Abbas: He who seeks out Death is terrified when Death calls.   825
Catharine: Not those who seek relief in the grave.
Shah Abbas: Eh? A knife over us?

Catharine: No, over these breasts.

Shah Abbas: Control your crazy anger.

Catharine: Control your evil desires.

Shah Abbas: We have, to be sure, remedies for defiance at hand.

Catharine: Use flame, stake, and steel.

Shah Abbas: Even diamonds can be broken.   830

Chorus of the Imprisoned Maidens

Chorus

The heated flame of weather
That consumes you, Gurgistan,
That turns you with your leaves, branches, and trunk
Into swirling, sizzling ashes,
Will, unfortunately, not yet cease—   835
Even if everything cracks and smolders
And, exploded by thunderbolts,
Vaporizes and smokes through the air.
Even though the bright fires
Were doused with mixed blood—   840
Where the collapsed walls
Sizzled in the purple tide,
And half-rotted corpses
Were torn from disrupted graves.
Yes, what suddenly had to pale   845
Was flung in its mother's face—
Yet it seems as if God's revenge
Still keeps watch over our necks.

Counter-Chorus

We, destitute of parents and friends,
Stripped of advice and comfort,   850
Left relatives of blood and marriage
Heaped upon the burning houses.
Alas! We were forced through the bones,
Limbs, bodies, rubble, and stench,
And fragmented marble,   855
Shackle, defiance, and the torture rack,
Between pilloried corpses
Into the land of the crude Fates,
Where we withered, like roses
Scorched by the sun's blaze.   860
Where, Princess of all women,
(Even if you now die of melancholy)
Still by your trust in God
You have earned the crown of honor
That (in spite of the shah and death!) adorns you,   865
That no power can wrest from you.

Chorus and Counter-Chorus

A spirit betrothed to God loses nothing if the world
Perishes in an instant!
He has his kingdom within himself, and rules, even if the crowns
Are snatched from his bejeweled hair.   870
He sits upon a stable throne
If all princes' thrones are smitten into grey dust.
By means of this, which frightens men,
His unwavering courage is discovered.

Like a cedar, besieged by an angry north wind,   875
Overcomes with a trunk as firm as a rocky cliff:
What the hellish grave sends up
To a heavenly heart
Is (however heavily it may oppress others!)
To it but a playful joke.   880

The Second Act

Shah Abbas. Seinelcan. The scene changes to the royal chamber.

Shah Abbas: Then the Russian finally let himself be persuaded?

Seinelcan: Not without a struggle! Yet since there was no other means to
    Lay down the sword, he conceded this point to us,
    And so in this respect we have attained peace.

Shah Abbas: In one respect peace! Oh peace, when we wage war!   5
    When night and day we lie under attack on the battlefield!

Seinelcan: One of our enemies has now become our friend!
    Now all of our power, which we formerly divided, falls
    Upon him who still threatens us. He, whom two powers do not constrain,
    Will not let one power wrest the glorious victory away.   10
    'Til now the Turkish camps were attacked with divided force:
    Henceforth all Persia fights.

Shah Abbas: Where it cannot conquer.

Seinelcan: What? Doe he not hope for victory? He, before whom
                         the whole world trembles?
    He, at whose very word the earth's foundation quakes?
    Before whom the enemies' power and assaults have always failed?   15
    Who can count more triumphs than years, than days, than hours?

Shah Abbas: And now is defeated.

Seinelcan: Who will be able to bind the lofty thoughts,
    The inexhaustible courage, the virtue,
    That lives in your heart?

Shah Abbas: Lived! And now no longer.
    It languishes! It perishes! It dies.

Seinelcan: What aggravates the honor   20
    Of your great soul?

Shah Abbas: This which no sword will subdue.

Seinelcan: Can Osman fight against us with an advantage?

Shah Abbas: How unfortunate! You don't understand the wounds of my heart.

Do you think that Osman will break our mighty powers?

This child! Whom we are used to commanding victoriously?   25

Whose land we besiege with ashes and arrows?

Who will stand beneath my foot, weighed down with chains?

And will yet tread the bitter path of Bajazeth?*

No! Osman? No! Wrong! They are much sharper claws

That cut through my breast right into my heart.   30

It is another enemy who tortures my soul,

Who mauls my body and gnaws at my limbs.

Seinelcan: It is, as I understand it, your royal worries.

Shah Abbas: Is it possible that our sorrow is still concealed from you?

Seinelcan: A great heart is not frightened by a great burden.   35

Shah Abbas: A deeper pain has taken hold of our limbs.

Seinelcan: Does Your Majesty find himself burdened by sickness?

Shah Abbas: An inner fire has consumed our core.

Seinelcan: Can no doctor provide counsel?

Shah Abbas: The doctor seeks our death.

He jokes about our anxiety and laughs at our distress.   40

Seinelcan: Can anyone dare to do such a thing?

Shah Abbas: You see it! We simply have to perish in most profound despair.

Seinelcan: Let this fire be quenched by his blood

And the skill of other doctors.

Shah Abbas: No one else can extinguish the blaze.

Only the hand that injures us knows how to find a cure.   45

Only the one who caused the wounds can heal them for us.

Seinelcan: To whom has heaven's resolve granted such mighty power?

Shah Abbas: To Princess Catharine, my heaven—

Most gracious enemy! Unsurpassable beauty!

Head that deserves Euphrates, Volga, and Tigris to crown you!   50

Prisoner who captured us! Who bound us in chains!

Charming if she weeps! Fresh if her anger stirs
And defends her honor. She is not overcome
By him who forces everything! She doesn't submit to the fierce raging
Of raw passion. We have, to be sure, your country,   55
Yet you (revenge upon revenge!) have seared our heart!
Princess! We confess it! You have fought against us before,
Yet your eye conquered more than your fist!
Still, when your noble spirit began to speak,
Shah Abbas was completely lost. We lack understanding;   60
We lack reason; what's more, we even lack the powers
Strong enough to bind your soul to our spirit.
The great empire stands at our beck and call;
We ourselves are at your service and yet find nothing but ridicule.
Seinelcan: Oh feverish pestilence of Persia! Is this what oppresses Abbas?   65
    Why not remove this monster from the world straightaway?
Shah Abbas: Oh blind one! You don't understand what love can do!
    Come here, deluded man! Look closely at your prince!
    Observe his face, his ever burning desire,
    His paled lips, and ever fresh tears—   70
    Behold the one often threatened by Chaldea* with flame and sword,
    Who feared no enemy's anger, yes, not even death,
    Who has controlled the world where day begins and where it fades away,
    Who penetrated South and North with weapons
    And sprang on the head of nations with proud feet;   75
    The mighty power of proud love holds him in bondage.
Seinelcan: Is it possible that this woman—who is but the ruin of Persia,
    Who so passionately sought to bathe in our blood,
    Who plays with her enemies and injures us in a hostile way,
    Who arrogantly opposes the conqueror himself,   80
    Who, filled with superstition, is accustomed to praying to a cross,
    Who, my Prince, isn't even worthy of appearing before you—
    That she could be the cause of this pain?
Shah Abbas: What? Can you dare to curse to us,
    The one whom your born prince chooses to look upon with desire?

And admires with awe? Can a knave dare   85

   To slander what is dear to us? Have you so soon forgotten

   Who Abbas is and who you are? But come, and tell us honestly,

   If you've ever seen a woman that resembles her!

Seinelcan: My Prince, I concede that no one is to be found

   Whose beauty, whose reason—

Shah Abbas: whose art surpasses hers.   90

Seinelcan: Whose virtue—

Shah Abbas: and whose breeding—

Seinelcan: whose splendor—

Shah Abbas::   whose fame—

Seinelcan: Is not far below hers.

Shah Abbas: Oh, flower of all flowers

   What alabaster compares to the snow of her brow?

Seinelcan: The tender lily must yield to her noble cheeks.

Shah Abbas: The ivory of her nose—

Seinelcan: her lips of coral—   95

   Her eyes like brilliant stars—

Shah Abbas: Her heart of steel!

   Only her heart is too hard. How superbly does she move about?

Seinelcan: Majesty personified is seen in her bearing.

Shah Abbas: Wisdom adorns her head.

Seinelcan: And eloquence her mouth.

Shah Abbas: Alas! How it wounds my timid heart to death!   100

Seinelcan: The salve for the wound is in the prince's hands.

   The one who causes this ache can also soothe the pains.

Shah Abbas: She can! Yes, if she will!

Seinelcan: When forced one usually does,

   If a serious intent is sensed, what one ought to do of free will.

Shah Abbas: Love cannot be instilled through force.   105

Seinelcan: How many wish of her that she could be forced!

Shah Abbas: She has nothing to do with the many. What remains untried?

   What hasn't been ventured? Yet without a single fruit.

   She would sooner wish to suffer fire, stake, and greatest despair

Than let a single hair of her honor be cut off.   110
She would collapse, if this valued treasure were taken from her by force—
From repentance and zeal, if not by her own hand.
Seinelcan: Time will reverse her arrogance, unexpectedly, yet.
Shah Abbas: It can indeed change beauty, but not our suffering.
Seinelcan: A woman changes easily.
Shah Abbas: What can be more obstinate   115
Than a stubborn woman?
Seinelcan: Her pride roots in more deeply
Because Your Majesty greets her as if he were her servant:
Your favor strengthens her defiance. As soon as this outrage is atoned,
The loss will be mourned. What is scorned, is sought after,
If time and means are gone. Let the prince strike from his mind   120
This pleasant image!
Shah Abbas: What are you saying?
Seinelcan: This: let him only pretend
As if his heart...   *Shah Abbas:* Oh bitter hell!
Seinelcan: Has torn the bonds and . . .
Shah Abbas: What then?
Seinelcan: ...that he is free from love.
Your delusion will soon fade away.
Shah Abbas: Ha! Mere fantasy!
Can the flame be doused, when the house and roof are burning?   125
Can flashing lightning be hidden in the murky night?
A word, a quick glance, a sigh destroys
What fabricated hate and feigned anger produce.

Imanculi. Seinelcan. Shah Abbas.

Imanculi: Your Royal Highness, the Russian has just arrived.
Seinelcan: He has paid very close attention to the appointed time.   130
Shah Abbas: Imanculi, call together the princes of the different
                                                      nations, right now!
Seinelcan, you make sure that the ambassador appears.

Shah Abbas with the Princes from Persia. The Ambassador from Russia.
The stage setting portrays the Royal Audience Chamber.

Ambassador: The long awaited day, most powerful of heroes
    Ever to be crowned by Persia: Prince, whom posterity
    Will laud with fame—the oft desired day   135
    That unites the Volga and Euphrates* and, after the thunder
    Of warring weapons, reveals to us the pleasant sun,
    The great pleasure of peace, the joy of countless people—
    The day is finally here, on which the vast nation
    Of Russia makes an offer: extend your trusted hand   140
    As a brother and fill with most joyous spirit
    Your favorably inclined heart that, filled with firm goodness,
    Offers itself as a pledge to us. Let hostile defiance vanish!
    Now the strong North and rich South unite.
    Whoever lives near or far! Whoever hears of the pact,   145
    Will both honor with earnest terror one power,
    And fear, whom he hates, and observe with trembling,
    How much both splendid realms increase through unity.
    Grant then, highest Prince, since I depart joyously,
    That I be allowed to boast about what he, who seeks only trouble,   150
    Will envy. Grant that it be made known,
    That the czar* will always be friendly to you and that the shah,
    Until death, will stand for our czar. Grant that I may report
    That the worthy Persian lacks no virtue,
    That so much favor was shown to me at the great court,   155
    Even ingratitude itself inclined to thankfulness and praise.
    Yet, before I finally turn back, oh glory of heroes,
    It is necessary that I, with urgent entreaty, make a final request.
    It is really more my czar pleading through me. He who has
                        granted so much,

Who loves the general peace more than great advantage,   160
Hesitates to release a woman from her chains:
A woman, who once wore the crown in Iberia,
And now grieves in captivity. It may be that she wronged
The one who now still punishes her; that she resists
The higher majesty; we don't seek to justify this,   165
Much less to defend her debt at length.
The czar firmly believes that Abbas would forgive more
Than a woman could incur, however guilty she might be.
He vouches (if vouchers are sought) henceforth for offences
That she might plot. And if you, too, should wish to speak to the czar,   170
Your Royal Highness, about something that you might want,
Firmly assure yourself of this; you will not seek in vain.

Shah Abbas: What our brother czar has promised without any deceit
We, for our part, intend to keep forever
Strong, firm, and unbroken. Your well-intended effort   175
Deserves more honor than the shah himself knows how to give.
Long live the most powerful monarch of the Russians!
She whom you desire free has (as deemed by law)
Scorned realm, crown, and life. Yet we shall let it happen,
That before evening she still might see herself free   180
As the czar so eagerly seeks. God the Almighty praise him!

Ambassador: Long live and rule Shah Abbas, the sun and joy of the Persians!

Shah Abbas. Seinelcan. The scene changes to the Royal Chamber.

Shah Abbas: Oh, dear and more than costly peace that we have purchased!
Oh, most gruesome loss this heart has ever suffered!
Tyrant of our soul, will you escape Abbas' hands?   185
Should you be sent back home, for the sake of Persia?
You, whom blood and war could hardly put in shackles!
You, for whom our soul so wretchedly has thirsted!
So that your Gurgistan, cheering, would see you crowned

And gossip that my arm was too weak for a woman?   190
Does neither good behavior nor pain move a trembling woman?
Must Shah, after so much victory, be either beggar or executioner?
Must Russia rage first against our country, and then against
                                                    us personally?
Must it, first enemy, then friend, by fighting and by pleading
Wrest from our hands this which we love and hate?   195
Must tranquility elude us both in battle and in peace?
Ha, peace! And why did we hear of peace?
Why has this dream deluded the wise mind?
Peace be gone! To arms! Let blood and burning prevail!
It's kingdom versus kingdom! With a vigorous hand let us   200
Tear up what has been written! Throw everything away
That Volga [*Russia*] and Tigris [*Persia*] concluded, since it only buys
Our sorrow and disgrace. How can we rage so blindly,
When we are the most guilty for our misery?
What is imputed to Russia that we actually spoke?   205
Where was our good sense, when we so quickly promised,
Thoughtlessly, needlessly, what the ambassador sought?
Let the czar ask! But only if Shah has the power to deny.
Just as Russia has the right to ask for this woman's release,
Abbas has even more right to cast his fury upon her.   210
Upon her, who frivolously destroyed those who were true to us
And defied this crown, and scorned this sword,
And scoffed at this throne; who sought protection abroad,
Who still derides us daily and curses us in her shackles.
(Vent anger, righteous revenge!) Let the whole world behold   215
What it means to defy Abbas! Harsh thunder falls
Upon her condemned head! Even dying, she shall feel
How hot the anger burns, that neither her own blood
Nor, indeed, even her death can cool! Prisoner, you are done for!
You have the brief remnant of hours as a benefit,   220
While we consider how to end your time.
You shall atone for your realm, for your son, and Meurab, too.

For Meurab! But, alas! How does that dog concern you?
Is there a justice so harsh, that it can punish someone
Who knows not of guilt, much less is guilty himself?   225
Granted, too, you avenged your husband and his father,
And for your kingdom set yourself against us!
You sharpened your sword with justice—this we admit.
Princess! Oh, this heart! This heart must break in sorrow!
Your judge must speak for you and also for your faults!   230
Princess! Oh, the wrath of heated anger subsides,
As soon as your sweet name appears upon my lips.
Shall Shah then, greatest joy—oh! Shall Shah then leave you?
Does his favor deserve nothing but unyielding hate?
This great land, this vast realm, is it too small for you?   235
Would you prefer to be free than to be our princess?
Fine! Be! Be free! And take this valued proof
With you away from Persia; that all locks yield
If they are forced by love; and think of him who loves you
And who gives you, worthy woman, dear treasure, to yourself!   240
Go and show everyone that Abbas does not consider
His own life as worthy as you, and yet gave you to yourself,
For whom Abbas himself is too base! Go and show to all
That Abbas keeps his word and is master of himself.
Go, noble spirit, depart! Help unite Euphrates and Volga
                                        [*Persia and Russia*]!   245
Go, be a pledge of peace, an end to the spilling of blood
That grieves Persia and Russia. Go! Bring both of us peace
And henceforth spend your time in greatest pleasure!
Yet without you can Shah, can Shah himself live on?
Shah, to whom heaven won't grant you, you joy of the world?   250
Does then Shah himself allow that you escape his realm?
And (if this fantasy isn't wrong) perhaps move on to others
Who are less than he? Oh, what meaning do those things have
That here make princes famous? That here make princes glorious?
And what is their joy but merely empty splendor?   255

People pay heed to their glories, not their burdens.

They only look upon their face, not their hidden pains,

Not the raw torture of their hearts overwhelmed by anxiety.

They wish us good luck for peace; we find nothing but strife.

All Persia rejoices in bliss; here bitter sorrow rages.   260

The Russian is our friend, and yet inflicts these wounds upon us

That the enemy cannot. The princess is bound up,

And forces him who bound her. Like a storm-wrecked ship

Upon a wild sea first plunges into the black depths

Of the horrible abyss, then courses through blue breezes   265

With full sail, then rushes past the narrow gorges

Of jutting cliffs; so are we dealt with by despair,

Promises, zeal, love, hate, revenge, torture, and death.

Behold the soul's terror! Whither are we coerced?

We are, by our own words, compelled to carry out this deed   270

That our spirit curses! They make and break the decision.

He isn't doing what he wants to do, and doesn't want to do what he must.

Seinelcan: Most powerful Monarch! If a servant may venture

To propose advice to the Prince on such a ponderous matter:

So let happen, I openly request, what his worthy prosperity   275

And the welfare of all commands me. I would sell my life

For Abbas' crown and head.

Shah Abbas: We know your loyalty—

Tell us what you think. Speak without fear or intimidation.

Do you, in your conclusion, also set the prisoner free?

Seinelcan: Your royal Majesty: indeed her guilt is great,   280

Yet greater is the favor that Abbas offers her.

And even greater yet, her defiance that shuns this favor.

How is it that his noble spirit esteems her so fine,

Who scorns the kingdom of Persia and the king himself?

But what? Will she then be sent from here unpunished?   285

Can a harsher sentence than freedom be conceived?

(If, indeed, it is freedom to avoid one who honors us,

One who heeds an imprisoned woman as if she were a goddess).

She, who out of arrogance forgets who Shah is and who is she,

Will rightly measure her lot only when she is away from here,   290

And she'll feel that here in prison she was more than free,

But there in Gurgistan, is more than just imprisoned!

Shah will undoubtedly not find himself without pain,

Yet we know that Shah, whom no one ever conquered,

Can overcome himself! Separation and time   295

Will extinguish all the flames. One conquers in love's strife

If the enemy is not seen. I do not praise the hero* now,

Whom Trebizond mentions with glory and Istanbul

with trembling bespeaks.

The Bosporus' great city was then in his hands;

When his vainglorious heart caught fire for Irene.*   300

The fire took upper hand; his lust for waging war ceased,

His bravery fell asleep and died amid so many conquests

'Til his Mustapha awakened him, as if from a dream,

And loyally informed him that the camp was filled with grumbling.

"Well," he said, "call hither the people who serve us,   305

And who shamelessly dare to censure their top commander.

This day shall be the judge between us and them

If our passion or we ourselves are unworthy of the regiment."

As soon as the army gathered, Mehmed [*Sultan Mehmed II*]

himself appeared

With Irene at his side, bedecked with sparkling rubies   310

And dazzling with bright splendor. Yet her face was glowing

Even more than the gold of her clothing and the diamonds' brilliance.

Whosoever was present was astonished at the sight of this sun

That melted the coldest ice with but a single beam.

Everyone lowered his guard and forgave the prince   315

And cried out that there could be no ground to rebuke his love!

"It is she alone," spoke Mehmed, "who could inflame us so.

Yet learn that nothing should be able to bind us body and soul,

That Mehmed is always his own!" Before anyone was quite aware of it

His sabre was already bare, his fist was in her hair,   320

The blade was in her neck! Here they saw her dead body,
And there, in his hand, they saw her cheeks' roses pale.

Shah Abbas: In doing this he was inhuman, just like you.

Seinelcan: It's not my opinion that one should do as Mehmed did:
Only (what seems a lot easier) that you willingly release someone   325
Who doesn't want to stay and cannot be kept.

Shah Abbas: Keep? What? Who will lead . . . who will help her
                                                    from this place?

Seinelcan: Oh, Your Majesty. And your explicit word.

Shah Abbas: Uttered before considered and spoken in great haste!

Seinelcan: The Persian's mighty Prince has never broken his word!   330

Shah Abbas: We were over rushed, as clearly could be seen.

Seinelcan: This approaches much too closely the majesty of the Prince.

Shah Abbas: Is this, so dear to us, being taken from our hands?

Seinelcan: For something even dearer, in order to obtain peace.

Shah Abbas: Oh dearly acquired possession! Oh, cherished pledge!   335

Seinelcan: Yet what is dearer to your majesty than your country?

Shah Abbas: By our own decree you've been ruined for us, Princess.

Seinelcan: What if, as is human, she had died a long time ago?

Shah Abbas: Then that would be the fault of providence, not us.

Seinelcan: Heaven sends this, too. So bear it with endurance.   340

Shah Abbas: Yet who will bind the wounds that she inflicted upon us?

Seinelcan: Time, which can find a way to heal all wounds.

Shah Abbas: Oh why are we ourselves not mindful of a way?

Seinelcan: Gold bound freedom itself.

Shah Abbas: Here it is powerless.

Seinelcan: Those who've been set free can be ensnared once more.   345

Shah Abbas: The lion is rarely caught that has once escaped

Seinelcan: Let's see if perhaps something can be gained by delay.

Shah Abbas: Then what about our promise "She'll be free before evening?"

Seinelcan: What if, free herself, she wants to tarry here?

Shah Abbas: She? Who seeks nothing more than fleeing far from here?   350

Seinelcan: Offer everything to her.

Shah Abbas: To her, who disregards everything?

Seinelcan: The tree that stood so long falls with the final stroke.

    What can it harm if at last you venture all

    And offer her fame, honor, power, yes, even offer her crowns!

Shah Abbas: It would only be in vain, indeed for the very last time!   355

    Yet grant us a moment's rest! A remarkable thought just occurred to us.

Chorus of the Princes Murdered by Shah Abbas

First Chorus

The mere handful of years

That the light of heaven grants us on this earth

Races to the black-draped bier.

This life is drowned in terror and in tears.   360

Flowers, before they're even found,

Have often vanished by midday.

The dew has barely moistened the field

And is gone when the sun rises.

A spark has barely delighted the eye   365

When it vanishes into its night.

A ship sails on the sea,

A bird on the heights,

The shadow over the land,

The storm's wind over the sand;   370

Arrows are barely seen as they pierce the severed air;

Yet nothing leaves even a trace of its rapid course behind;

As swift, yes swifter, flees this life

That we finish before we commence.

We are hardly born into this light   375

And are already chosen by death,

Which we often suffer unbeknown!

We come and are bid to depart.

Counter Chorus

Yet Shah the murderer severed
The short thread* and thrust sword and tongs   380
Into our breast: he blew out
The spark of our life before time so decreed.
Of what use was it to run from his sword
When secret poison could take us anyway?
What did it help to offer him our hand,   385
Since he harassed his friends more than his enemies?
We fell by furious raging:
More are devoured by assassination.
He broke with a cruel hand
Even the bond of blood: 390
He often scoffed oath and alliance
And tread on what fell and what stood.
Yet dying was easy for us, for he first embittered our death
With all kinds of torture. His wrath was kindled like hell's smoldering.
Pillory, mortar, spear, lead, axe, and stake,   395
Cane, saws, flame, slashed cheeks,
Exposed lungs, bared hearts;
The endless writhing in pain
When our guts and tongues were ripped out,
That was what exhilarated Abbas' eye.   400

Chorus and Counter Chorus Together

Oh Judge of this world! Counsel of princes!
How long willst Thou look on?
Does the tyrant, in spite of time! In spite of Justice and God!
Still enjoy peace on his throne?
Willst Thou, Lord of the world, not awaken   405
And make an end of this raging?
Willst Thou not avenge our death?

Willst Thou no longer pass judgment?
Do not so many thousand sufferings
Affect Thy heart any longer, Judge? 410
Willst Thou allow that at the nod of one man
Entire kingdoms drown in blood?
Solemn Judge! Take vengeance!
Wake up! Great God awaken!
Wake up! Wake up! Wake up! Wake up! 415
Revenge! Revenge! Revenge! Revenge!

The Third Act

Catharine. The Ambassador from Russia. The scene is the Queen's chamber.

Ambassador: Your Royal Highness, if ever the well-being of Russia

                                    pleased you,

Which, after such a difficult war, is now at peace;

If, like us, before this you were even more than well aware of

Whether our czar's good fortune ever created authentic desire

For your throne: then let yourself now be moved   5

To somewhat cast aside your oppressive sorrow

And wish for this effort and sovereign contract

That binds us and Persia, which this momentous day

And your affection implores. So it is! We are reconciled!

The thunderous roar of weapons, the storm cloud, has withdrawn,   10

The furious justice of swords will be totally removed

And yield its place to noble peace!

How fortunate I am! I'm now permitted to honor you with the news!

Yet why do I let you hear only of our joy?

Why do I behold your bitter misery for so long,   15

When this day can bring more comfort to you than to others?

Princess! Our happiness is the source of your joy;

Oh, may no unpleasant sorrow embitter the sweet delight!

This day, pregnant with joy, shatters the dungeon's lock

And the shah frees you from your chains at our request!   20

My prince, who always hoped to unlock your prison,

Greets you, no longer a prisoner, with freedom,

And wills that together with us your troubled country,

And King Tamaras, who extends his outstretched hand

To your right hand, will also rejoice from the heart: 25

That the anguish you have suffered will renew itself in joy:
He wishes your spirit will be strengthened by the many

                         crosses you have borne

And that you will have even more good fortune than you and

                              Tamaras desire.

Catharine: The powerful leader of the Russians indeed makes it understood

That his mind, like his rank, approaches heaven,   30

Since he, like God, also shows himself sympathetic

And bends down from his throne to our dungeon.

We really don't know how to thank God nor him,

Whom his virtue thanks. If someone can rejoice

In the harsh restraints of unspent anxiety;   35

Then believe us, Lord Ambassador, that neither the long lament

Nor the compounded pain nor the tearstained cheeks

Nor what the wrath of time still inflicts upon us

Could hinder the joy that your peace has brought to us.

Yet you, in your joy, are considerate of our sorrow   40

And bid us to be free and let us feel our own joy.

Believe sir, believe, that this means linking us anew forever

To him who did so much for our well-being.

We shall remain indebted to you, and shall be your czar's maid.

Ambassador: Your Highness, I am more indebted to good fortune   45

That through me he serves her, who performed miracles

When she held the scepter; who is beheld with wonder,

Since the glory of her virtue, in spite of all bondage, blooms!

Catharine: We know of nothing like this to be recognized in us.

Ambassador: She who won't praise herself, eternal fame knows

                           to acknowledge.   50

I would wish for one thing more: grant that

Your highly deserved acclaim and the honor of our czar

Be increased by a description of the terror that burdened your spirit

And bound your body.

Catharine: What you now request

Is a mere pittance for the favor that your prince demonstrates toward us!   55

My eyes reveal to you, even if my lips are silent,

That nothing except pure agony, except woe and fierce pains,

Except murder, perjury, hate, betrayers' insane teasing,

And a deluge of blood and greatest tyranny

And executioner, fire, and stake can be shown to you!   60

Yet since you aren't terrified by an exceptionally frightful horror

That even a hardened Turk can only observe in a swoon,

Your request will be granted. It's only too well known to you

That, unfortunately, we are too weak to properly stifle,

With an ever-armed defense, the threatening presence of the Turks   65

And the Persians' rigorous fighting—they surround us east and west.

Therefore, as she indeed was forced, Georgia sought protection

From those who could do harm: and Istanbul [*Turkey*]

                              pursued its own advantage

From the vulnerability of Tiflis. We, for whom the Caspian's waves

And Persia's border form definite boundaries,   70

Greeted Isfahan [*Persia*]. Yet where we sought protection,

The sword, eager for murder, was sharpened at our throats.

The blood-storm first began to rage in Tiflis,

When the pressured prince sought to shake off the burden.

In vain! His weak arm was shackled and ensnared   75

By Turkish power. When he was murdered by poison,

Prince Alovassa inherited his father's throne and crowns.

Ahmed [*Turkish Sultan 1603-1617*] helped him up, and

                              gave the gentle son

Wise Meurab, who conducted himself so gallantly

That he filled the entire country with his fame   80

And (filled) all hearts with favor. When Abbas noticed this,

He feared that if he didn't soon pay heed,

That Ahmed, by such means, was strengthening his state,

Gurgistan might likewise worship Istanbul's power.

Thus he suddenly offered us an alliance and protection.   85

Prince Alexander could refuse him neither the one nor the other.

The proximity of the Turks was indeed too suppressive for us,

Yet the Persian's quarrelsome army frightened us even more.

Ambassador: Given that, Georgia was really trapped between

two oppressors.

Catharine: The shah sought a closer pledge and so that no inadequacy   90

Would appear on our side, our prince quickly sent

Prince Constantine, his first-born child,

To Persia's capital: Constantine, whom Abbas so deceived

That, bewitched and deluded by Ali's [*Shiite leader's*] illusion,

He renounced God, baptism, and the cross. Oh, unexpected pain!   95

Oh wretched shaft, that penetrated his father's heart

Into his very soul! He tore the grey hair

From his balding head and longed for his coffin.

He disinherited his fallen son without delay,

And gave the realm and crown to David, his youngest child.   100

To David, to whom we had been married such a brief time,

And, unfortunately, counted but a few years of deepest devotion;

From whom Prince Tamaras, our first and only child,

Was conceived in chaste marriage, who now perceives our bondage

And feels all our pains. He had hardly begun to blossom   105

When, at the shah's command, he also had to trek to Persia

And serve as a hostage for us. But he remained free and firmly

Stood with his Christ and renounced the mad pestilence

Of Ali's superstition, no matter how fiercely Abbas raged,

No matter how much he promised him gifts and land and favor.   110

Ambassador: Oh, steadfast soul!

Catharine: Just as resolutely as he [*Tamaras*] conducted himself,

So did Constantine blindly carry on, who, like a symbol

Of depravity, should teach all people living and those yet to live

That those untrue to God also never honor their own kin.

Ambassador: Whoever has already ignored the law of heaven   115

Has never respected the conventions of nations or human agreements.

Catharine: Shah Abbas incited him against his father's life

And his brother's throat. He swore to give him subjects

And Alexander's realm. Yet he could only rule securely

If he would first behead his father   120
And skewer his brother's heart onto a bare dagger.
Indeed, it was his father, who awakened him to the danger,
For he promised the golden crown to his other son.
His brother had become his enemy, for he would inherit the throne.
Alas! Can thirst for a scepter so delude reason?   125
Alas! Can greed for a crown so dishonor the soul
That, when this disease awakens, they blindly disregard
Related blood and the fury of their conscience?
They decided to murder them both. The king was summoned in writing
Together with my husband.

Ambassador: Did Abbas perpetrate this?   130

Catharine: They [*Alexander and David*] both set out with
                                        four thousand men
To the betrayer's court. He received them in friendship.
The assassin himself concealed his brash plan
With a haze of fickle love. He sought to gain
Their true hearts (so it seemed) ever more and more,   135
And invited them to a banquet, at which, following extended honor,
He stabbed his father's breast with his own hand
And (oh, horror!) broke his brother's neck,
Who fell onto the table and, in this palace of murder, bespattered
Both host and guests with his gushing blood.   140
The double murder resounded. The court grew delirious
With trembling and with rage. The shah himself didn't dare to praise
What had been so masterfully executed according to his own wish.
 Yet he needed new intrigues and sought to expedite a ruse
With power. When, at his command, there appeared in the court   145
Those who ventured to come along from Gurgistan to serve their king
In Persia, he spoke to them sadly:
"Dearly beloved, it disturbs us greatly that in Isfahan
You lost your leader and king. Yet, who is there who doesn't know
How easily midst wine and wrath people can fight and spill blood.   150
This tragedy stems from quarrelling: the quarrel arose from

Simple misunderstanding and hasty words.
Yet although the princes are gone, the state still endures.
Here is Prince Constantine, who will love you, his people;
Begotten in your country, first son of the king,   155
His one and only heir. The crown of Gurgistan is
Justly acknowledged to him as his rightful inheritance.
Be eternally true to him and lead him undivided
Into his inherited realm and live in tranquil peace."
Thus he spoke, and gave Constantine five thousand Persians.   160
The news came first. We thought we were lost
When word of our husband's father's fall and our husband's death
Oppressed our listening ears and spirit: when Abbas' evil band
Followed the brother-murderer into home and church
And declared war against God himself. This heart had determined,   165
As certainly as everyone trembled, that the blood he had spilled
Would be avenged by his downfall and death.
We didn't let our people and weapons rest,
And we immediately mobilized twelve thousand men,
Whom we secretly hid where a narrow route passes   170
Through high stone cliffs uphill into our country
And which a forest fills with deep shadows.
The Persians' tents appeared not far from these cliffs.
It could be observed how army upon army arranged
                        themselves into formation
Ready to attack us.
Ambassador: What did Gurgistan do?   175
Catharine: We offered Constantine negotiations and peace.
He was told that with our sincere request
We were ready to receive him at our court and throne;
That he should not use foreign power to seek the realm
That was duty bound to him with such unity. Yes, that we alone,   180
Without an army, planned to welcome him in his tent,
Since the fair sex and modesty permitted this for princesses.
Because we wished to show him personally the things

Upon which his crown and our welfare

And the troubled state depended. Therefore would he please arise　　185

And come to the open field without a great entourage

Since we, accompanied by a few of our people,

Offered to kiss his hand.

Ambassador:　　　　　　　　What did your ambassador accomplish

With this proposal?

Catharine:　　　　　　　　　　As much as we desired.

The murderer, disarmed of people and assistance, ventured　　　190

To the chosen place and, still warm from the blood

Of princes, hotly burning with the passion of mad flames,

Proposed his crown and marriage to us. We, in order to

Justly take revenge, proved that he would not lack power

Even if the Persian army did not penetrate the land　　　　　195

And his subjects were ruined by a foreign nation.

We pretended to be ready to live according to his wish

And didn't refuse to give him our body.

He found (so it appeared) even more than he ever had sought.

Yet soon (as he deserved) he found the fruit of his mad evil;　　200

For, when blinded by the appearance of vain illusion

He hurried to his camp and turned his back to us,

Our folk charged and oppressed him

So that he gave up his false soul in an instant.

His camp was quickly besieged by our army.　　　　　　205

Prince Alexander's men, who, compelled, had come back with him

From Persia, and who strengthened his force,

Began to bathe their sharply whetted blades in Persia's blood,

Which was flowing in the fields, as soon as they became aware of

The patricide's death. The stream pressed on, filled　　　210

With corpses, and then clogged. In short: whatever didn't belong to us

Or was not saved by hasty flight, perished.

Ambassador: In what frame of mind did the shah hear about the

　　　　　　　　　　　　　　relentless revenge?

Catharine: As soon as the news reached his ears, he sent

 Our only child, our Tamaras, back to us   215

 And with most beautiful words congratulated us on our victory.

 Yes, he praised us for resolutely avenging our husband and his father

 And bound us further to keep our pledge

 And be true to Persia, as we'd been 'til then.

 He also wanted to see Tamaras married as soon as possible. 220

Ambassador: What am I hearing? Heaven help us!

Catharine: Whom wouldn't he deceive?

 Whom wouldn't he rock to sleep with his hypocrisy?

 Yet Shah Abbas was false, and below this veneer

 He sought the son's fall and the mother's bitter pain;

 He saddened both of them for a while with new anxiety 225

 Because our Tamaras loved the flower of Teflis.

 The girl whom he chose for his bride

 Surpassed, indeed by far, the others in good breeding and beauty—

 So that also Alovassa, who met her too late,

 Was dangerously scorched by her glance,   230

 And he sought her heart, which had already been given to our son.

 He expressly charged that we had overtaken him with too much haste,

 That Tamaras could not justly take from him the one,

 Who, as his subject, belonged only to him.

 And even if Tamaras had her word first   235

 Teflis belonged to him, and Alovassa's crown

 Would cancel all pledges. It was hoped they would reconcile,

 Yet due to love and anger neither prince could yield to the other.

 The bride herself fled to a safe castle.

 The countries' tranquility ceased. The princes rushed off 240

 And each took to the field with the intention of defeating the other

 And risking everything, to the last drop of blood, for the prize.

 The battlefield was occupied and all the people armed,

 When in an instant the whole proceeding changed its course.

 For Alovassa (Perhaps his army persuaded him!   245

Perhaps friendship drew him to this deed!) --
As man against man and lance against lance were aimed at
                                                one another:
When the drums and trumpets resounded in the air,
And the great armed column moved in a single wave
Like when the northeast wind bids the ripe grain to yield—   250
Alovassa sent notice to our tent and bid us to consider
Whether this quarrel should be settled by swords or by conciliation.
He thought it was extreme that in order to kiss a woman
So much innocent blood would be spilled like water:
That both of them, who now burned with hate and zeal,   255
Just a short time before always had met one another
With the bond of true friendship, united for God and country:
That Christ blessed their alliance with mild grace,
Which would now be ruptured fruitlessly by an angry sword
For the benefit of the Agars [i.e., *Muslims*].   260
Indeed Alovassa did not lack courage or conquests
But it pained him that his friend would be defeated by him.
Further, he didn't desire this bride for love alone:
He did it on command. The shah, whom he trusted,
Provoked him to this deed and in all his correspondence   265
Bade him to go through with it and to kill Tamaras right away.
Finally, Alovassa warned Tamaras that he ought to proceed
                                                with caution,
For otherwise what the Persian desired so eagerly might happen.
We were numbed by these words, for the shah, as often, had
Secretly commanded this by means of a faithful messenger.   270
"Go forth," cried Tamaras, "and tell your king
That if he can prove Abbas' handwriting to us today
We will be willing to surrender." Without hesitating he sent us
The Persian's death-warrant. We rushed to thank him
And in the same exchange of letters the Persian's own hand   275
Was put before him. Thus this affair came to light.

Ambassador: Oh heaven! Should a man think this of Abbas?
  What did Alovassa do?
Catharine: He quickly was persuaded
  And came to Tamaras' tent sooner than expected
  And he spoke: "Look, my brother. Does the hellish world   280
  Breed such a raging pestilence, that it strives to wound us both
  By our own quarrelling? Does the shah bid me to hone the sword?
  And does he incite you against me? Does he seek through our blood
  The ruination of our countries? No! Believe that I'm too honorable
  For such assassination. God must prevent this!   285
  Renounce all enmity and let us rage no longer.
  Take the princess away and give me your hand
  As a sign of your favor and brotherly pledge.
  Leave the betrayer's court. If Isfahan doesn't want to be of use
  Then Istanbul can protect us, in spite of cunning and power
                                    and weapons!"   290
  Prince Tamaras embraced his worthy guest with joy.
  The discord was silenced, the burden of cruel war
  Was transformed into the joy of a wedding, and all former
                                    murder-trumpets
  Now summoned Tamaras to his bridal banquets.
  New pacts were made and the Bosphorus [*Turkey*] was approached   295
  Because nothing but perjury could be hoped for from the
                                    Tigris [*Persia*].
Ambassador: How did Abbas accept this?
Catharine: This plan remained so secret
  That the slightest mention of it never reached his ears
  Until the Turkish prince made known to him through an ambassador
  That he proposed to use Gurgistanian strength for his army, too.   300
  Yet first he wanted to know
  If they were not already in contract with Abbas
  And if he had a claim or a right to these people.
  The shah laughed into his hand and since he decided
  To scorn Istanbul directly, he promised the ambassador   305

That without fail his allies—
The Prince of Teflis himself and the Prince of Gurgistan—
Would be present to speak and answer, since he expected
Their presence in Isfahan in eighty days.
The ambassador decided to wait out such a short delay.   310
The shah immediately informed both us and Teflis
That he wanted both prince and army to appear at his court.
In response the princes let him know without flinching
That they relied on Osman, not the shah,
And that neither with an army nor much less in person   315
Did they intend to appear before Abbas' throne at his command.
The shah, whom this scorn pained beyond endurance,
(When the ambassador ridiculed his arrogance
And left, laughing, as he set out for home in Istanbul),
Swore by the highest power guarding over princes   320
That from that moment on he would never rest
Until he had completely eradicated this impudent scorn
With flame, murder, dagger, and our ruination
And had refreshed his wilted honor with liberal bloodshed.
He wanted to go to battle himself, and began to rant violently   325
At everyone who would not praise his intention.
Duke Alovard, who tried to dissuade him from it,
Was secretly murdered with poison in his food.
In a furious rage, he ordered Curtzi Bassi whipped,
And, after repeated humiliation, had him locked in a tower.   330
When Bassi's wife begged him not to leave the country,
He angrily bit a finger off of her hand—
Indeed, he had all of Gurgistan besieged in such haste
That it was impossible for us to raise protection and assistance.
So it is when a ship dashes on jagged cliffs   335
And the entire cargo cracks open with the first impact.
Yet, once again, we sought (stout-hearted amid the terror)
To risk our life for the blood of Georgia.
As soon as we had sent away our son and his wife,

And already had seen the Persians' tent from the mountain,   340
We proceeded directly to the tyrant's feet
And intended to kiss his hand in deepest humility.
He, whose fierce anger dashed all his senses,
Was impassioned with lascivious lust when we pleaded to his cruel power
With tears, when we offered to appease his raging fury   345
With our own body.
The ever-changing flush in his face revealed
How violently his soul was inflamed with revenge and love.
He spoke to us in a friendly way (yet his favor was embittered)
And asked why our child didn't appear.   350
"Indeed," he said, "it's all the same. If, in honest truth,
You want the seriously breached treaty renewed for
Your realm and yourself, then oblige those who will be named to you
To recognize the treaty with us by taking an oath.
This is what we desire. If you agree to the proposal,   355
Then it will not be difficult at all for Gurgistan."
We agreed to everything. At his demand,
Fifty of the noblest men had to be granted swiftly to him,
To whom, as soon as they had sworn to commit themselves,
He gave permission to return home immediately.   360
Yet he didn't want anyone to turn homeward or leave the camp
Until after the guest banquet, which went on late into the night
With heaps of food and rich abundance.
Oh night, black as hell! That flew up from the abyss!
And awakened incessant darkness in this breast!   365
That shrouded Abbas' cruelty and perjury!
The fifty, whom he now allowed to leave for home,
Were the ones, whom his men stabbed to death as they first set out
At his very own command. He took us along, imprisoned,
And has kept us until this very day. Since Tamaras escaped   370
He seized Alovassa, whom he bound with chains
And quickly sent to Persia's capital with Meurab.
A man mounted the throne [*of Georgia*], who, although born

Of Greek princes' blood, nevertheless long ago renounced Christ.
To him he entrusted both realms. It's not unknown to you   375
How Alovassa had to relinquish his life by poison!
Who doesn't know how Meurab's wife was violated right here?
How the shah treated Meurab's son and little daughter
Right before Meurab's own eyes? Until Meurab was driven so far
That he scorned the Lord's cross for Persia's favor.   380

Ambassador: So it is! Yet now he has repented this grievous event
And with impassioned revenge brings joy to himself and his country
And horrifies Isfahan. Thus does a hero stand up more courageously
After the first fall! Thus is metal tempered
By smelting: thus does the runner who at first holds back in a tough race   385
Soon overtake the dashing pack
As if he were flying. How much has happened because of him
Your Majesty will soon see with us:
When your crowned son, with tears on his cheeks,
Expresses his profound joy and embraces you with a kiss!   390
When your redeemed realm will throng toward you
And shout through the air: "Long live Catharine!"

Shah Abbas.
The scene changes to the royal pleasure garden.

The decision is finally certain! The heavy yoke will break
  In which we've labored for so long!
Today the Shah will at last refresh or avenge himself   395
  Before the moon shall rise.
Before the sun must fade away, the Shah will find
  Pleasure or tranquility!
Forgive it, burning love, but lust for revenge incites us!
Stop, revenge, stop! It is love that can hinder us.   400

We're tired of the words that seemingly have bound us:
She shall be free before evening.
We've found the proper salve for this burn:
    Free from the pain of long imprisonment
She shall mount our throne really **free today**   405
    And if not, then she'll lower herself into her grave.
Indeed, Princess, you're free! Now choose: joy or sorrow.
Abbas proposes this to you: his marriage bed or death.

Can anyone rightly accuse us of this, oh heaven,
    To which we are forced by fate?   410
Although wounds may be healed by plaster or iron,
    It's the grim plague that's compelling us!
  You yourself, Princess (if only you can be convinced!),
    Cannot blame Abbas
Since he, who until now has loved you without any result,   415
Sincerely seeks his own prosperity in your welfare.

Alas! On the other hand, must you be saddened by such severity?
    Is such a brief time limit set for you?
Indeed, they love us not, who are forced to love us!
    The hand is cursed that wounds us.   420
  What if you would prefer to choose death
    In order to torment us even more?
  Is it possible that she can ever love us,
    When she was condemned already to brutal pain by our hand?

Shall Tigris [*Persia*] and Volga [*Russia*] then curse our perjury?   425
    With you, most unfortunately, our honor dies!
If the Russian Prince gets this for his noble attempt,
    Will anyone who draws a breath trust us again?
  Will not all posterity cry out against us
    And angrily spit upon us?   430
  Who will not begin to doubt the new union
That, with so much effort was barely brought into being?

Ha! What do we contemplate? Who would dare
    To rebuke what seems fair to us?
Isn't divine justice accustomed to going hand in hand with the king,   435
    Because what the king thinks is just?
  Suppose, too, that we perchance besmirch ourselves,
    Royal purple must hide it.
  Majesty and the sun are both so blinding,
  That one is recognized as seldom as the other to be black.   440

Can anyone in his right mind scorn the power of love?
    It is she who holds us bound!
Doesn't the crown oblige us to look out for Persia's salvation?
    That will fall with the woman's freedom.
  Pardon the one who triumphs and is also crowned,   445
    Yet whom a woman scorns!
  Revenge, love, and scepter are what our heart battles.
  Revenge, love, and scepter are what triumph over us.

Shah Abbas. Imanculi

Shah Abbas: Is that Imanculi coming? Good! Go quickly and tell
  Gurgistan's queen that Abbas will grant her   450
  The freedom that she seeks and also his crown,
  But that she must do that which we have hitherto requested.
  The scepter is before her: if she decides to believe
  What Persia teaches and considers Abbas, who honors her,
  Worthy of marriage. If the proposal doesn't suit her,   455
  Then let be performed in haste (and with loss of her head)
  What this document bids you. Don't appear again
  Until the deed is done. Oh, what horror grips
  This injured breast! Wait! Go! Oh, no!
  Stop! Come here! Yes, go! For, finally, it must be.   460

Chorus of the Imprisoned Maidens

Sweet land that we greeted
   When the light of day first smiled upon us,
That, with us, yearns for freedom
   And suffers in Persian bondage:
      Now let your enduring lamentation cease   465
      And let your trembling turn to delight!

Lift your shattered limbs
   Gladly up from the ashes!
Compose new songs of joy
   Because now, in a cycle come full course,   470
      Your prosperity will greet you
      And bless you with utmost delight.

Although your scepter, staff, and crown
   Sank into the dust a short while ago:
After all that, the One who controls realms and thrones   475
      Puts an end to all your anxiety!
      And now wants to return to you
      That through which alone you can live.

Harsh Persia be blessed!
   Call out: Happiness to Georgia!   480
Heaven! You have poured forth!
   Winds, now lie down to rest.
      Let us with joyous laughter
      Begin the journey home.

Today you see us for the last time,   485
    Splendid Shiraz! Fare thee well!
Even if Isfahan didn't forecast it
    God still has returned us.
        We will have no fear at Sirvan
        Where they build towers out of skulls.*   490

From the noble skulls of dead men,
    Whom the cruel sword devoured.
 Let us ourselves take comfort
    Where the chaste princess [*Ameleke Kanna*] once sat,
        Who much preferred to surrender her life*   495
        Than her virginity.

You nymphs who spring to her
    Around the peaks of stony cliffs,
Who sing to her around the green tips
    Of ancient palms: 500
        Let yourselves be heard far and wide
        For the honor of your Catharine.

Praise not only her triumphs
    And her never failing courage:
Not only her traits so rich in honor   505
    And her never tainted blood.
        Sing that she overcame in terror
        And was always free in chains.

Sing that she scorned the cruel raging
    Of incited anger;   510
That she disdained the embellished praising
    Of enamored desire;
        That she, although she was imprisoned,
        Found her realm and self within.

The Fourth Act

Catharine. The scene changes to the Queen's room.

Catharine: As when the turbulent air of a thunderstorm has moved on,
　　When after the flash of lightning the night of clouds has vanished,
　　And the feeble flock of doves refreshes itself in the sun,
　　Drying back and wing, which the falling rain has drenched,
　　In its warmth, while coaxing the frightened young　　　　　　　5
　　From the cleft of the cliff with melancholy cooing:
　　So do we finally hope, after pain and cruel abuse,
　　After prison and bereavement, to see fresh air.
　　Thus we step forth together, we mistreated women,
　　And let ourselves be seen dampened with our own tears.　　　10
　　Thus we seek to cast the burden that has oppressed us so gravely
　　From our shoulders, and to tear from our breast
　　That which consumes our spirit. And yet! How many have perished,
　　In groaning, anguish, and pain, before they found the light
　　That drives away our night! That breaks open this gate,　　　15
　　That lifts us from the funeral bier and proclaims us to be free!
　　How many have expired in the dungeon's stench?
　　How many have perished before the dungeon could be reached
　　While still on the march? The robbers' acquisition
　　　　　　　　　　　　　　　　　　[the captured Georgians]
　　Collapsed, exhausted by dust and sun and thirst and chains!　　20
　　A child, half-dead with thirst, suckled lukewarm blood
　　From the dead breasts of its mother. Dying eyes bade
　　Farewell to a friend, who couldn't even press them closed,
　　Because both his guard and chains begrudged him this brief duty.
　　Into a single chain were looped here the living, there the departed,　　25

And here those who wanted to die. Some sank down exhausted,
Whose strength and spirit had departed. Buried in the same sand were
Those half-dead and the dead; smashed against the wall were
Those who fainted in the cruelest pain in their mothers' arms,
And unborn fruit was excised from pregnant wombs.   30
Here, fields were found filled with lanced corpses;
There, a bleeding woman saw her husband meet his death.
The flame that served at night for torchlight
Did not singe palaces nor what greens on meadows;
The band of those from Gurgistan whom Abbas conquered   35
(Though more by tricks than power) burned in this self-same blaze.
Yet blessed those, whom the fall of the fatherland shrouded!
Who stained neither their conscience nor their body
Except with the pure blood that flowed from their wounds,
That was spilled for freedom, compatriots, and church and God.   40
Oh blessed they, whom the torrent of the first fury consumed!
Oh blessed, whoever was granted death on the way to Persia!
Who never entered the Persians' realm, nor the city of their princes,
Nor the fortress of their king, nor the palace.
Whose precious child was never misused before his eyes!   45
Who was not asphyxiated in extreme torture near burning embers!
Who was not impaled in the grave before he suffocated!
Who did not deny the Saviour out of a desire to live!
How many has the tyrant not impugned through threats,
                                      defiance, and pleading,
Through gifts, desire and force, and torture!   50
And then finally suppressed! Who wouldn't wish for death,
Rather than this continuous agony and incessant misery?
Lord, that Thy poor maid still stands unharmed
Is Thy deed and not the deed of men. Our body is in chains;
But our spirit finds itself free, strengthened by many a cross,   55
Yet, because Thou dost watch over us, it [our body] is not
                                      consumed by fire.
Thou seest that neither death nor the loss of my crown

Nor the decline of my realm nor this in which I live,

This house of terror, nor the splendor Persia promises us,

Nor the torrent of tyranny that strikes and breaks everything,   60

Can tear me from Thee. If, then, the chain shall break;

If Thou willst bring us home again from great suffering;

So grant that our ship, which sailed on the billows,

Does not wreck on a calm sea or in the port.

If my freedom would serve to increase Thy endless praise,   65

So grant, that crowned, I might honor Thee, my King.

But if I haven't offered enough for my church and country,

And Thou willst have my body: here I am, Thy maid.

Salome. Catharine.

Salome: The prince of the great court (Oh, long awaited hour!)

Is looking for Your Majesty. Now we have found   70

What we have longed for so often. He'll free us on behalf of Abbas.

Catharine: Control your emotion! Your joy is much too great!

The shah will not sell us freedom so cheaply.

Why do tears run down both of our cheeks?

Alas! What a strange burden oppresses this breast!   75

What depresses our weary spirit and subdues our new happiness?

This melancholy is surely a prelude to new suffering.

Salome: Thus it is when hope struggles with fear in one heart.

Catharine: We don't hope too much, nor fear too greatly.

Go, let the prince enter.

Imanculi. Catharine.

Imanculi: The prince, whom victory and honor   80

And power and justice serve, most royal of women,

Allows her to behold his heart and generous favor through me;

And he gives her crown and realm, which she lost previously,

Before strange fortune pledged itself to her downfall,

So that she may arise, as if from the grave, even more splendid   85
And find a scepter through loss of throne and scepter.
Thus does the light of the world set in the Gulf of Guinea [*Africa*]
And rise again with new splendor when the jagged peak
Of the cliff pales. Thus does winter's raging rob
The flowering of splendid gardens. When gentle breezes blow   90
Everything grows more beautifully. Seed is sown
That multiplies a hundredfold, if the desired warmth
Of the sun brings forth a harvest. She has left the country
That really is too inadequate for her. She holds the fortune imprisoned,
That imprisoned her. Shah Abbas grants her   95
The land between the Black and the Caspian seas.
                              Yet this is still too trivial
For her, who deserves to receive more from Abbas:
From Abbas, whom she, most Royal Highness, captured.
All of Persia is conceded to her and the shah offers her his hand
That bears the scepter of Persia as a genuine pledge   100
Of royal marriage! I would like to wish the crown,
The ensuing freedom, the throne of the fates,
And the profound joy and incomparable marriage
Ever-blooming happiness and an ever-expanding realm!
Catharine: That Imanculi bent so low in devotion   105
    To greet a poor imprisoned woman in greatest distress
    Is recognized with deepest gratitude by the one who can only thank
    With a bound spirit. The king offers us
    What Catharine will never be willing to accept,
    And indeed must never accept. Filled with longing, we wish   110
    That Abbas would listen to us. If he would break apart our chains
    And grant us Gurgistan, then we would truly be free
    And fall at his feet and kiss his hands
    And swear fidelity and service until our death.
    Yet he wills that our spirit declare itself not Christian: 115
    And thus freedom with Persia's crown becomes too dear for us.
    We praise his feeling, which wants to honor us so deeply,

Yet unfortunately our spirit can hear of no freedom

That severs us from the One who is united with us,

Who gave us this life and counts our every hair.   120

Much better that this flesh languish in a thousand pains!

Much better that this blood from a dissevered heart

Stain the earth and executioner than that the realm be scorned

Wherein no misery exists that pains us in this world!

Imanculi: Your Highness, why will she exclude the favor   125

That is above the world's favor? What can she deny to the shah,

Who gives her own life to her? Will she let this opportunity pass?

Can her Christ really be so important to her?

Catharine: Let the prince inform us! What does the shah think

he can give us?

What does he have in mind for us? Whom does he seek to elevate?   130

Of what use are honor plus fortune? Assuming that it happened,

That Abbas would see us separated from Christ's camp!

Whither would he want to go with us? If he bids us to freely enjoy

What rich abundance put in the treasury;

What friend and subject and conquered power brought   135

By free will or on command and greatly pressed,

It would only serve to fill the empty mouth

And to cloak the nude body with clothing.

While we are now true to Jesus and remain Abbas' maid

Neither bread nor clothing, which every slave receives,   140

Are denied to us by the shah. We are shown his chamber

And called to his bed, in which, with terrible lament,

We would be bound to him with shame and scorn in place of sleeping,

Like the others whom he favors. Or be it, too, that he would

Honor us by nothing but a firm bond and love   145

And would kiss us in holy marriage and increase our fame

On Persia's golden throne; what gain would that be?

We would be called queen. But we are that already!

And just so that a crown may be set upon our head

We mustn't damage our right of conscience nor the favor of God.   150

It is also a vain effort to tantalize us with

Earthly pleasure since we are free, since our still tender breast,

Not consumed by terror, has allowed us to rejoice

Refreshed with abundance: that which isn't allowed we consider

Nothing but filth, humiliation, and a curse. Yes, our faith

                            and bearing   155

Are terrified by the frenzied joy and that which the king's hand

Shows the weary soul. Our honor is bargained for!

We are offered smoke and haze. They try to suppress the

                         doctrine of the Highest

With a trinket! And for the mere wind of time,

To rob our possession of holy eternity   160

That God of all Gods (who hath never broken His oath)

Hath promised us, his poorest maid, in abiding grace.

If we (yet sooner let heaven fall for us!

First this flesh would have to stand on burning flames!),

Excited by sweet passion, defied by cruel threats,   165

Sought to avoid death and God's covenant,

Then who in Gurgistan, when fear seized him,

Wouldn't be encouraged to apostasy by our example?

What? Would a weak child or a tender maiden think:

"Shall terrible pain torture me until the stake?   170

If Catharine herself chose the throne, not the cross,

And lost the crown of faith, rather than her body?"

No, dearest ones! If ever fear should overcome you,

Seek to steadfastly follow after your queen.

Accept a prison for a palace; instead of freedom, embrace chains;   175

For prosperity, choose privation, and exchange that which can delight

For torment! Risk friend and flesh and years!

Fear no flame! Leap onto the funeral bier!

Kiss the swords that are driven through your breast and throat

If the one treasure of holy faith abides with you.   180

Imanculi: Your Royal Highness, it is difficult for an illusion to die!

Catharine: He who dies for the truth can nevermore perish!

Imanculi: The Persian, Jew, and Christian nevertheless honor one God.

Catharine: The Persian and the Jew ridicule God's son.

Imanculi: Yet how could a son be born unto God? 185

Catharine: Shouldn't He be fertile, who made the earth fertile?

Imanculi: He was a mortal man, whom you make equal to God.

Catharine: Who brought time and eternity into His power.

Imanculi: You say that he died suffering on the cross.

Catharine: And that through death He gained life for us. 190

Imanculi: That his pale corpse was hidden in a grave.

Catharine: That He awoke on the third day by His own power.

Imanculi: Whoever is dead lies and sleeps until God will sit in judgment.

Catharine: Who [*Christ*] will lay the enemy at the feet of this judge.

Imanculi: Has any prophet been awakened from his tomb? 195

Catharine: Yes, the one through whom God hath made prophets.

Imanculi: Does she trust so very much the one who has forsaken

her 'til now?

Catharine: No father is used to hating his child even if he punishes him.

Imanculi: How long will he allow you to continue in this grief?

Catharine: A moment passes quickly and will not fade for eternity. 200

Imanculi: Let us make use of time and the world while we're still here!

Catharine: In an instant the world and its splendor will go up in smoke.

Imanculi: God grants to men their pleasure in this instant.

Catharine: Except for God, we are not conscious of any pleasure at all.

Imanculi: Even he who doesn't love pleasure tries to avoid torture. 205

Catharine: Whoever is an enemy of this life is not afraid to suffer.

Imanculi: Suffering and death run contrary to nature.

Catharine: Life and death are firmly tied together on one string.

Imanculi: Death embittered by sharp pain seems horrible.

Catharine: The harder the thunder strikes, the quicker the

storm is over. 210

Imanculi: A king is greatly incensed by ridicule aimed at him.

Catharine: We honor Persia's leader, yet honor our God even more.

Imanculi: The one who paled on the cross and gives nothing but crosses.

Catharine: Who, through the cross, provides strength to the
                                        souls that He loves.
Imanculi: She loves what gives crosses and hates what gives crowns.   215
Catharine: The cross gives us the crown that no one takes or wrongs.
Imanculi: It is a false illusion that deludes your mind.
Catharine: We have heard the truth from God's mouth.
Imanculi: In that case, the truth is much too difficult.
Catharine: Enough of that. Let the prince say something else to us!   220
Imanculi: Does she want [*to hear*] what I myself am terrified to say aloud?
Catharine: One must always choose the lesser of two evils.
Imanculi: Let her choose, while she still can, a great benefit
                                        instead of an evil.
Catharine: We'll do it! And we'll gladly risk our handful of blood for good.
Imanculi: The false appearance of good is often deceptive.   225
Catharine: Vanity will not triumph over the one whom God strengthens.
Imanculi: Alas! Then does she want from me the king's harsh decision?
Catharine: Why does he conceal it from the one who must suffer it?
Imanculi: Princess, forgive me! I'm forced to carry out this task!
Catharine: We perceive it! What we've always agonized over is coming!   230
Imanculi: It is the king's idea, but the words, indeed, are mine.
Catharine: But quickly! The delay intensifies and sharpens the cruel pain.
Imanculi: Princess, must I aggrieve you so violently?
Catharine: Delight, great prince!
Imanculi: She can postpone death!
    She holds her life, her welfare, and her death in her hand.   235
Catharine: Oh, death! Longed-for death! Oh welcome promise!
Imanculi: The gruesome manner of dying is more gruesome
                                        than dying itself.
Catharine: God Himself had to acquire His realm through gruesome pain.
    Be not afraid, honored prince! Make known the pains to us.
    We find ourselves prepared.
Imanculi: Read this order.   240
Catharine: Oh, joyous message! Oh, loosened bonds!
    Oh, delivered crown! Oh, cast-off shame!

Oh, freedom of my soul! Oh, long anticipated peace!
Oh, eternal kingdom! Oh, fatherland! Welcome!
Martyrdom (we confess!) appears unbearable indeed, 245
Yet what can a spirit that Jesus strengthens not venture!
Through Him, even a child has scoffed the executioner's defiance!
Without Him, human strength has cracked even without adversity!
Farewell, honored prince! Let us end the struggle
And enter into peace.

Imanculi: If only I could alter the disaster! 250
If it were in my power, nothing would be too difficult for us.

Catharine: That we know! This blow proceeds from Shah Abbas!
Yet the prince can still connect us with a final favor:
Let him allow that if a priest can be found here
Who, with us, honors Jesus, he may appear at the palace 255
As a witness of our faith and sustenance during our pain.

Imanculi: I willingly submit! Yet if she could be moved,
If she would consider for a final time the joy and the terror,
If she …!

Catharine: No more of that! We thank Abbas
For offering us his crown after so much sorrow 260
And the prolonged stench of the dungeon; and because we refuse it,
He causes us to seek the crown of eternity.

Imanculi: Then farewell, honored lady! Worthy of a better fate.

Catharine: What befalls us today is the highest fate.

Catharine

Oh, Master and General of Thy legions! 265
  Thou who fought the battle for us
    And through Thy blood blessed what God had cursed
I fall before Thee!
  Accept what I shall now spill for Thee in sacrifice:
    My blood, stained indeed by sin. 270

Yet through Thy blood what must flow from these veins
For Thy honor will become pure and good.

Weak flesh quakes at the thought of misery
   And trembles in the face of bitter despair!
   The fresh spirit calls out to death   275
Ready to bear the fear of fears!
Alas! that I am only granted to die for Thee but once!
   The brief pain is not at all worthy of
   The honor that Thou bestoweth upon me,
That my so worthless nothingness must perish for Thy glory.   280

Perish? No! What is ventured for Thee,
   My bridegroom, is saved!
   They have deplored the loss
Who grow old in the pleasure of the earth.
Who wouldn't entrust what time will eventually take
                           from us anyway   285
   As a gift to the one
   Whom we, immortal, will behold
And who will honor us when the world will be ashamed.

Oh Saviour! Let me not waver now!
   Now that the final enemy pursues me   290
   And tortures me with all kinds of martyrdom!
Oh, stand by me in this bondage!
Offer me Thy hand and help me to overcome.
   Alone I am much too weak:
   With Thee I will find, through fear and woe,   295
The victory, the light, the way to Thee, my Saviour.

My oppressed realms! Be blessed!
   God offereth me higher crowns.
   This what the world cannot give,

Freedom, has greeted me today.   300

My prison! Consecrated with sigh-filled tears,

   Which my blood, too, shall bespatter,

Farewell! Now my soul is at peace

For in this hour it feels its long yearning satisfied.

Catharine and Salome with all the Ladies of the Court.
The Hooded Executioner with the soldiers and executioners.

Catharine: Salome, we are free! The Highest doth tear the bonds   305

   Of long imprisonment asunder! And leadeth us from the land

   Where death and martyrdom rule into the wished-for realm

   Of ever-constant joy! We leave this corpse

   To the shah as a ransom. The spirit is commended to Him,

   Who will deliver us out of misery into the fatherland.   310

   Observe the image of the sufferer:

   And receive, oh dearest, our final good night.

   You have courageously borne the heavy yoke with us!

   The thunder that struck us has also struck at you!

   And yet your faithfulness remained unmoved by storms,   315

   Even though we already lay in the dust of our throne!

   Accept our gratitude for this service that we now cannot repay!

   We (if only it could be so!) would not spare our blood

   If you could be helped! Alas, but our crown

   Tumbled with our freedom! Fortune robbed wealth and throne   320

   And treasure and money! We have retained nothing

   But our bound body that shall now turn cold!

   Alas! Learn how the pleasures of earth suddenly vanish

   And how all of our hopes stand on unstable ground.

   Ignore what the world or Abbas might offer you   325

   With magnanimity. Only pure morals

   Accompany the spirit summoned before the court of justice

   When God pronounceth final judgment on what we've done.

   Farewell! Mourn not for us! We are not to be wept over!

The Lord! The Lord of Lords will appear to us full of joy—   330

We pass through darkness to God, the Light of Lights.

Burden not our death with your tears.

Grieve for those who enjoy themselves here in spite of their sins

And who set their foundation of hope on transitory wealth.

It's not a time for weeping; believe instead it's worthy of rejoicing   335

That our bridegroom bestoweth upon us the martyr's crown.

Salome: Alas! Did Russia, did Persia promise us this?

Catharine: The shah didn't break his promise for the first time today.

Salome: Help! Jesus! Help! Shall this now be our journey home?

Catharine: Yes indeed! Yes! We are going to God and entering life.   340

Salome: Must Your Majesty depart from us so miserably?

Catharine: What Jesus doth send must be endured without resistance.

Salome: I think God doth turn His gracious ear from us.

Catharine: Be patient, Salome! Do not accuse the Highest.

Salome: I am ready to lose my life with her.   345

Catharine: God doth bid only us alone, not you, to martyrdom.

Lord, we go willingly. What zeal inspires us!

Who is there that has reason to weep for us?

Are we denied the crown? We are just beginning to live

And to defy Persia and death! Who wants to forfeit courage?   350

Behold! Jesus doth go before us! One moment weighs heavily

But eternity delights. Cross, knife, tongs, and oven

Are rungs toward honor. The dream is now fulfilled

That, when worry and sleep enshrouded us last night,

Pointed to this outcome. Gurgistan's realm is gone!   355

From the crown we have only thorns as gain!

Only thorns, that, when all pleasure had vanished,

Just like rose petals, we still found in our hair.

The tears fell like pearls into our lap,

As our eyes' fountain incessantly flowed.   360

Our purple garb was torn asunder, the scepter was broken into bits,

When we were pressed from our throne into dust and bondage.

Meurab, Russia, and Tamaras struggle in vain

To alter our sorrow, that blooms without ceasing

And daily becomes more fertile. The one who finally attacked us   365

And tore us from the thorns, and (as it appears) wounded us,

Is (without a doubt) Death. The joy that enveloped us

As the rapid storm of foul weather passed over

Points to the blessed realm that Jesus hath won for us.

Rise! God will give us the crown, when we, like Him, have died!   370

Salome: Alas! How agonized Tamaras, the worthy prince, will be:

Who, unfortunately, counted every day and moment!

Who every hour wished to kiss his mother's hand:

His mother, who (Oh God!) here must shed her blood.

Oh, great prince! All that has been endeavored was in vain!   375

Your steadfast zeal bears, sadly, bitter fruit.

Catharine: If he loves God above all else, as everyone should,

Then this demise cannot sadden his heart.

Should he be unable to lose his mother for God,

Then he is not our child and means nothing to us.   380

Farewell! Time is fleeing! Accept this last kiss,

You, whom I embrace, yet enclose in my heart even more.

The One who doth take us from the world and from your side

Hath determined already how and when you shall follow us.

Cassandra, take this ring; you; this string of pearls: 385

Salome, the diamond; Serena, the sapphire.

Accept as a farewell the jewels from our hair,

The chains and any other jewelry left to us,

And remember our death. With this, may God be with you!

Should the Highest still bring you back to Gurgistan,   390

Then witness to Tamaras and all the people of the land

That he will not perish, who can die as did we.

Executioner: Princess, you are wanted in the great hall.

The priest has been summoned.

Catharine: Let us leave the valley of sorrow.

Let us depart from hell! What need is there for tears?   395

What are you doing?

Ladies of the Court: Worthy Lady, we wish death for ourselves.

 I. Lady: Shall Your Majesty depart from us so deplorably?

 II. Lady: So deplorably perish?

III. Lady: Oh, more than bitter suffering!

IV. Lady: Until now I have only grieved for my country and parents—
    She was both of them to me: she, who offered solace to us   400
    When our hearts were breaking. With her the burden,
    Princess, was not so heavy for us. It seemed that no catastrophe
    Would be unbearable for us in her presence.
    Now new pain grips our souls
    And rips open the wounds that time has barely healed.   405
    The fire of fear breaks out and hope is abated.
    What am I saying? She is gone! Who will help us now?

Catharine: God, who is Father of all, who can save orphans from the mire
    And widows from the dust and the dead from the bier
    If He will. Believe that He will protect you   410
    And be true to Him forever.

Salome: Alas, can it not be possible
    That for our consolation we attend her suffering?

Executioner: Three and not more may accompany her to the hall.

Ladies of the Court: Oh, let us come too!

Executioner: I cannot exceed my orders.
    My head would be the price.

Catharine: Lay your spirit to rest   415
    And upset us no further with melancholy weeping.
    We have lived long enough and can ask for nothing
    That the great world is still capable of granting us.
    We have guarded church and crown with counsel and sword:
    We've governed Armenia, ravaged Persia,   420
    Avenged the tragic fall of our husband's father and the blood
                  of our beloved:
    We've broken the yoke of blind love and the arrow of Death,
    And we mount the bier in the bloom of our years:
    We mount in victorious splendor our immolation altar

Where we commit our flesh as a sacrifice   425
To Him, who let Himself be crucified for us.
Earth smells foul to us. We enter into heaven.
Dearest ones, do not mourn! The pain is without pain!
The tongs barely weaken our firm mind.
You will not be allowed to witness our death?   430
Patience! You will serve us here in this room even more.
Fall at God's feet for us! Pray that He may hear us
And Himself help us struggle and grant us strength in our fear:
Pray that He can forgive committed sins which soil us
And comfort us in death and save us from all sorrow.   435
Farewell with this kiss until eternity.

Chorus of the Virtues, Death, and Love

The Virtues

Frightened mortals, what trembling seizes you
When your tender flesh is tortured
And swords are sharpened on your throats?
How can you be so despondent over whatever can kill?   440
Must not this lifeless life be given
To the years as plunder?
Why then is that which must be lost so beloved?
How is it that you still won't give up
For this, which eternally can delight,   445
The restlessness, this burden, the tears, the vexation!
Tremble before the One who can hurl body and soul
Into the depths of the terrible abyss
With one angry gesture
And shorten for you that which lives forever.   450

Death: This arrow that is moistened with the blood
Of God Himself,
Who embraced me for your good,
Heals when it wounds.

Love: This arrow that pierced the heart   455
          Of God Himself,
          Kills fear and torment and pain
          And torture's duress.
Death: Though this torch lights the way
          For you out of this world: 460
          It leads from the bier
          Into the canopy of heaven.
Love: This torch's burning glow
          Kindles the spirits
          So that it is possible to appear   465
          Before God with flaming courage.
Death: Whoever fears this bow
          Knows neither the world nor self:
          Whoever sees through the earth correctly
          Wishes nothing more than me.   470
Love: Whoever doesn't love this bow
          Knows neither self nor God
          And will remain sorrowful here and there:
          Indeed is dead while alive.
Death: In my white gown of honor   475
          God Himself was shrouded
          When He stilled the suffering of your souls
          Through his own suffering.
Love: My purple gown was dyed
          In the blood of the Highest   480
          When on the cross He bequeathed to you
          A never ending blessing!
Death: If I close your eyes,
          Then in fact you end
          This quarreling without rest: 485
          This battle without honor!

Love:	He whose eye and light is paralyzed	
	By the power of my flame	
	Sees in the highest holy splendor	
	The countenance of God.	490
Death:	You, who languish in bonds,	
	Turn to me:	
	I will pry open the dungeon's might,	
	I will open barricade and door.	
Love:	If you wish yourselves free from bonds	495
	Come only to me!	
	Love blasts the chain in two,	
	Breaks through steel and stone.	
Death:	If you loathe this vale of tears	
	Offer me your hand.	500
	I lead from the torture chamber	
	Into the fatherland.	
Love:	If you hasten to the realm of delight	
	I go before you!	
	To me this path is known	505
	That can be trod.	
Death:	What is stronger than Death?	
Love:	Love prevails even more!	
Death:	Death ends sorrow and woe.	
Love:	Love crowns with honor!	510
Death:	Death cancels everything!	
Love:	Except Love!	
Death:	If his arrow is at full speed--	
Love:	Love breaks it.	
	Pure love reigns forever.	515
Death:	Confirmed by me.	
Love:	It wears the grace of the eternal crown.	
Death:	That was bestowed by me.	
	Did I not force God Himself?	
Love:	After I bound him.	520

Death: Whom I forced on the cross.

Love: I offered you my hand.

Death: Virtuous love is only recognized in Death.

Love: Whoever loves is not separated by Death from Love.

Death: He loves without deception, who loves unto Death.   525

Love: Whoever dies loving is not saddened by Death.

The Virtues

Whoever loves unto Death will stand forever

And cannot perish in Death.

It helps not to struggle and resist:

The end crowns all things.   530

Whoever has begun must finish

If he wants to sing the victor's song.

Whoever is true to God until burning at the stake:

Whoever doesn't shy away from the tongs or sword:

Whoever exchanges state and throne for the grave: 535

That selfsame person will attain the most splendid crown of honor.

The Fifth Act

Cassandra. Serena. Ladies of the Court. The Eunuchs.

Cassandra: Oh blessed they, whom the fall of Armenia has buried!
    Oh blessed they, whom the Persians put to the stake!
    Oh blessed they, who perished in the fire of Gurgistan!
    Who suffocated in the smoke, who didn't postpone the dismal end
    Until today: here's to you, if you have died!   5
    Woe! If your weak spirit has vanished but for a short while
    And then must find itself revived in this place of execution,
    In this river of tears, in this sea of martyrdom!
Lady of the Court: Help, eternally high God! What misery is at hand.
Cassandra: Those who witnessed the raw pain of the Queen   10
    Lost reason and sense when they saw the flames,
    But she remains undismayed, who is indeed near death,
    But is not yet able to die.
Lady of the Court: Bring vinegar to help soothe her!
    Bring salve! She is beginning to feel the fresh air.
    Seren!
Serena: Oh, Queen!
Cassandra: Seren! She's coming to!   15
    Alas, Seren, heaven is keeping you and me
    For a greater catastrophe; for those destined to suffer more,
    Terror doesn't allow escape by simple fainting.
Lady of the Court: How is the queen bearing her martyrdom?
Cassandra: She scorns insolent Death: God Himself offers her His hand.   20
    Don't detain me with questions. Seren can tell you
    How horrible Persia is, how cruelly the shah orders torture.
    I'm in a hurry to see the end of this struggle.

Serena: Where am I? How is she? Oh, what has happened to me?

Oh, my Queen! Can the sun still shine   25

And the heavens not flash with lightning? When will the world perish

If no thunder strikes now? When will the earth split open

And swallow the cliffs, if it remains free of trembling

At this tragedy? When will revenge awaken,

If Thy light won't penetrate the universe now,   30

Prince of all Princes? The miracle of this age,

The pure woman who already conquers eternity

In her courage, confronted pain and death

With brave composure. She felt a blaze from within

Through which she caught on fire. She was still undaunted,   35

Even though the band of murderers themselves mourned

                                        her bitter suffering.

One of them trembled at her courage, while another watched her face

As if he were paralyzed, for similar to the light of the sun

When it is setting, it seemed far more pleasant.

The majesty of her eyes compelled the Persians to leave;   40

Her alabaster brow; her rose-white cheeks;

The snow of her pure throat; and what captured the shah,

Her eloquent mouth, brought tears to everyone's eyes.

She thought of her God, and with a deaf ear

Rejected the salutation of the prince, who in commiseration   45

Ventured to persuade her. When the priest's blessing

And intercession for her were permitted, she turned aside

And spent in prayer the limited amount of time

That the meager respite allowed. Whoever intended to strengthen her

Became strong through her courage; the closer death approached her,   50

The more joyous her heart grew; she mounted the throne

And grasped the scepter as she transformed the nation's scorn

Into honor and power: thus have I seen her

When she took to the battlefield, when she cleansed the Persians' abuse

With precious blood and triumphantly returned   55

And enthusiastically embraced her crowned son.

Lady of the Court: She will be resplendent with new victory
before the face of God!

    Her Jesus will embrace her now as she has wished!

Serena: The murderers attacked her like ferocious lions.

Lady of the Court: Who can hear of this murderous deed without anguish?   60

Serena: Her clothes were torn off. Her immaculate limbs

    Were publicly exposed; she cast down her cheeks,

    Covered by a blush of shame, and considered it most painful of all

    To be an object of unchaste eyes and a wanton spectacle.

Lady of the Court: Thus did her Redeemer Himself have to die exposed.   65

Serena: Her tender hands and feet were bound in fetters,

    And her arms, body, and knees were lashed to the stake with chains.

Lady of the Court: Her King departed from this valley of sorrow
on the wooden cross.

Serena: She stood like an image made of purest wax:

    Her hair fell about her neck, casually loosened,   70

    Partly fluttering in the breeze and partly hanging down, as if weighted,

    While her every heartbeat pulsated on her breast.

    The executioner pressed hard into her with glowing red tongs—

Lady of the Court: Did merciful God decree such a cruel deed?

Serena: —And gripped her shoulders. Steam rose in the air;   75

    Steel hissed in her blood; her flesh melted like snow

    Into which a flame falls. Yet she, while having the smooth muscles

    Pinched and lacerated from her arm bones,

    Cried out—

Lady of the Court: Heaven help us!

Serena: "Savior, grant me patience!

    I accept this pledge of everlasting grace   80

    In deepest humility: I, who with patent sins have earned

    By my guilt the flames which Thy wrath incessantly bids

    To ignite, am not worthy of the grace

    Of suffering for Thine honor: it is a sharper sword

    With which Thy grave severity is accustomed to punish depravity.   85

    What did Thy spirit not feel when Thou passed on before me,

When Thy soul collapsed in curses and the terror of death
And found itself abandoned? My pain is but child's play!"
Lady of the Court: Thus can God's power be seen in His children.
    Thus is the strong spirit accustomed to strengthening weak flesh.   90
Serena: Pieces [*of flesh*] were now hanging down from both thighs
    When she was dealt two cruel slashes in her breast.
    Blood gushed everywhere, and doused the flame and iron:
    Her lung was exposed. Her spirit began to depart
    Through the exit newly opened by this cruel fury.   95
    I was stricken with horror. The ringing in my ears,
    The cold sweat of my brow, and the trembling of my limbs
    Suddenly took the upper hand. My melancholy eyelids
    Gradually became rigid. I was aware of nothing more
    And was brought, I know not how, to this place.   100
Lady of the Court: Arise! Since we are allowed to bury her dead body,
    Let us provide her service with a final kiss and tears.
    Come, wrap what remains of her exposed bones
    And mangled body in pure silk.

The Chief Executioner, Salome, Catharine, the Priest, the Executioners.
The scene changes to the front court of the palace.

Chief Executioner: Hurry, stack the wood pile! Bring pitch,
                        bring bundles of sticks!   105
Salome: Alas! Don't rage even more furiously.
Chief Executioner: I must!
Salome: Alas! A little more gentle!
Chief Executioner: You! Fetch the dying woman before she's completely gone!
Salome: God, Thou who seeth all, dost Thou not see our misery?
    Alas! At least allow the Queen to faint beforehand.
    What has the burning of the tongs left to the fire   110
    But half-consumed bones? Oh, grant final peace
    To such noble blood. Grant to the Princess
    What no enemy has ever denied his enemy out of malice.

Allow that she, mourned by us with final farewells,
   May have a simple grave.
Chief Executioner: It cannot be any other way!   115
Salome: Oh, hearts of steel! Oh, more than ferocious pain!
   Princess! Alas, my light! Alas, but a little while ago my bliss!
   Princess! Good night! Oh, does the sun still shine for us
   And the earth not rupture?
Catharine: Welcome, sweet death!
Priest: Princess! Remember Jesus' final suffering.   120
Salome: Princess! One word more!
Catharine: We have overcome.
   Through death we have found life itself.
   Oh Jesus, come!
 Priest: He cometh. He extendeth His hands to her.
   He offereth her His kiss!
Chief Executioner: What are you gawking at? Make an end of it.
Salome: Alas! Let up for a little while!
Chief Executioner: Hurry! Throw her on the flames!   125
Salome: Alas, why can we not die together, Princess?
Priest: Princess! She is gone! Mourn for her no longer
   Whom the Highest now doth comfort, who exchanges weary toiling
   For sweet tranquility. If her body now must perish,
   Let the remaining ashes be cast as dust to the blowing winds.   130
   Believe that for the Lord nothing vanishes from His world,
   Which is our most beautiful grave. One blessed with the
                            inheritance of heaven
   Sleeps as softly in the sea as in the deepest earth:
   More so than do those who are in gold and marble.
   Where will the vain splendor of great crypts stand   135
   When the structure of this earth must perish in flames
   And God will appear?
Salome: Appear, Judge of all things!
   Appear, Avenger! Alas, appear!
Priest: In the meantime, let us keep watch.

Salome: Alas, my Savior, why do I not fall asleep instead?

Priest: One must be ready no matter how, when, or where God doth call.   140

Chief Executioner: Get out! You are not allowed to tarry any longer.

    This whimpering is futile. If you want to escape the wrath

    That offers you this spectacle, then pay more heed

    To the hand that can kill and bring life to the dead.

          Shah Abbas, Seinelcan, Imanculi.

          The scene changes to the Royal Hall.

Shah Abbas: Run! Rescue her! Are you just going to stand there?

          Hurry! Hurry! while there's still time to hurry!   145

    If it's not already too late! If the blow can be averted!

    Repeal the punishment and sentence! Faithless one, did you not

    Think of us and yourself?

Imanculi: What have I done beyond

    What Shah Abbas expressly ordered me to do?

Shah Abbas: Shall I not rip your heart from your breast,   150

Your thoughtless heart? Which didn't even consider

    That heated jealousy, if it's accustomed to prevailing,

    Is not to be followed so blindly every moment?

Imanculi: Whoever undertook to judge the Prince himself?

    He commands. We can do nothing but carry out what he orders!   155

Shah Abbas: Then must all our joy flee with this day?

    Must our heart perish because of you, you bloodthirsty scoundrel?

    Must our humiliation arise from this flame because of you?

    And does the executioner still appear in our sight?

    Are there no more prisons? Are there no chains?   160

    Straightaway, Hali! Tie him up!   (*Abbas departs.*)

Imanculi: Oh strange course of events!

    Even as I carry out what the prince so strongly commanded

    This storm is raging on me. He clears away whatever he can

    With our hands and then attacks us ourselves,

As soon as the deed is done. We commit outrage for his benefit,   165
   And he washes himself clean of his own guilt with our blood!

Seinelcan: In this instance you have obviously acted too hastily.

Imanculi: He issued the command to me under penalty of death.

Seinelcan: The instructions of princes are very strange and difficult to grasp.

Imanculi: And he who doesn't understand them must let himself

                be bound like this.   170

Seinelcan Patience! And listen to this: often much is done only for appearance.
   You know what Russia seeks! This could be your good fortune.
   The Prince can also be served faithfully in chains.

Imanculi: He who has become so tarnished has never shone again.

     The Russian Ambassador, Procopius, Demetrius.
    The Priest with the charred head of Queen Catharine.
      The scene changes to the Ambassador's apartment.

The Priest: So it is! As I stated! The flower of women is gone!   175
   The sun of Armenia and the prize of Gurgistan!
   The miracle of all times! Now she has overcome
   Even as she perished. She has found the crown
   Even as her flesh disintegrated. This vale of tears, the earth,
   This house of terror, was no longer worthy of her great spirit: 180
   It therefore sought a course through so many vicious rifts
   And pressed through both breasts. To it the flame was sweet!
   It was not afraid in spite of the tong's torture,
   That indeed wounded her tender body but not her courage.
   Whosoever can bid farewell in such a way deserves no pitiful mourning.   185
   Whosoever can appear before Jesus so stained with blood
   Does not heed your tears. Thus are the world and death struck down,
   And eternity defied and violent despair scorned!

Russian Ambassador: Is this then Abbas' word? Is Persia thus to be trusted?
   Air! Heaven! Earth! Sea! Who will not be horrified at it?   190
   Does no thunder sound that will strike the murderers
   Who plotted this betrayal? This game of murder?

Does Persia's soil not tremble, oh righteous God,

When such horror inhumanly rages?

Has Abbas lost his reason? Bloodthirsty, bestial tiger!   195

Do you recall your oath and lofty promise?

Has a tyrant ever so raged against a woman?

Has a woman ever been so afflicted with torture

That is worse than death? Whoever so punishes a knave?

Does beauty, does reason, does youth, does her fair sex,   200

Does royal lineage, or does the pleading of my czar

Count for nothing to this beast? Arise! Abandon the murder-mills

Of the mad executioners! Is this the new bond,

The sign of true favor, the mighty pledge of peace?

Miserable wretch! Must I, because I want to free you,   205

Loan myself unwittingly to be a tool of your torture?

My pleading, Queen! My pleading made it so

That you were murdered in such haste! So shamefully!

Prince Tamaras! Do I bring your mother to you again like this?

Not even the noble body and distressed limbs?   210

Nothing but a frightful head that articulates without a tongue

How miserably I fulfilled your wishes in Persia!

Alas, with what tears you will receive this gift!

This brow without flesh! The shriveled cheeks!

The teeth no longer lovely! The ruby lips,   215

The splendor of golden hair and the shining eyes are gone!

Will you, saddened prince, will you be able to believe me

That the shah so cruelly had you robbed of your mother;

That the head of Persia so lightly jokes with promise and oath,

That here neither rank nor friend nor foe is heeded?   220

No! No! Alas, the whole burden of guilt will be laid upon me.

Your sighing heart and the deluge of your tears

Will reproach me for what the shah, not I, has perpetrated.

Yet I, too, am guilty for imprudently beseeching the mad lion.

Thou henceforth holy soul! Thou, who now rules other realms   225

With higher power! Thou head of the holy body! (*He kisses the head.*)

Thou, who adorneth this head with crowns of honor

And refresheth the rejoicing spirit on Thy throne,

Reveal who is guilty here! You, too, heroes of Gurgistan,

Help proclaim the horrifying demise of your queen.   230

And always and freely bear witness before the nations

That neither honesty nor truth exists in in Persia.

The Priest: Witness rather with what courage the queen conquered,

Who battled fear and desire and death while dying from torture

And yet triumphantly overcame. Bear witness that she scorned   235

All splendor and the cumulative agony of the Fates.

Begrudge her not her happiness with such bitter tears.

She is resting in this port for which everyone yearns!

She is where we are going, and from heaven's home laughs

At the earth's vanity and Abbas' raging.   240

Believe as well that your kingdom, for which this blood has flowed,

Is like a burned field that has been watered by the rain;

And the oppressed church, that this dew moistens,

Will now bear more fruit than if it had gone unharmed.

Believe, that provided the delight in which they   245

Who (like the worthy spirit) steadfastly overcome,

                                   will find themselves—

Provided that this delight will still allow anything to

Be known of our sorrow: the Princess in the Highest

Will also remember you and bring before the eyes of God

Your conquered land and accumulated misery.   250

That she—

Russian Ambassador: Who is there?

Servant: My Lord, the shah's advisor wants to see you.

Russian Ambassador: Indeed! Aren't we even granted respite for a few tears?

Do they still seek to delude us anew?

Do they seek to maliciously ascertain how we feel?

(*As these words are spoken, the Queen's head is covered with a white silk cloth.*)

Let him come, let him know what consumes my soul   255

And perhaps even more than he desired to know.

The Russian Ambassador. Seinelcan with several servants, who
proceed bearing various gifts. The Ambassadors from Georgia
(Procopius and Demetrius) depart.

Seinelcan: Since Shah Abbas has heard that having completed his tasks
    The Ambassador has decided to return home to Russia,
    He wishes for him abiding good fortune for such a journey
    As his virtue merits: he who untied the knotted rope   260
    Of discord through reason and effort,
    Who found peace for the countries and fame for himself,
    And he offers him farewell gifts as an expression of his favor
    For such useful efforts.
Russian Ambassador: Seinelcan is certain, I know,
    That I cannot be bought by anyone with gifts.   265
    A spirit kindled by fame heeds no vessels of gold—
    Yet, that Abbas wants to honor me with his favor
    And sends this as a pledge surpasses all belief!
    I only wish that the one be granted to me
    Whom the czar so eagerly bid me to request from Persia,   270
    Whom even today Abbas promised me when I urgently implored,
    Indeed, whom he even promised to our czar himself through me.
Seinelcan: We wish it were possible to give you this woman.
Russian Ambassador: What? Why isn't it possible?
Seinelcan: She is no longer alive.
Russian Ambassador: What is the prince saying? Is this what
                     Abbas promised me?   275
Seinelcan: The shah is furious with the one who had her burned to death.
Russian Ambassador: What? Are you allowed to burn a queen whom
                     the shah sets free?
Seinelcan: He who is guilty shall pay for his mistake with death.
Russian Ambassador: Can the shah be tolerant with you in this deed?
Seinelcan: It happened, unknown to him, through strange hatred.   280

The prince, who was ordered to the fortress of Shiraz by the king,

Acting alone and in secret, out of embittered jealousy,

Has committed this heinous deed (in order to avenge his son,

Who remained true to Gurgistan when Tamaras was driven

                                          from his throne),

With the intention of quickly escaping   285

Into Osman's nearby tent before her lifeless body

Smoldered on its ashes. Yet no! It was discovered.

How hot the prince's [*Abbas'*] wrath was kindled by this fire

His [*the offender's*] dungeon already proves. And his wretched end

Will verify with what sincerity the infuriated hands   290

Of the prince [*Abbas*] are prepared to draw the sword of revenge

On those who strive to undermine his power.

Russian Ambassador: It is more than obvious how easily the shah

                                          starts to fume:

It is very obvious how one sweats out his soul here in fire.

The Princess' stake bears witness that harsh tyranny   295

Cannot be mollified by gifts, pleading, and profit.

In supposing to reconcile Persia and Russia

Am I allowing the head of Russia to be scorned in my person by

                                          your defiance?

Do you seal the bond with the death of this woman,

Over whom peace was made? What is the use of promise?   300

Whom and what shall be trusted in Isfahan

If Abbas' word no longer can be built upon firmly?

So be it! Scoff at oath and spit at heaven—

But remember that this flame can ignite the empire!

Seinelcan: It seems easy to me to dispel the delusion   305

That the Ambassador creates; yet let him convince himself

More through deeds than words. The prince has indeed been trapped:

The state is filled with new fear. The shah, who sends me to you,

Laments the violent incident. I can say it expressly:

I! who heard him myself lamenting the queen.   310

What? Or do you think he doesn't understand the meaning of an alliance?
That he doesn't take his promise to heart?
No, for sure! Abbas can't be joked with in this way.
The princess has been killed! And indeed through bitter pain!
Is the murderer then free? Is it unheard of among you   315
That (in spite of the czar's word) burning revenge disables those
To whom the head of Russia had granted full freedom?
Even those whom he bid to live in palaces next to him
Were often attacked by immorality! It was not asked if it occurred,
But only if, when it occurred, it was also tolerated!   320
Does the Ambassador wish to cite this as an offense?
Does he wish, now that golden peace is already seen in bloom,
To topple what has been achieved? Then let God and the world judge
If there is cause that the corpse-filled battlefield
Ought to behold us all in arms. If the shah lets justice sleep   325
And doesn't rush to punish this murderous deed according
                                        to its merit,
Then cry out to the heavens, tear the bond asunder,
And draw your swords! Yet both choices are open to you!
Just consider if hereby the deceased would be awakened:
It concerns much more those who still remain in fetters.   330
She was a foreign woman. Your own gain could be great.
Many thousand Russians will be freed for one woman!
Also, so that you can feel how we really think,
Shah Abbas will let you take them with you out of Persia
Along with those remaining from Gurgistan and Tiflis.   335
Don't throw your own fortune so carelessly to the wind!
Russian Ambassador: The matter has been considered!
                                        What we hope to gain
Costs you as much as us. If your lands are open,
Then ours are also free! Your prison is not empty
And ours are filled. If your scale weighs heavy,   340
The Russian's is not light. Whoever is guilty must feel it.
Unless Abbas quenches this fire with blood,

His words are just in vain!

Seinelcan: It shall happen yet today!

   You will see the murderer's head on your table!

   Shah Abbas, Catharine. The scene changes to the Royal Hall.

Shah Abbas: Is Catharine dead and the Shah still alive?   345

   And doesn't heaven,

   Armed with the glow of brimstone-bright light

   Want to strike fire upon this head?

   Has the Shah, Princess! Has the Shah made such a mistake

   And torn his own heart to pieces with your torture?   350

   What does it help that tears were flowing down our cheeks

   Even as deeply hued streams ran from your wounds?

   Princess, take revenge! Set fire to my soul

   With ever-renewed regret and pains!

   Does Abbas have a heart of stone?   355

   Oh, tender one! Could not your pleading, coupled with your tears,

   Curb the mad, raging flame of zeal?

   Yet why can we not penetrate the abyss

   And wrest you from the austere prison of furious death?

   Alas, we ourselves! Princess! We hurled you into such a prison   360

   You miracle of nature! You honor of your age!

   Was your friendly countenance

   Destroyed in the burning glow?

   Did your lovely charm perish in smoke?

   Princess, the raging fire   365

   Did not so monstrously consume the snow of your limbs,

   But rather it was this flame that curses our soul

   With ever-burning remorse.

   The torch of sweet love never stirred our hard heart!

   Revenge appearing as love led us astray!   370

   Not revenge either: the flock from hell

   With hair of snakes and armed with trouble,

They carried wood to this fire
And tried to fell us into the grave through your death!
Oh, horror! Oh! What appears before our eyes?   375
Is it you, former joy of our heart?
How horribly the severed breast hangs!
Your bloody tears summon heaven to judge us!
Pull out! No, don't pull out
Her singed hair.   380
We wish for our grave
And run for the funeral bier.
Behold how she extends her exposed arms to the harsh Judge,
And hear how she awakens sleeping revenge with incessant calling.
Behold! Behold! The sky is bursting!   385
The clouds are torn asunder!
Righteous Justice assists her cause!
It is Justice itself that pronounces our final sentence.
Princess! Alas! We see her standing before us!
No longer stained with the crimson of her own chaste blood   390
She has inherited a higher realm
Than this one, that must perish with us.
Her lovely face is transformed into a brilliant sun—
Her heart forgets the raw pains and is astonished with new joy.
She is covered with more beautiful flesh: 395
The noble life of her tender limbs
Defies all beauty that this great world
Contains within its boundaries.
She is resplendent in garments beside which snow isn't snow!
A throne is placed for her in the star spangled heavens.   400
Say nothing more of sparkling gems;
The crown that innocence places on her pearl-studded hair
Is far beyond anything treasured by Euphrates or Tigris [*all of Persia*].
Princess, alas! Who will mourn your fortune?
Except the Shah! Upon whom your fury runs high,   405
And flashes all around with bright flames!

Princess, alas! Princess! Alas, we burn!
Fire! Fire! Fire! Fire! Fire crackles in this heart!
We explode, we melt, set aflame with sulfur matches!
Princess, look! Princess, we confess   410
Without scepter, on our knees and wringing our hands,
That we aggrieved you unjustly,
That we committed a deed against you
That every age throughout all ages will call heinous.
Princess, demand revenge!   415
Alas! Alas! Alas!
Run! Kill the murderers who laid a hand on her!
Away, scepter, away! The Shah himself is guilty here!
And does heaven still have patience with us?
Is this hand paralyzed that once moved West and East?   420
Come, come my sword! We have power to punish ourself!
What is happening? Is Shiraz collapsing? Where are these
                                        weapons grating?
Why the sounding of trumpets?
Who is drawing swords to kill us?
The earth's surface roars and trembles!   425
What is it that rages behind us?
What? Or does vain fantasy terrify us?

(*Ghost of Catharine appears*)

Princess! Alas, we fall to our knees—
We, before whom the entire East has bowed down!
Forgive the one who shows his remorse with ever-bitter grief!   430
Catharine: Tyrant! It is heaven that seeks your ruin.
God doth not let innocent blood call out in vain.
Your laurel wreath withers! Your conquering is over.
Your lofty fame vanishes! Death already reaches out his hands
For your condemned head. Yet before you perish   435

You must behold your Persia standing in the flames of war,

Your house infested with the dark poison of discord,

Until, stained by infanticide and incest,

Unbearable to foe, friends, and yourself, you will hand over your life,

After the gruesome horror of pestilence, to the Judge.   440

(Ghost vanishes)

Shah Abbas: Justly so! Princess! Such is right! Attack our victor's wreath!

Make war on Persia's peace! Tear away whatever can protect us

With a mighty hand. Give up, now that you've paled,

The stubborn arrogance to which Abbas often succumbed.

On the altar of fire, the theater of your pain,   445

Let us ourselves be a sacrifice to ease your fury.

Yet there is no revenge more bitter, nor one that can grieve us more,

Than that we, my enemy, always must love you, even when

you are dead.

Notes appended by Gryphius to *Catharine of Georgia*

Brief Notes of ANDREAS GRYPHIUS about
Several Obscure References in his *CATHARINE.*

In the First Act:

l. 15 (See p. 159, above): Refers to the noteworthy words of Seneca in *de Tran-quilitate, chapter 11.* "What kingdom is there for which ruin and a trampling underfoot and the tyrant and the hangman are not in store? Nor are such things cut off by long intervals, but between the throne and bending at another's knees there is but an hour's space." Take a look at the whole chapter very carefully, keeping in mind that this tragedy [*Catharine of Georgia*] was written long before the regrettable demise of Charles Stuart, King of Great Britain. But when a crowned person of serene royal highness* read these lines about three years ago while in a state of deepest melancholy, she scratched these lines little by little with her fingernail in the same copy of *Catharine* in the hands of a friend of a relative.

[*Note*: Gryphius added this final sentence to Version B, 1663. The probable reference is Countess Elisabeth-Charlotte of the Palatinate (1597-1660), mother of Frederick William of Brandenburg (the "Great Elector") and sister-in-law of Elizabeth Stuart (1596-1662), the sister of Charles I, King of Great Britain. She was acquainted with Gryphius while at her widow's retreat in Crossen on the Oder through his elder brother Paul, who was superintendent there.]

l. 34 (See p. 160, above): Juvenal in the Tenth Satire: ". . . Death alone proclaims how small our poor human bodies are!"

[*Note*: Decimus Junius Juvenalis (58-140 A.D.) was a Roman orator and satirist. In fuller context, the citation of Juvenal reads: "One globe is all too little for the youth of Pella (Alexander the Great): he chafes uneasily within the narrow limits of the world, as though he were cooped up within the rocks of Gyara or the diminutive Seriphos; but yet when once he shall have entered the city fortified by the potter's art (Babylon), a sarcophagus will suffice him! *Death alone proclaims how small are our poor human bodies!*" (Emphasis added). Translation by G.G. Ramsay.]

l. 58 (See p. 161, above): Those who first ventured across the unknown ocean to the new world now and then named new coasts and islands after themselves, their masters, and their friends. Take a look at the maps of the *Strait of Magellan, Brazil, Florida, the Caribbean, Canada, etc.*

l. 60. (See p. 161, above): In Michael Florent van Langren's *Summary Outline of the Moon* specific places and parts are labeled with the names of the most famous princes and astronomers. There are, among others, the passages of honor, of labor, and so forth. In this connection I can't gloss over remembering the well-mannered words of her most serene highness and incomparable Princess Elisabeth, Countess of the Palatinate on the Rhine. When the same copper engraving was sent to her by its creator, she praised him for being so generous to her because although his king had deprived her of her paternal land inheritance, he (van Langren) had still granted her a place on the moon. Now she expected from him a means to take possession of the same. Shortly thereafter, van Langren's effort was completely overshadowed by the illustrious work of Johann Hevel. Which was soon followed by Eustatio Divini with his summary outlines in 1649 and Hieronymus Sirsalis in 1650, and finally, as far as I know, the work of Giovanni Battista Riccioli with the assistance of Francesco Maria Grimaldi (1651).

[*Note*: Michael Florent van Langren (1598-1675) was a third-generation Belgian cartographer and astronomer. His *Map of the Moon* appeared in 1645. Although he was the first to assign names to lunar features, few were widely accepted because they were so closely linked to the Spanish court, where he served as Royal Cosmographer and Mathematician to King Philip IV of Spain. (The moon crater *Langrenus* is one of the few names he proposed that is still in use.) Princess Elisabeth (1618-1680), a friend of Descartes and Leibniz, was the daughter of Frederick V of the Palatinate (1596-1632) and Elizabeth Stuart (1596-1662). Gryphius was possibly acquainted with the Danish mathematician Johann Hevel (1611-1687), since they both studied at the *Gymnasium* in Danzig (later Hevel was a councilman and mayor of Danzig). Both were also at the university in Leiden during 1634. Hevel published his results in *Selenographia* (1647), a work earning him the epithet "founder of lunar topography." Eustatio Divini (1610-1685) published a print of the moon (1649) that documented the advancements offered by his telescopes. Based on his observations of the full moon in March 1649 using two telescopes with micrometer eyepieces involving a grid of wires, he was able to draw moon spots in their exact position. Hieronymus Sirsalis (Gerolamo Sersale, 1584-1654) produced an image of the full moon made in July 1650 and published in 1651. Giovanni Battista Riccioli (1598-1671) devised the modern system of lunar nomenclature first published in his work *Almagestum novum* (*The New Almagest*), Bologna 1651. With over 1500 folio pages, Riccioli's two-volume work is divided into ten books that cover all topics related to contemporary astronomy, including illustrations drawn by his colleague, Francesco Maria Grimaldi (1618-1663). The majority of names and their allocated formations remain unchanged to the present date (*Mapping and Naming the Moon: A History of Lunar Cartography and Nomenclature*, Ewen A. Whitaker, Cambridge University Press, 1999, p. 61.) In citing Langren, Hevel, Eustatio Divini, Sirsalis, Riccioli and Grimaldi, Gryphius offered a complete and up-to-date summary of contemporary lunar cartography in his explanatory note.]

l. 107. (See p. 162, above): See Act III, Scene 1, in which the Queen relates her complete life story.

l. 128. (See p. 163, above): Tamaras is the biological son of Queen Catharine and is the ruling King in Georgia.

l. 305. (See p.169, above): Consider the poem about roses by Ausonius that is never praised highly enough (Idyll XIV).

[*Note*: Decimus Magnus Ausonius (c. 310-c. 395) was a Roman poet, rhetorician, statesman and scholar. The poem *De rosis nascentibus* ("On budding roses"), long attributed to Ausonius, includes the lines: "I saw such rose-beds as Paestum cultivates/ smiling all dewy at the new-risen harbinger of light./ Upon the frosted bushes a white pearl glimmered here and there,/ to perish at the earliest rays of day." The authorship of this poem, often listed among the collection of *Idylls* by Ausonius, has long been considered dubious. Translation by Hugh G. Evelyn White in Ausonius, Loeb Classical Library, Vol.2 (Cambridge, Massachusetts: Harvard University Press, 1985), p. 277.]

l. 332. (See p.170, above): Pearls signify tears according to dream interpreters. Pseudo-Salomon (*Somnia Salomnis*) Book 5: "Who came to the understanding himself to believe that bundles of pearls signify sadness or vigorous weeping." Chapter 14. Astrampsychus, in Oneirocrit: Οϊ μάργαροι δηλοῦσι δαχρύων ῥόον. Pearls signify streams of tears. Precisely these words are of the dream interpretation of Nicephorus, Patriarch of Constantinople. Although Achmet and Artemidorus are of a contrary opinion. See Cardanus in *Synesianis*. P.C. Hooft in the Biography of Henry the Great: "Oók had sy ghedrómt, (Queen Maria Medices) toen men besigh vvas met hare króón van ghesteente op te maken, dat alle de gróte demanten vvaren verandert in Perlen." (*"She had also dreamed [Queen Maria Medici] while they were busy with the hewing of her crown out of stone, that all the large diamonds were changed into pearls."*)

[*Note*: The *Somnia Salomnis*, a pseudo-Solomon text, appeared in this first century AD Jewish-Greek literary tradition. Astrampsychus is a legendary priest, magician, and poet from Egypt or Persia. Attributed to him are the *Sortes Astrampsychi* (*The Lots of Astrampsychus*, a third century AD Greek-language Roman oracle book), an astrological book, a love spell, and a dream book. The latter, *Oneirocritica*, deals with the interpretation of dreams in 101 Greek iambic verses: verse 55 ("Pearls are symbols of a flood of tears") is the verse to which Gryphius refers. The work of Astrampsychus was republished by

Johannes Meursius (1579-1639) as *Astrampsychi Oneirocrition* (Leiden, 1608 and 1630). Nicephorus Gregorus (1295-1360) was a Byzantine astronomer, historian and scholar. His writings include commentaries on Senesius' treatise on dreams (see below). The works on dream interpretation by Achmet, son of Sereimi (Ahmad Ibn Sīrīn 633-728) and Artemidorus Daldianus (2nd century), together with those of Astrampsychus and Nicephorus, were published by Nicolas Rigault (1577-1654) in Paris as a four-part edition with Greek and Latin texts in parallel columns: *Artemodpro Daldiani & Achmetis Sereimi f. Oneirocritica. Astrampsychi & Nicephori versus etiam Oneirocritici... Lutetiae (Paris), 1603.* Hieronymus Cardanus (1501-1576), an Italian doctor, mathematician and philosopher, wrote *Explicatio somniorum synesiorum*, to elucidate the fifth century work *De insomniis (On Dreams)* by Synesius of Cyrene (c .373-c. 413), a Greek bishop of Ptolemais in the Libyan Pentapolis. Pieter Corneliszoon Hooft (1581-1647), renowned Dutch poet and historian, first published his biography of the French King Henry IV *Hendrik de Grote* in 1626, with six further editions by 1664 (Amsterdam)].

l. 442. (See p. 173, above): Tiflis. Another royal residence city in Armenia.

[*Note*: In several instances Gryphius refers to Georgia/Gurgistan as Armenia (see his *Content* summary preceding the printed drama, in which he refers to "Catharine, Queen of Georgia in Armenia"). Although some Iberian territories, namely the southern and south-eastern provinces, were briefly conquered by the Kingdom of Armenia in 189 BC, Georgia has never been a part of neighboring Armenia. On the contrary, in 1124 the Georgians conquered a large portion of Armenia and the Georgian Kind David IV ("David the Builder," 1073-1125) also became the official king of the Armenians, incorporating Northern Armenia into the lands of the Georgian Crown. During the reign of Queen Tamar (1166-1213), previously Turkish-controlled Southern Armenia also came under Georgian control. Armenia remained a part of the Georgian empire before the Mongol invasions (1236 ff.). Following St. Lazare, Gryphius uses the spelling *Tefflis* for the royal city in Kartli, formerly Iberia. See additional comments in *The Historical Source*, above, pp. 142-45.]

l.580. (See p. 177, above): See lines 269, 270 and following in Act III.

[*Note:* Gryphius here draws attention to *Abbas'* similar treacherous deceit via the use of a messenger to "dishonorably kill one prince by the other" when *Abbas* instigates a potentially deadly wedding dispute between the Princes Alovassa and Tamaras in Act III, 269 ff. (see p. 212 above).]

l. 744. (See p. 183, above): Isfahan: The royal capital city in Persia that has been extensively described by many and has been highlighted on account of its splendid incomparability.

In the Second Act:

l. 28. (See p.190, above): Bajazeth. His story is more than well-known and has been described in detail by Leunclavius and others.

[*Note*: Johann Löwenklau (1533-1593), a German legal scholar, classicist, and historian born in Westphalia, traveled widely in Europe and the Middle East, visiting numerous royal courts. He lived in Turkey for many years prior to his death in Vienna. He is the Latin translator (from the Greek) of Book 2 by Achmet, son of Sereimi (Ahmad Ibn Sīrīn 633-728) in the *Oneocritici* of Nicolas Rigault (Paris, 1603), a work that he had previously published in a separate edition in Frankfurt am Main, 1577. (See Explanatory note to I, 332, above.) Löwenklau's account of the Turkish Emperor Bajazeth, who came to power in 1389, appears in Book 6 of his *Historiae Musulmanae Turcorum, De Monumentis Ipsorum Exscriptae,* Frankfurt/M. 1591 (See German edition: *Hansen Löwenklaus Neue Chronika türkischer Nation* Frankfurt/M 1590, 1595*).* Christopher Marlowe's lively portrayal of Bajazeth's fate in Part I of Tamburlaine (written c. 1587, first printed 1605) depicts the clashing of Persian-Turkish powers that also lies at the political heart of Gryphius' *Catharine* and would most likely be among his referenced "others."]

l. 71 (See p.191, above): Chaldar: formery Chaldäa, famous enough from the ancients as well as from the holy scriptures.

[*Note*: Babylonian Chaldea appears in the Old Testament and in the writing of both Greek and Roman historians (e.g., Strabo, Horace, Cicero, etc.). Since the political and military might of Chaldea ended when the last king of Babylon was deposed by the Persians under Cyrus II in 539 BC, *Shah Abbas'* dramatic reference to this region of lower Mesopotamia serves to imply the broad geographic spread of his conquests rather than an actual physical encounter with them.]

l. 136 (See p.194, above): Volga. The famous river in Russia, which some consider to be the Ptolemaic Rha, runs between the people of Russia and the Tartars into the Caspian Sea. Also line 136 The Phrat River, earlier name of the Euphrates River, flows between Turkey and Persia into the Persian Gulf, or the El Catif Sea.

l. 152 (See p.194, above): The usual title with which the Russian honor their grand prince. According to some it is derived from the Latin CAESAR.

l. 297 (See p. 199, above): The hero. This is Mohammed II, who conquered Trabzon and Constantinople, which the Turks call Istanbul.

[*Note*: Mohammed II (1432-1481), Sultan of Turkey (1451-1481), conquered Constantinople in 1453. In 1461 he conquered Trabzon (formerly Trebizond), which is located on the Black Sea in the northeast region of Turkey.]

l. 300 (See p. 199, above): Irene: This sad and horrible murder is told by various authors: the author Icariae has described it in detail, but most superlative of all is Ludovicus Cellotius, S.J. in his extremely beautiful Latin poem, which, along with others, was published with his poetic works.

[*Note*: The collected works of Cellotius (1588-1658) appear in *Ludovici Cellotii Pariensis et Societ. Jesu Opera poetice*, Paris, 1630.]

l. 380 (See p. 202, above): All books are filled with the drastic and horrifying death penalties of ancient and modern Persians. See Purchas and the Persian journeys of Olearius. The description by the delegation that was sent to Shah Abbas by Rudolph II reports that Shah Abbas, in the presence of the Ambassador himself, struck a prisoner dead with his own hand.

[*Note*: The English cleric Samuel Purchas (1577? -1626) first published *Purchas His Pilgrimage: or Relations of the World and the Religions observed in all Ages and Places discovered, from the Creation unto this Present* (London, 1613). His four volume collection *Hakluytus Posthumus, or Purchas His Pilgrimes* (*London, 1624, 1626*) incorporated *The Principal Navigations* (1589) of Richard Hakluyt (1552-1616). Gryphius was most likely acquainted with the complete works of Samuel Purchas in the Dutch translation published in 1655. The *New Oriental Travelogue* (*Neue Orientalische Reisebeschreibung*) of Adam Olearius (1603-1671) appeared in 1647 (2nd edition 1656). Rudolph II (1552-1612) was Holy Roman Emperor (1576-1612).]

In the Third Act:

l. 490 (See p. 220, above): Where they build towers out of skulls. Near Sirvan the remains can be found of a tower built of stones and the skulls of those felled noblemen whom the king in Persia conquered and had immured as a memorial. See the *Journey* of Johann Cartwight [sic]. Also the same of Anthony Jenkinson in his second journey in Persia made in the year 1562. Although several are of the opinion that he modified his anger and instead of human heads had the heads of dogs set in (the tower).

[*Note*: John Cartwright describes the tower of skulls in *The Preacher Travels to the Confines of the East Indies through Syria* (London, 1611). Samuel Purchas includes Cartwright's report (*The Journey of John Cartwright*) in his *Pilgrims*. Also included in the collections of both Hakluyt and Purchas was the first British account of travel in Persia, a trade report written for the Muscovy Company by Anthony Jenkinson (1529-1610/11).]

l. 495 (See p. 220, above): There the chaste princess. Ameleke Kanna, the daughter of a Persian king, took her own life with a knife not far from Sirvan, when she, after swearing an oath of chastity, was forced by her father to marry a Tartar prince. Because of this, the Persians founded in her memory a cloister for young women, in which her demise is commemorated near her grave annually by the virgins of this country. See Cartwight's [sic] *Travels*.

[*Note*: In the lines following his description of the tower near Sirvan, Cartwright describes castle ruins "about a mile" beyond. He writes: "And a little further off, was a Nunnery most sumptuously builded, wherein was buried (as they told us) the body of *Ameleke Canna*, the Kings Daughter, who slew herself with a knife, for that her Father would have forced her (shee professing chastity) to have married with a Prince of Tartary: upon which occasion the Virgins of this Countrey doe resort thither once a yeere to lament her death." (*The Journey of John Cartwright* in *Purchas His Pilgrimes* (London, 1626), I. B.9, Ch. 4, p. 1428.]

Gryphius did not append any notes about "Obscure References"
to the Fourth or Fifth Acts of *Catharine of Georgia*.

ILLUSTRATIONS

Eight copperplate illustrations were made by Gregor Bieber, artist, and Johan Using, engraver, to commemorate the festival production of Gryphius' *Catharine of Georgia* at the Court of Duke Christian von Wohlau in 1655.

Title page of the eight engravings made for the festival production in 1655

Relevant program text is affixed to a pillar, with Queen Catharine and Shah Abbas positioned to reflect their respective roles: the Queen ignores Abbas' defiant offer of an earthly crown, instead directing her gaze towards heaven where a cherub-like messenger offers the martyr's palm and eternal crown.

Catharine of Georgia, Act I, Prologue of Eternity

Following the explicit staging directions offered by Gryphius, this first engraving to depict a scene from the *Trauerspiel* presents a stage "strewn with corpses, crowns, scepters, swords, and other insignia of earthly vanity. Heaven is revealed above the stage; hell, below. Eternity descends from heaven and comes to rest on the stage." In the final lines of an extensive monolog, Eternity describes her return ascent to heaven: "Theater of mortality, farewell! I am borne away on my throne." (*Catharine* I, 81)

Catharine of Georgia, Act I, Scene 2

In a palace garden of Shiraz, Demetrius and Procopius, two Ambassadors from Georgia, discuss the plan to free Queen Catharine via the request from the Russian Ambassador.

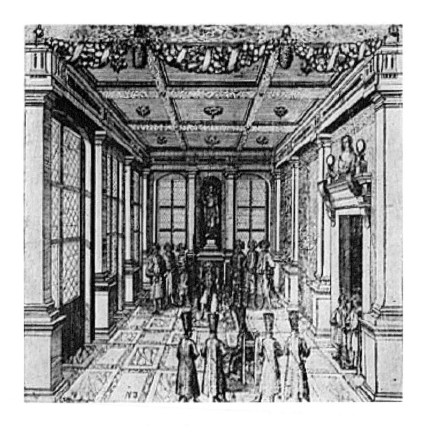

Catharine of Georgia, Act II, Scene 3

Shah Abbas and Princes of Persia meet with the Russian Ambassador in the royal audience hall.

Catharine of Georgia, Act III, Scene 3

In this scene, which Gryphius describes as set in "the royal pleasure garden," Imanculi, one of two Privy Councilors to Shah Abbas, receives from him the fatal document that he must present to the Queen to elicit her final decision regarding the Shah's proposal.

Catharine of Georgia, Chorus of the Virtues, Death and Love following Act IV

The Virtues (see background) introduce and conclude the verbal contest between Death and Love, depicted here with the emblematic bows, arrows, and torches to which they refer.

Catharine of Georgia, Act V, Scene 1

The engraving depicts the torture of Queen Catharine as described in the drama in great detail but not actually carried out on stage.

Catharine of Georgia, Act V, Final Scene

Crazed with sorrow and rage at his final act against Queen Catharine, Shah Abbas envisions the martyred Queen even before she appears as a ghost on stage, holding the martyr's palm of victory over death.

SELECT ANNOTATED BIBLIOGRAPHY

1. Editions of *Leo Armenius* and *Catharine of Georgia*

Gryphius, Andreas. *Gesamtausgabe der deutschsprachigen Werke*. Eds. Marian Syrocki and Hugh Powell. Neudrucke deutscher Literaturwerke. 8 vols. Tübingen: Niemeyer, 1963-72.

> *Leo Armenius* appears in volume V; *Catharine of Georgia* appears in Volume VI. Extensive bibliographic information and editorial commentary supplement both dramatic texts.

---. *Catharina von Georgien. Abdruck der Ausgabe von 1663 mit den Lesarten von 1657*. Ed. Willi Flemming. 4th rev. ed. Tübingen: Niemeyer, 1968.

> Flemming's pioneer publication of the 1663 version of *Catharina* in 1928 was the first and remains the only readily available copy of Gryphius' final 1663 text as used for my English translation. The first edition of this seminal publication contributed to the early twentieth-century re-awakening of interest in Gryphius and German Baroque literature. In addition to the annotated dramatic text, it offers key biographical insights and updated critical commentary in a brief but comprehensive introduction. 107 pages.

---. *Catharina von Georgien. Trauerspiel*. Updated bibl. Ed. Alois M. Haas. Reclams Universal-Bibliothek Nr. 9751. Stuttgart: Reclam, 2008.

> This bibliographically updated version of the original 1975 edition provides an inexpensive copy of the 1657 version of Gryphius' second historical tragedy. Footnotes identify changes made by Gryphius in his revised

1663 version, upon which my English translation is based. Bibliographic references include both modern editions of the tragedy and literary criticism of *Catharine* as well as general studies of Gryphius. Editorial commentary includes information about the drama's sources and history together with a narrative that identifies key developments in literary criticism regarding the play. 159 pages.

---. *Catharina von Georgien: Sprachlich modernisierter Text der Erstfassung von 1657.* Eds. J.E. Oyler and A.H. Schulze. Bern: Peter Lang, 1978.

This instructive guide and modernized German text of *Catharine* assists readers in approaching the original German text of Gryphius. A divided bibliography identifies 1) recent editions of *Catharina*, 2) works pertaining to *Catharina* and 3) general literature regarding works of Andreas Gryphius. 179 pages.

---. *Leo Armenius. Trauerspiel.* Bibl. updated 1996. Ed. Peter. Rusterholz Reclams Universal-Bibliothek Nr.7960. Stuttgart: Reclam, 2009.

This readily available edition of Gryphius' first historical tragedy includes the German version of Cedrenus (historical source used by Gryphius) as it appeared in Willi Harring's 1907 study (see Harring entry below, p. 281), together with useful notes, commentary, and a bibliography provided by the editor. 147 pages.

---. *Leo Armenius."* Trans. Janifer Gerl Stackhouse. *German Theater Before 1750.* Ed. Gerald Gillespie. The German Library, Vol. 8. New York: Continuum, 1992. 99-137.

This first published English translation of selected excerpts from *Leo Armenius* introduces Gryphius as one of six pre-1750 German dramatists presented in English through sample translations from their dramatic works. 244 pages.

2. Critical Works and Sources in English ·

Benjamin, Walter. *The Origin of German Tragic Drama*. Trans. John Osborne. London: Verso, 2009.

First appearing in 1925, Benjamin's study of the baroque *Trauerspiel* or "mourning play" exhibits the difficult and esoteric qualities of thought that later defined his modern engagement with literature, aesthetics, and philosophy. In translation, his investigation of 16th and 17th century German dramatists, along with Shakespeare and Calderón, often provides a first introduction to Gryphius for non-readers of German. 256 pages.

Blunt, Wilfrid. *Pietro's Pilgrimage: A Journey to India and Back at the Beginning of the Seventeenth Century*. London: J. Barrie, 1953.

Blunt offers rare insight into the eastward travels (*Viaggi*) of voyagers in the early seventeenth century primarily through his retelling of the letters written by Pietro della Valle. In addition to this first-hand account of the life, actions, and unpredictable personality of Shah Abbas I, Blunt includes lesser-known information about the imprisoned Queen Catharine of Georgia in selections from letters written during della Valle's simultaneous residence in Shiraz (June-August, 1622). 320 pages.

Flannery, John M. *The Mission of the Portuguese Augustinians to Persia and Beyond (1602-1747)*. Studies in Christian Mission 4. Leiden and Boston: Brill, 2013.

In the context of his history of the Portuguese Augustinians' 1602-1747 mission to Persia and India, Flannery describes the complicated relationship of Shah Abbas I with various Christian groups that provides new background information to the better known report of Pietro della Valle (see Pietro della Valle, below, pp. 284-85). His descriptions inform the reader interested in additional facts that might have been known to Gryphius when he articulated the role of Ambrose as the final religious attendant of Queen Catharine. Flannery's study also offers new assessments of political relationships and historical events related to the martyrdom of the Georgian queen. 128 pages.

Gillespie, Gerald. "Time and Eternity in Andreas Gryphius' *Catharina von Georgien*" in *Garden and Labyrinth of Time: Studies in Renaissance and Baroque Literature*, 169-91. New York: Peter Lang, 1988.

Gillespie's English translation and updated revision of his earlier study "Andreas Gryphius' *Catharina von Georgien* als Geschichtsdrama" (Ed. Elfriede Neubuhr. Darmstadt: Wissenschaftliche Buchgesellschaft, 1980. 85-107) appears in this book as the seventh chapter of twelve. In its entirety, this thoroughly documented book delves with great curiosity and insight into diverse and often lesser known aspects of Renaissance ideals and Baroque originality. In his *Catharina* chapter, Gillespie demonstrates how Gryphius entwines the personal qualities and political roles of his protagonists within diverse near-contemporary political phenomena to portray "the inner world of heart, mind, and soul and the outer world of history as temporality" (p. 184). This, in sum, produces a new image in the *Catharine* play of "the human being who exists *only* in time's toils" (p. 188). 335 pages.

Hardin, James N., ed. *Translation and Translation Theory in Seventeenth-Century Germany* (*Daphnis: Zeitschrift für mittlere deutsche Literatur*, 21.1). Amsterdam and Atlanta: Rodopi, 1992.

Hardin's preface summarizes the papers in this collection that were presented at the 1990 Chicago meeting of the Society for Renaissance and Baroque Literature, all of which elucidate both famous and lesser-known German literary translators and their work. His lament regarding "the lack of first-rate English translations of German seventeenth-century literature" (p. 2) holds true to the present day and also serves to inspire my current, if humble, attempt to remediate this situation. 156 pages.

Juvenal and Persius. *Juvenal and Persius with an English Translation by George Gilbert Ramsay.* London and New York: William Heinemann and G. P. Putnam's Sons, 1928.

> This volume contains all sixteen satires by Juvenal together with translations from the Latin by G.G. Ramsay. Ramsay's English version of Satire X, the satire cited by Gryphius in his explanatory note to *Catharine*, Act I, line 34, is entitled "The Vanity of Human Wishes." Now in the public domain, the work is readily available online. 415 pages.

Metzger, Erika A. and Michael M. Metzger. *Reading Andreas Gryphius: Critical Trends 1664-1993.* Columbia, S.C.: Camden House, 1994.

> The authors lead the reader on a chronological path through multiple and diverse critical responses regarding the work of Andreas Gryphius from his death in 1664 until publication of their book in 1993. In this pioneering effort to clarify changing trends in Gryphius criticism and scholarship for the English-speaking world, they supplement their concise but cogent analysis of specific critics and critical trends with a useful bibliography that offers separate chronological listings both of published works by Gryphius (1634-1994) and of critical works cited (1653-1994). 155 pages.

Newman, Jane O. *Benjamin's Library: Modernity, Nation, and the Baroque.* Ithaca: Cornell University Press, 2011.

> In the chapter "Allegory, Emblems, and Gryphius' *Catharina von Georgien*" (pp. 170-84), Newman scrutinizes how Walter Benjamin recognized Gryphius' dependence on these literary devices to construct his *Trauerspiele* as "modern tragic dramas" or "mourning plays." Within the broader context of her analysis regarding developing historical and national views of the German Baroque, Newman focuses here on interpretations of the changing *crown* emblem that weaves through the text and staging of *Catharine*. 237 pages.

Perur, Srinath. "Hunting for a Georgian Queen in Goa - The Travelling Hand: A 17th Century Royal Martyr, Portuguese Friars, a Ruined Augustine Church and a Search that Stretched on for over 25 years!" *The Mint on Sunday,* Updated 11 April 2016. Available online.

> Perur's journalistic coverage of recent events regarding the remains of Queen Catharine of Georgia provides up-to-date information on a centuries-old dilemma that also attests to continued and current international interest in the fate of the Georgian queen.

Powell, Hugh. "Observations on the Erudition of Andreas Gryphius." *Orbis Litterarum* 25.1-2 (1970): 115-125.

> Powell clarifies how the poet-dramatist's comprehensive knowledge of multiple languages and his exposure to a wide variety of influences through study, reading, and travel underlie his acquisition of an encyclopedic knowledge that informs all of his work.

Sommerstein, Alan H., and Isabelle C Torrance. *Oaths and Swearing in Ancient Greece.* Berlin and Boston: Walter de Gruyter, 2014.

> Source of information regarding false oath sworn to Hippias as cited in *Leo Armenius*, II, 291 (See footnote 46, p. 62 above). 473 pages.

Spahr, Blake Lee. *Andreas Gryphius: A Modern Perspective.* Columbia, S.C.: Camden House, 1993.

> Spahr's erudite but very approachable presentation of Gryphius' life and works leads the reader through critical analyses of his poetry, tragedies, comedy, celebratory plays, translations, and other works. A comprehensive bibliography completes this useful book. 168 pages.

Stackhouse, Janifer Gerl. *The Constructive Art of Gryphius' Historical Trage-dies.* Berner Beiträge zur Barockgermanistik 6. Bern: Lang, 1986.

> The author examines three conventional dramatic forms (choruses, poeticized monologs, and visionary phenomena) to clarify how Gryphius worked with a variety of source materials to construct artistically his four historical tragedies that would establish a procedural mode of drama construction followed in Germany until the end of his century. This book includes a list of works cited. 194 pages.

Whitaker, Ewen A. *Mapping and Naming the Moon: A History of Lunar Cartography and Nomenclature.* Cambridge [U.K] and New York: Cambridge University Press, 1999.

> Ewen A. Whitaker (1922-2016) played a pivotal role in lunar map production that enabled NASA's first lunar missions and the selection of landing sites for the Surveyor and Apollo missions. His lifelong research in the history of lunar selenography (mapping surface features of the noon) and nomenclature presented in this summative work testifies to the thoroughness and accuracy of Gryphius' knowledge as presented in his explanatory note to *Catharine,* Act I, line 58. 242 pages.

White, Hugh G. Evelyn, trans. Ausonius. Loeb Classical Library, Vol. 2. Cambridge, Massachusetts: Harvard University Press, 1985.

> The Appendix of this volume contains White's English translation from 1921 of "On budding roses" (*De rosis nascentibus),* the renowned poem long attributed to Decimus Magnus Ausonius (c.310 - c.395), to which Gryphius refers in his notes to *Catharine,* I.305. As noted by White (p. 271), however, the poem's authorship is unclear and in some manuscripts is erroneously attributed to Virgil. 367 pages.

Wiggin, Bethany. "Staging Shi'ites in Silesia: Andreas Gryphius's *Catharina von Georgien.*" *The German Quarterly* 83.1 (Winter 2010): 1-18.

> Wiggin's inclusion of illustrations from the 1656 expanded edition of Adam Olearius' travels in Russia and Persia (1647) and from the Bieber/ Using engravings of a 1655 production of Gryphius' *Catharina* (Act II, Scene 3: see above, p. 268) provides useful visual information that supplements her discussion of how Gryphius sought to portray stark cultural differences among the Persian, Russian, and Georgian characters in his *Catharine* tragedy.

3. Critical Works and Sources in Languages other than English

Bodin, Jean. *De la démonomanie des sorciers*, 4th ed., Paris: Paul Frellon, 1598.

> The text of my English translation of Bodin's "horrible tale" (see above, p. 131) appears in this 1598 French edition of his work on p. 155.

Flemming, Willi. *Andreas Gryphius: Eine Monographie.* Stuttgart: Kohlhammer, 1965.

> Flemming crowns his unique lifelong Gryphius scholarship in this comprehensive and insightful capstone monograph. Useful for students and scholars alike, it provides a treasure trove of information about the Silesian poet/dramatist and his works. 231 pages.

Goethe, Johann Wolfgang von. *Werke.* Ed. Erich Trunz. 7th ed. 14 vols. Hamburg: Christian Wegner, 1965.

> Goethe recaps episodes from Pietro della Valle's travel diary to Persia and India in notes written to clarify how this work influenced his *Westöstlicher Divan / West-Eastern Divan* (i.e., Collection of Poetry). He concludes his detailed report on della Valle with an apology for having included so much information even as he acknowledges that della Valle's powerful

presentation "first and most clearly" introduced him to those unusual characteristics of the Orient that led to his Divan poetry. *Werke*, II, 228-42.

Harring, Willi. *Andreas Gryphius und das Drama der Jesuiten.* Halle: Niemeyer, 1907.

Harring's thorough comparison of the *Leo Armenius* tragedies by Joseph Simon and Andreas Gryphius (pp. 53-74) includes the historical account of Cedrenus, the primary source of both dramatists (pp. 53-58) and a scene-by-scene summary of Simon's Latin play (pp. 561-66), with the Jesuit's entire original Latin play included in an appendix (pp. 74-126). Harring convincingly demonstrates that Gryphius borrowed many elements from the conjuration scene appearing in Ludovicus Cellotius' 1630 drama *Sapor admonitus* (IV, 13) for his *Leo* tragedy (IV.2), including the name *Iamblichus* (p. 42-48). 178 pages.

Homan, Johann Baptist. *Map of the Persian Empire and all of its Provinces (Imperii Persici inomnes suas provincas nova tabula geographica).* Nuremberg: n.p., c. 1724.

Homan's map clarifies the geo-political terminology for the region between the Black Sea and the Caspian Sea as denoted by Gryphius in his *Catharine* tragedy. The map identifies the greater region of Caucasian Iberia, together with Armenia, Georgia, Gurgistan, and the city of Tiflis. Map held by the Library of Congress available online at https://www.loc.gov/item/2004629239/. Also see above, p. 144.

Kaminski, Nicola. *Andreas Gryphius.* Stuttgart: Reclam, 1998.

Kaminski's comprehensive review of Gryphius' life and works includes critical analyses of *Leo Armenius* and *Catharine of Georgia* with reference to recent Gryphius scholarship before 1997. Complete bibliography, 264 pages.

Kaminski, Nicola and Schütze, Robert, editors. *Gryphius Handbuch*. Berlin and Boston: Walter de Gruyter, 2016.

> This substantial volume of almost a thousand pages offers a comprehensive selection of critical essays that detail the life, work, critical aspects of the work, and the reception of Andreas Gryphius from the seventeenth through the twentieth centuries. Extensive bibliographies complete this massive but useful compilation for students and scholars alike. 933 pages.

Kayser, Wolfgang. *Kleine deutsche Versschule*. 9th ed. Bern and Munich: A. Francke, 1962.

> Kayser leads the reader through a concise but comprehensive history of verse forms in German poetry that includes useful sample illustrations of the Alexandrine line (as favored by Gryphius) in this succinct volume of 123 pages.

Kircher, Athanasius. *Oedipus Aegyptiacus*. 3 vols. Rome, 1652-54.

> Kircher's three-volume work presents esoteric text and illustrations based on his renowned and eclectic late-Renaissance scholarship. His sources included Chaldean astrology, Hebrew Kabbalah, Greek and Latin mythology, Pythagorean mathematics, and Arabian alchemy. An original copy of *Pantheon Hebraeorum* is available online on Google Books. Scroll to Chapter XV, p. 334, for the image described by Gryphius in his explanatory notes to *Leo Armenius*, IV.81. Also see above, pp. 128-30.

Leubscher, M. Johannes Theodor. *Ad Virum Nobilissimum et Amplissimum Christianum Gryphius, Gymnasii apud Vratislavienses Magdalenaei Rectorem & Professorem Celeberrimum . . . Socerum summa observantia Sancte Venerandum, De Claris Gryphiis Schediasma*. Brigae Silesiorum (Brieg, current Brzeg, Poland): G. Gründerum: 1702. Reprinted as "Andreas Gryphius [=De claris Gryphiis Schediasma Brigae Silesiorum] (1702) in *Text + Kritik* 7/8 (Mar.1980): 12-23.

This second biography of Andreas Gryphius, written almost forty years after the poet's death, appears in the context of Leubscher's panegyric written for his father-in-law, Christian Gryphius, the eldest son of Andreas Gryphius, on the occasion of Christian's 54th birthday. Leubscher taught at the Magdalene Gymnasium in Breslau, where Christian Gryphius then served as head. He utilized personal anecdotes related by Christian, material from the poet's own diary, and the earlier published biography of Stosch (see entry below) to craft a monument of praise for the unrivaled artistic, legal, and scholarly works of the celebrant's father.

Malingre, Claude. *Histoires tragiques de notre temps.* Paris: Collet, 1635, and Rouen: Davé and Ferrand, 1641.

Malingre included his account of Queen Catharine of Georgia as the sixteenth narrative in his collection of short biographies first published in 1635. Although his text served as the primary source for the historical, political, and geographical details taken up by Gryphius in his *Catharine* drama, it is the only primary dramatic source of any of his tragedies that Gryphius does not acknowledge in his attached explanatory notes. 890 pages.

Stieff, Christian. *Schlesisches Historisches Labyrinth Oder Kurtzgefaste Sammlung Von hundert Historien Allerhand denckwürdiger Nahmen / Oerter / Personen / Gebräuche / Solennitäten und Begebenheiten In Schlesien Aus den weitläufftigen gedruckten Chronicken und vielen geschriebenen Uhrkunden [...] mit vielfältigen neuen Beyträgen zu der alten und neuen Schlesischen Historie / verfertiget.* Breslau and Leipzig, 1737. Reprinted in "Andreae Gryphii Lebens-Lauff." *Text + Kritik* 7/8 (March 1980): 24-31.

The final of three early Gryphius biographers, Stieff borrowed heavily, as he acknowledged, from the earlier biographies of Stosch and Leubscher. As a favorite pupil of Christian Gryphius, son of Andreas, Stieff likewise served as head of the Magdalene Gymnasium in Breslau. In "Andreae Gryphii Lebens-Lauff," the final of one hundred chapters in a collection that presents the biographies of one hundred learned Silesians, Stieff endeavors to confirm Gryphius' enduring place in European literary history and thereby validate Silesia's cultural importance.

Stosch, Balthasar Sigismund von. *Last- und Ehren- auch Daher immerbleibende Danck- und Denk-Säule / Bey vollbrachter Leichbestattung Des weiland Wol-Edlen / Groß-Achtbahren und Hoch-gelehrten Herrn Andreae Gryphii.* Glogau: n.p., 1665, and Leipzig: Schlovien, 1683. Reprinted as "Stosch, Balthasar Sigismund von, "Danck und Denck-Seule des Andreae Gryphii (Leipzig: Johann-Erich Hahn, 1665)" in *Text + Kritik* 7/8 (March 1980): 2-11.

The first of three early Gryphius biographies, printed one year after Balthasar Sigismund von Stosch (1635-1677), at the age of twenty-seven, delivered his eulogy at the poet's funeral in the Evangelical Lutheran Church of Glogau. Stosch combined praise and consolation as rhetorical guides to his eulogy that begins with an extensive, poeticized tribute to the famous poet followed by a *curriculum vitae* that balances his acknowledged achievements with lesser known information garnered by Stosch from Gryphius' own handwritten diary.

Susini, Eugène. "Claude Malingre, Sieur De Saint-Lazare, et son Histoire de Catherine de Géorgie." *Éudes Germaniques* 23 (1968): 37-53.

Susini includes the entire text of the original French version by Claude Malingre in this article that establishes Malingre's narrative as the primary source relied upon by Gryphius for his *Catharine* drama.

Valle, Pietro della. *Della conditioni die Abbàs Rè di Persia.* Venice: F. Baba, 1628. 93+ pages.

This first of della Valle's published reports based on his six years in Persia features information about his experiences resulting from close contact with Shah Abbas over this extended period and also includes his commentary on the imprisonment of Queen Catharine. Gryphius probably read this report by della Valle in 1646 while visiting in Rome. Della Valle's most remarkable details about Shah Abbas, however, appear in his eye-witness accounts recorded in the letters he sent home to Italy during his lengthy travels in Turkey, Egypt, the Levant, Persia, and the west coast of India. (1614-1626). These thirty-six letters, containing more than a million words, were not published until *after* Gryphius had finished *Catharine* (1647): Vol. I of the letters first appeared in 1650, with Vols. II and III following in 1658.

APPENDIX

Translator's Notes

Reading Gryphius

Until now audiences throughout the English-speaking world or those unfamiliar with seventeenth century German have lacked direct access to reading a play by Andreas Gryphius. While descriptions of his contribution by both critics and defenders have surfaced over time, from Johann Christoph Gottsched (1700-1766) and August Wilhelm Schlegel (1767-1845) to Johann Wolfgang von Goethe (1749-1832) and Günter Grass (1927-2015), from brief summaries in reference books and German literary histories to countless online references, relatively few have *read* the actual work of Gryphius. *Reading* an original play instead of only reading *about* it enables the reader to access, explore, experience, and appreciate this key figure of seventeenth-century German literature. Unencumbered by the barrier of a foreign language, the reader can understand the unfamiliar and often confusing geographical, historical, and political background information necessary to appreciate his plays. Thus assisted, the reader can encounter firsthand how the poet as dramatist employed emblematic forms, symbolic imagery, and lyrical composition to proclaim his ethical and spiritual beliefs.

I have chosen to translate the third and final versions of *Leo Armenius* and *Catharine of Georgia* as published by Gryphius in 1663 because I believe they best reflect both his intent and his poetic mastery. Because many, if not most, currently available German editions offer earlier "unpolished" versions of the plays, it is important that readers of my English translations be aware of his many textual emendations, corrections, and additions that appear only in the 1663 or

"C" versions. Although an exact accounting of such changes would interrupt the readability of my translations, I have provided footnotes to indicate major additions of new material (lines) or characters not present in earlier versions of the plays.

Translating the Historical Tragedies of Andreas Gryphius

The compelling spirit and powerful grasp of the German language that Gryphius summoned to write his four historical tragedies reveal his mastery of meter and rhyme that first brought wide recognition to his earlier lyric poetry. In addition, it underlies some of the challenges faced when attempting to translate his work from the original German.

From the start, my objective has been to make difficult German text less difficult for those encountering seventeenth-century German for the first time and to make the dramatic voice of Gryphius heard by those who do not read German at all. I have followed a translation theory that contains both formal and dynamic approaches. For those dramatic lines where contextual ideas or the transfer of specific information requires a clear and precise rendering of the German into English, my approach seeks to relate fully the content and complete thought (formal approach). However, for other dramatic lines that may contain ideas, idioms, or expressions that can benefit from creative and resourceful insight, I have tried to supply the most appropriate and natural imaginative English words (dynamic approach). Throughout my translations, the mutability rate of great languages underlies my attempt to reach an intelligent compromise between contemporary international usage of English and some of the special qualities and terms in English that are closer to the cultural age out of which I am translating. In many respects I have followed the explicit rules for translation offered by Johann Burckhard Mencke (1674-1732) in his *Ernsthafte Gedichte* (*Solemn Poetry*), first published in 1706. Mencke supplied the literary translator with five concrete suggestions: "1) be clear 2) consider the matter being translated: if it is scientific then it must be exact, if literature it must be natural . . . 3) what one may omit and add—emendations are permitted but should not be obvious 4) how to deal with foreign names and idioms, proverbs etc. 5) the creative aspect of translation is touched on, the fact that imagination is required." [73]

In my attempt to clarify the content and meaning of the plays and, above all, to make reading them a pleasant and stress-free experience, I have eschewed the attempt to mold my translation into Gryphius' own use of meter and rhyme schemes, which primarily involve his distinctive rhymed *Alexandrines*. This 12-syllable meter that usually appeared in rhymed couplets was the most popular form of verse in German Baroque poetry. The term *Alexandrine* originates from the rhymed metrical scheme used by the French poet Ronsard in his *Song of Alexander*. Two major influences converged to align Gryphius with the Alexandrine form that he favored in both his lyric poetry and his dramas. On the one hand, non-Germanic literary forms prevalent in contemporary Europe exerted a profound, if not definitive, influence on the options available to Gryphius. By the time he began to write lyric poetry and to translate modern European dramas into the German language, French and Dutch models had introduced him to the Alexandrine form that is prevalent from his earliest to his most mature writing. Simultaneously, a new national identity of preferred German literary style affirmed his adoption of the Alexandrine line, first for his lyric poetry and subsequently throughout his dramatic works. Like all German poets of the mid-seventeenth century, Gryphius employed and developed the Alexandrine form as canonized by Martin Opitz (1597-1639), the renowned "father of German lyric," in his influential *Buch von der deutschen Poeterei (Book about German Poetry),* first published in 1624. Opitz, himself a poet laureate of Germany, died of the plague before he could witness Gryphius' meteoric rise to become the foremost lyric poet of Germany and the father of German drama. Nevertheless, the Alexandrine consecrated in his guide book for German poetry remained the dominant verse form used by Gryphius and his contemporaries.

---

[73] Johann Burckhard Mencke, *Ernsthafte Gedichte* (1706), as quoted by James N. Hardin, ed., in his preface to "Translation and Translation Theory in Seventeenth-Century Germany," *Daphnis: Zeitschrift für mittlere deutsche Literatur,* 1992, 21, 1:6.

Appendix

Anatomy of the Alexandrine Line

Understanding the line form favored by Gryphius for his dramas reveals much about the pattern of thought present in both the monologs and dialogs of his characters, who often represent diametrically opposed philosophical, political, and religious convictions. The lyrical *form* of the Alexandrine serves to enhance the *meaning* of each line, because it brings a balance of opposition into play. The uninterrupted flow of this rhythm and rhyme pattern establishes a smooth symmetry of counterbalance and strength that embraces all of the dramatic lines formed in its mold. Each Alexandrine line contains six accents, with a distinct pause, or *caesura*, at the line's center. The rhythm itself projects and controls the line's meaning, for the first half (the first three accents) stands in opposition to the second half (the final three accents), with reliance upon the line's center pause (*caesura*) to separate the opposing concepts.

The Alexandrine line requires that the content or idea to be expressed be "molded" into rigid lines of 12 syllables (if ending in a word of one syllable, a masculine ending), or 13 syllables (if ending in a word of two syllables, a feminine ending). The lines are arranged either in rhymed pairs (aabb) if their endings are masculine, or embraced rhyme quatrains (abba) if the first line ending is feminine. When explaining the Alexandrine form in his *Kleine Deutsche Versschule* (A *Brief Primer of German Verse*), Wolfgang Kayser notes the powerful influence of this meter on poetic creativity by quoting from a letter written in Jena by Friedrich Schiller to Johann Wolfgang von Goethe on October 15, 1799.[74] Schiller reminds his good friend of the difficult constraints imposed by all aspects of the Alexandrine line when he discusses Goethe's current effort to translate into German Voltaire's *Mohammed* (*Le Fanatisme, ou Mahomet Le Prophete, Tragédie par M. De Voltaire*), a five-act French tragedy composed in Alexandrines that was first published in 1736. Schiller writes: "The nature of the Alexandrine is to divide into two equal halves and the peculiarity of the rhythm to form a couplet out of two Alexandrines, which not merely determine the whole language, but also

---

[74] Wolfgang Kayser, *Kleine deutsche Versschule*, 9th ed. (Bern and Munich: A. Francke, 1962), 32.

determine the whole inner spirit of the pieces. The characters, the sentiments, the actions of the personages, everything is thus classed under the rule of contrast; and precisely as the musician's fiddle directs the movements of the dancers, so the double nature of the Alexandrine affects the movements of the mind and thought. Demands are perpetually made upon the understanding, and every feeling, every thought, forced into this form as into the bed of Procrustes."[75]

My English translation of the Gryphian plays written in Alexandrine verse forgoes forcing a matched rhythm and rhyme scheme that would attempt to reflect accurately Gryphius' Alexandrine compositions. Concerned about their ease of reading the plays, I have sought to provide readers with a useful key to understanding the content and ideas present in the original dramas. While it is crucial to appreciate Gryphius' lyric and poetic achievement in his elevation, indeed his perfection, of the Alexandrine in the German language, I believe that my goal of bringing his work to a wider audience is best met by adjusting the limitations imposed by the "iron bed of Procrustes" through the use of free verse that carries the message of Gryphius even though it lacks his original Alexandrine form.

Gryphius Beyond the Alexandrine

In additon to the ongoing structure of opposition embodied in the Alexandrine line that determines the inner tension carried forward in both lengthy monologs and extensive dialogs, Gryhius opts for alternative metrical and rhyme schemes to heighten and intensify choral commentary, philosophical reflections, or entertaining episodes added to the plot.

The total of eight choral interludes that apppear after the first four acts of *Armenius* and *Catharine* introduce a variety of lyrical forms by means of which Gryphius offers commentary external to the dramatic action or provides contextual information that authenticates the dramatic action. For example, the *Chorus of Princes Murdered by Shah Abbas* (*Catharine*, II.357-416) encourages the audience/reader to pause and reflect on action that has either occurred on-stage

---

[75] In Greek mythology, Procrustes, a son of Poseidon, forced his guests to spend the night "fitted" to his infamous iron bed. For this to occur properly, Procrustes either sawed off his guests' legs or stretched them out on a rack, using whichever method was necessary to fit his visitors' bodies into precisely the length of his iron bed.

or has been reported in spoken lines of the dramatic scenes. By lamenting their unjust misfortunes in rhymed speech that is at times quite natural in its meter, the murdered princes verify otherwise preposterous legendary tales that become totally believable through their realistic self–reporting. Because they relate, in more natural tones, their own personal experiences of atrocious trickery and murder under the cruel shah's murderous reign, their climactic call for divine justice can be fully understood. Concurrently, commentary reflecting the voice of Gryphius can be heard in this chorus that confirms Shah Abbas as an evil enemy of God and established world order as revealed by his desecration of those who rule by divine right. When the combined choruses offer their final appeal to God as the Solemn Judge, their plea approaches its crescendo as they roar "Take vengeance! / Wake up! Great God awaken!" And then, in an unparalleled dramatic frenzy, they deliver one of the most remarkable outbursts ever written by Gryphius. Their six-fold repetition of "Wache! / Wake up!" followed by their rhymed, four-fold repetition of "Rache! / Revenge!" is a powerfully released linguistic blow that has broken through any metric bonds such as those required by the Alexandrine form.

Numerous examples of philosophical reflections unconstrained by the Alexandrine meter appear in both translated plays. To cite but one example, Queen Catharine's prayer of gratitude appears as a five-stanza lyric soliloquy before she offers her final farewells to the Ladies of her Court at the closing of Act IV (*Catharine*, IV. 265-304).

The sole appearance of a conjuring magician in a drama by Gryphius occurs when Iamblichus the wizard summons a ghostly spirit from hell in *Leo Armenius* (IV. 24-160). The well-choreographed onstage movements of Iamblichus add dramatic appeal to live productions of the drama, while this inclusion of specific directions also entices the reader to participate directly in the magician's mysterious process of enchantment. A vast array of theatrical requisites is called forth by Iamblichus to heighten the bizarre, supernatural effort he has undertaken. The remarkable use of language in the Iamblichus scene of Act IV provides a showcase sampling of how Gryphius draws upon multiple meters, alternating rhyme schemes, the repetition of powerful rhetorical devices, and even inarticulate mumbling (between lines 128-29) with both mastery and purpose. Although much of the episode is couched in rhymed Alexandrines, at times Iamblichus departs from these couplets to intensify his incantations with both changed meters and alternative rhyme schemes. For example, his direct approach to the power of evil switches to octosyllabic dactyls to establish the intended solemnity of his formal plea (*Leo Armenius*, IV.61-65 ff.). Rhetorical repetitions abound throughout this persuasive chant, while unexpected departures from the regular scheme of rhymed couplets include three four-line abab segments (IV.93-96, 105-08, 109-12). The powerful language residing in his wizard's incantations demonstrates the German dramatist's poetic versatility.

Conclusion

Every translator reaches a point when the question "Am I finished now?" requires an answer. For over fifty years I have returned periodically to work on my translations of Gryphius' first two historical tragedies. Each review brings forth new possibilities that I previously had not considered, and the temptation to revise is ever present. Perhaps this is my personal testimony to the enduring quality and lyrical depth of the original German drama created four centuries ago by the first celebrated poet and dramatist to write in the German language. The historical tragedies of Andreas Gryphius have remained current until the present day. Their verse exploration of history, philosophy, religion, politics, geography, and human endeavor as staged by a host of extraordinary characters has earned a rightful place for him in the pantheon of German literary figures. I hope that my translations will assist in revealing the mastery of these plays while also inspiring a wider appreciation of their meaning, message, and form. It is with this hope for his first two historical tragedies that I will continue my translation of his final two historical tragedies: *Charles Stuart or Murdered Majesty* (1657, revised 1663) and *The Magnanimous Jurist or Aemilius Paulus Papinianus Facing Death* (1659), which I expect to offer in the future.

ABOUT THE AUTHOR

Janifer Gerl Stackhouse, Harvard Ph.D., has pursued her lifelong interest in Germanic literature with a primary focus on German drama of the seventeenth century. She has held teaching and research appointments at the University of California at Davis, Stanford University, and the University of California at Santa Cruz. She continued her Gryphius scholarship while serving nearly twenty years as associate professor of Humanities and academic dean at College of Notre Dame in Belmont, California, and is currently an independent scholar in Palo Alto, California. Her publications include *The Constructive Art of Gryphius' Historical Tragedies*, (Bern: Peter Lang Verlag, 1987) and excerpts from *Leo Armenius* by Andreas Gryphius (English Translation) in *The German Library: German Theater* before 1750 (New York: Continuum, 1992).

Printed in Great Britain
by Amazon

17726651R00174